RUSSIA'S WAR AGAINST UKRAINE

RUSSIA'S WAR AGAINST UKRAINE

The Whole Story

MARK EDELE

MELBOURNE
UNIVERSITY
PRESS

MELBOURNE UNIVERSITY PRESS

An imprint of Melbourne University Publishing Limited

Level 1, 715 Swanston Street, Carlton, Victoria 3053, Australia

mup-contact@unimelb.edu.au

www.mup.com.au

First published 2023

Text © Mark Edele, 2023

Design and typography © Melbourne University Publishing Limited, 2023

Cover design by Philip Campbell Design

Typeset by Adala Studio

Cover image by Roman Novitskii/Getty Images

Printed in Australia by McPherson's Printing Group

 A catalogue record for this book is available from the National Library of Australia

9780522879834 (paperback)

9780522879841 (ebook)

Kenya and almost every African country was birthed by the ending of empire. Our borders were not of our own drawing. They were drawn in the distant colonial metropoles of London, Paris and Lisbon, with no regard for the ancient nations that they cleaved apart.

Today, across the border of every single African country, live our countrymen with whom we share deep historical, cultural and linguistic bonds. At independence, had we chosen to pursue states on the basis of ethnic, racial or religious homogeneity, we would still be waging bloody wars these many decades later.

Instead, we agreed that we would settle for the borders that we inherited, but we would still pursue continental political, economic and legal integration. Rather than form nations that looked ever backward into history with a dangerous nostalgia, we chose to look forward to a greatness none of our many nations and peoples had ever known …

We believe that all states formed from empires that have collapsed or retreated have many peoples in them yearning for integration with peoples in neighboring states. This is normal and understandable. After all, who does not want to be joined to their brethren and to make common purpose with them? However, Kenya rejects such a yearning from being pursued by force. We must complete our recovery from the embers of dead empires in a way that does not plunge us back into new forms of domination and oppression.

Martin Kimani, Permanent Representative of Kenya to the UN, 22 February 2022[1]

CONTENTS

PREFACE

Since February 2022, books about Russia's aggression against Ukraine have proliferated. Why should readers select this one? What does this book do that others don't?

First, this is a book by a scholar, not a journalist, refugee, soldier, war correspondent or international observer. I am not a participant observer of this history. I would not recommend myself as a guide to frontline trenches. But scholars can see patterns and processes which participants often cannot perceive as clearly, hindered as they are by the myopia of human experience—particularly in times of war.

Second, this is the book of a historian rather than a political scientist or international relations ('IR') scholar. Hence, this book brings a longer-term perspective than most recent accounts. This longer-term framework is important, as both sides of the front line trace their histories back for over a thousand years, and such claims are often accepted as gospel by outside observers. Historians are also more inclined to see the contingency of events, but also their overall pattern which compels actors in a certain direction.

This is a book by an outsider written for outsiders. I am neither Ukrainian nor Russian, and while I have spent considerable time doing research in several of the successor states of the Soviet Union, I always remained a sceptical non-belonger. This book is not written for Ukrainians or Russians, many of whom will learn little new in its pages. Neither is it written for fellow scholars, although I hope that it will inspire or provoke them, should they happen to read it. Its main audience is the intelligent reading public in the English-speaking world who would like to understand how and why we got into this mess. For this reason, endnotes have been kept to a minimum. Bibliographic notes in particular have been replaced by the guide to further reading at the end of the book.

I would like to thank Erik Jensen and Peter Browne, the editors of *The Saturday Paper* and *Inside Story*, respectively, for the invitation to explain the background of the war against Ukraine to their readers. Marko Pavlyshyn believed that I might have something to say to a conference of Ukrainianists, which was daunting but educational. And Catherine Kovesi invited me to deliver the Kathleen Fitzpatrick lecture at the University of Melbourne only a few months into the war. Although I did not know it at the time, these various attempts to come to terms with what was happening set me on the path towards this book. When Nathan Hollier, then of Melbourne University Publishing, suggested I write it, I was thus well on my way. That I could finish the manuscript was due to Russell Goulbourne, Dean of the Faculty of Arts at the University of Melbourne, who agreed that he could do without his deputy for a month and a half in late 2022 and early 2023; and the indefatigable Richard Serle, who made sure the library remained up to date. My reading, thinking and writing were also in part supported by an Australian Research Council Grant (DP200101777). The editing of the final version of the endnotes was made possible by the Funding Arts Research Essentials scheme of the Faculty of Arts (FARE). Yana Ostapenko took on this task at the last minute, for which I'm very grateful.

Gorana Grgic taught a seminar with me, in the process introducing me to the work of Jeffrey Mankoff, which clarified some thoughts about empire and decolonisation I had been grappling with on my own. I would also like to thank the members of the *kruzhok* of Russia watchers, who flood my email inbox with their thoughts, observations and reading recommendations. You know who you are. While I mostly keep quiet in your sometimes animated discussions, you will notice many parts in this book where I draw on your expertise (or implicitly argue with your views). I could not have written this book without you.

That I turned from a Russianist into a historian of the Soviet Empire was to no small extent due to my encounter with Ukraine and its history. Yuri Shapoval and Serhy Yekelchyk were my first guides here, and more recently Frank Sysyn became an essential interlocutor. They contributed to this book in ways they might not appreciate. Frank in particular showed remarkable tolerance towards the attempts of a modernist to grapple with medieval and early modern history, and a Russianist trying to make sense of Ukraine. Serhii Plokhy's magisterial *Lost Kingdom: The Quest for Empire and the Making of the Russian Nation* (2017) has influenced my views deeply. Parts of my reaction to this book were published in H-Net Reviews in June 2018 (see http://www.h-net.org/reviews/showrev.php?id=51411), sections of which have been reused here. Conversations with Oleg Beyda and Filip Slaveski alerted me to some of the more apocalyptic potentials discussed in the final chapter.

Earlier versions of parts of this book were first published as the preface of the Spanish translation of *Stalinism at War*, released by Desperta Ferro Ediciones in 2022 under the title *Estalinismo en Guerra 1937–1949*, and presented as a book talk, with lively and helpful discussion, at the Carmel Institute, American University, Washington, DC, on 18 November 2022; others first saw the light of day as '"It's NATO, Stupid!" Two New Books Disagree about the Origins of Russia's War against Ukraine', *Inside Story*, 22 November 2022, https://insidestory.org.au/its-nato-stupid/; and 'The Long War of Soviet Succession: The War in Ukraine Is Part of a Long-simmering Conflict across Post-Soviet Europe and Asia', *Inside Story*, 19 September 2022, https://insidestory.org.au/the-long-war-of-soviet-succession/. Earlier versions of parts of chapters 1 and 2 were first presented as 'Soviet History with Ukraine Left In: What Difference Did Independence Make to the Writing of Soviet History?', keynote address at the conference of the Ukrainian Studies Association of Australia and New Zealand & University of Melbourne, 3–5 February 2022; and 'Failed Decolonisation: Russia, Ukraine, and Vladimir Putin', Kathleen Fitzpatrick Lecture, University of Melbourne, 19 May 2022.

Frank Sysyn and Sir Rodric Braithwaite read early drafts of this book. I cannot thank them enough for their comments, disagreements and encouragement. Readers should not blame them for my mistakes and misjudgements.

PUTIN'S WAR? AN INTRODUCTION

War

On 24 February 2022, Russia went to war against Ukraine. Throwing caution to the wind and shocking even his closest associates, Russian President Vladimir Vladimirovich Putin, just four months and two weeks after turning sixty-nine, ordered an all-out onslaught on the country, with which Russia had been engaged in a smouldering proxy war ever since 2014. After massive missile strikes designed to disable Ukraine's air defences, Russian forces advanced on four axes: from the north towards Kyiv, from the north-east towards Kharkiv, from the south-east towards Luhansk and Donetsk, and from the south to establish a land bridge between the Donbas and Crimea (illegally annexed in 2014) (see Map 1).

The plan's audacity would have pleased Hitler's generals: speed, shock and awe were of the essence. And it was nearly as optimistic as the German Operation Barbarossa of 1941: the plan was to disable the enemy in ten days, decapitate the country by arresting or executing the political leadership, mobilise pro-Russian Ukrainians to support the invader, suppress what was expected to be a minority of resisters, and take over vital infrastructure (heating, electricity, finance) to use as leverage for controlling what was expected to be an apathetic majority.

1

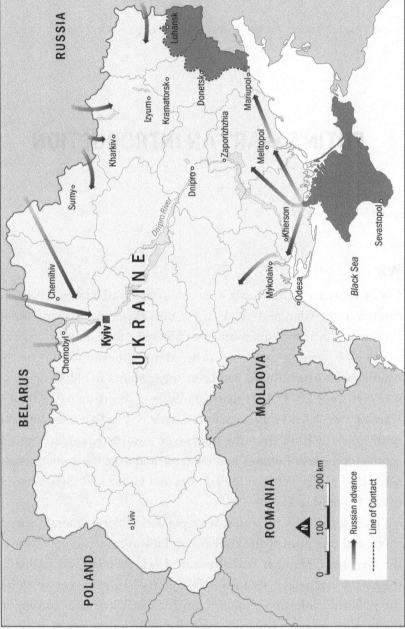

Map 1: The initial Russian assault, February 2022
* Dark grey: Russian-occupied Ukrainian territories at the start of the invasion.

Military leaders would be enticed to surrender by text message, leaving the armed forces headless. Ukraine would be occupied by mid-August in preparation for annexation or the instalment of a puppet regime.[1]

The next stages of the plan would have been appreciated by Stalin's secret police: once in control of the situation, special services would go through prepared lists to 'filter' the population. Four categories of political and community leaders were listed separately: Ukrainian patriots who were considered such implacable enemies of Russia that they needed to be physically liquidated; others considered less threatening but in need of intimidation; neutral leaders who could be bribed into collaboration; and, finally, pro-Russian leaders who were assumed to collaborate willingly. Also out of the Stalinist handbook was the plan to register the population, establish surveillance files on anybody deemed suspicious, and use 'filtration camps' to sort those to be deported from the rest. Once the population was under control, teachers and officials from Russia would be brought in to start a re-education campaign.[2]

Taking Kyiv, Ukraine's capital, was a central part of this plan to subjugate the country. In addition to two columns of tanks, trucks and armoured infantry carriers advancing from Belarus towards Ukraine's capital, there was also an airborne assault on Hostomel airport, just outside the city. As Kyiv's citizens descended into the more than 6500 bomb shelters the capital had prepared for such an eventuality, and while authorities handed out guns and Molotov cocktails to citizen-defenders, a group of choppers flew in from Belarus at low altitude to secure the strategic installation. With the airport secured, Moscow's war plan called for transport planes to bring in more elite troops to help take the capital and hence decapitate Ukraine.[3]

Because Moscow's strategy of shock, awe and terror depended on surprise, disorientation of the enemy, and deception, preparations had been kept secret. So secret, indeed, that even the troops who would execute the assault were told only at the last minute. In an extreme example of how to ensure low morale, the paratroopers who flew in to take Hostomel airport were only told once airborne that they were not in training, but flying into combat. 'The troops were fucking shocked,' recalled a survivor of the assault who would surrender to the

Ukrainians, 'especially considering we took fire in the air.' Two of the helicopters were shot down before their occupants could fast-rope onto the runway. Under heavy fire, the Russians managed to secure the air-field but were not able to suppress Ukrainian fire. The transport planes scheduled to bring in the main assault force thus had to turn around. The paratroopers dug in, waiting for reinforcements. They came later in the day in two transport planes but were shot out of the skies, killing some 300 elite troops. Fifty more paratroopers would be killed during the next few days of heavy fighting, eliminating about a quarter of the initial assault force. A mechanised counterattack eventually took back the airport, and a dozen of the survivors were captured. The attempt to take Kyiv in an airborne lightning strike had failed.[4]

The Russian troops, then, were often surprised by what they were asked to do; by the resistance they encountered; by the locals who blocked their path and abused them, telling them in no unclear terms to go home; and by the street signs which were quickly changed to show where the population wished them to head: '*na khui!*' (literally: 'to the cock', a Russian idiomaticity of the English 'fuck off'). They often could not read a map, did not know where they were going, had no idea how what they did fit into a larger plan, and were short on ammu-nition, fuel, food and other supplies. None of this helped morale.

Ukrainian troops, by contrast, had been preparing for such an onslaught since the initial Russian invasion of Crimea and Donbas in 2014. They had been fighting ever since, although the outside world had largely forgotten this 'frozen conflict' (which killed ninety soldiers in 2021 alone). Hence, the invaders confronted a battle-hardened force. Because pay in the military could not compete with the civilian economy, the army had struggled to retain its trained staff. That had the unintended but positive result that there were large numbers of well-trained soldiers in civilian clothes all over the country who could be mobilised without too much training. The Russian assumption that Ukraine could mobilise only 40 000 new troops beyond what they had under arms already was therefore way off the mark. And given that they defended their country, their homes and their democracy, they were much better motivated than the invading troops.

On what soldiers call the 'tactical level', then—that is, the cohesion, preparation and morale within the primary fighting units—Ukraine had the edge from the start. On the 'operational level', by contrast, where strategic goals are put into action by directing larger units, armies and fronts, the attackers had the advantage. As a result of the severe secrecy surrounding the preparations, Ukraine's leadership had not expected an assault from three sides but had prepared for a major onslaught from the Russian-occupied regions of Donbas in the east of the country. This was where their best troops, and most of them, were dug in. Kyiv, by contrast, was relatively unprotected.

The battle of Kyiv would last a month. It was a close-run thing. On the first day of the invasion, Russian special forces had broken out from Hostomel airport and gone on the move in armoured vehicles in the suburbs of the capital. Firefights broke out as close as 4 kilometres from government headquarters. Two groups of assassins—Chechens as well as mercenaries from the private Wagner army—had been deployed to Kyiv ahead of the assault with lists of targets, including President Volodymyr Zelensky. They did try to kill the president but were eliminated by Ukrainian defenders in the attempt. Zelensky, who had famously declined 'a ride' out of the city by his American allies, remained to post defiant video messages to the citizens of his country.[5]

With the airborne assault on Hostomel airport suppressed and the teams of assassins eradicated, the major threat remained, however: the columns of armour moving in two groups from the north towards the city (see Map 1), which, because of the successful deception by the Russian armed forces, was nearly defenceless: Russia had a 12:1 advantage in forces north of Kyiv. Things looked bleak.

Ukraine had never become part of the North Atlantic Treaty Organization (NATO), and its American and European partners had been reluctant to supply offensive weapons, lest Putin be provoked. Hence, Ukraine relied mostly on its own resources during the first phase of the war. Notwithstanding the prominence of shoulder-fired, NATO-supplied anti-tank weapons in both social media and mainstream coverage, the battle for Kyiv was won by Ukraine's own artillery and modernised Soviet-era tanks, not NATO weaponry. At the

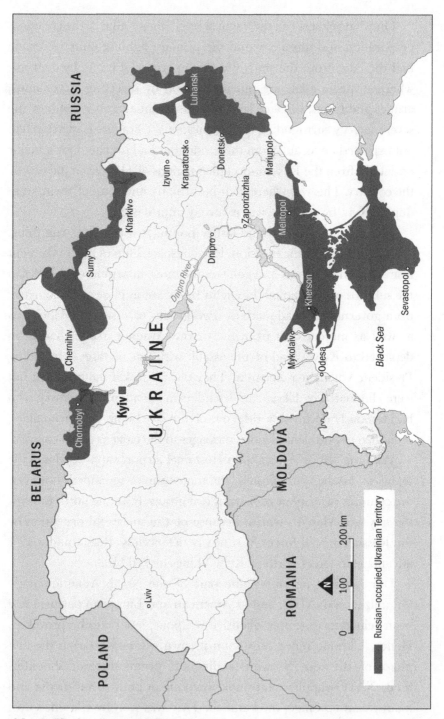

Map 2: The front lines on 27 February 2022

beginning of the conflict, Russia had an advantage in artillery pieces of only 2:1 and in tanks of 3.6:1, and Ukraine used these assets to their full potential. Two artillery brigades deployed in the north of Kyiv blasted the attacking columns with 'massed fire' using considerable stocks of ammunition built up in preparation for an all-out Russian assault. Likewise, the 'public obsession with anti-tank guided weapons' led to ignorance about 'the large number of main battle tanks' Ukraine fielded in the first phase of the war, largely as mobile artillery. It was these Ukraine-produced weapons and their determined crews which denied the Russian aggressor victory in 2022.[6]

As the Russian and Ukrainian armed forces used near-identical adapted Soviet-era equipment, the invaders needed to distinguish their vehicles from the enemy's to prevent that wonderful military euphemism 'friendly fire' (of which there was a lot, nevertheless). Hence, they painted their vehicles with large white symbols: the assault group heading out from Homel in Belarus was assigned a large 'V', the troops formed in Bryansk in Russia painted their vehicles with an 'O', the vehicles attacking from Crimea were emblazoned with a 'Z in a square', and those engaged in Donbas received the tactical sign 'Z'—the letter which would soon become the symbol of the invasion among both friends and foes.[7]

The columns daubed with the Vs and Os continued to drive towards Kyiv (see Map 2). With a superiority of 12:1, they should have been in a position to quash their opponents. But soon they ran into trouble. Contained to roads partially because the ground was already soft due to relatively warm weather, and partially because they had not properly maintained their vehicles for off-road driving, the invaders formed a 60-kilometre-long traffic jam all the way from the Belarusian border. Their mobility was limited by fuel shortages and breakdowns, but also by the artillery beating their forward units in Bucha and other suburbs of Kyiv. Ukrainian counterattacks followed. On 29 March, the invaders started to withdraw in orderly formation. The assault on Kyiv had failed and with it the original battle plan.

As Ukrainian troops moved back into Bucha and other suburbs, they found evidence of massive war crimes—executions, killing of civilians, rapes, torture. This hardened the Ukrainian attitude dramatically. If, at the start of the campaign, the political leadership was still willing to negotiate a return to the 24 February front line, from now on only a total withdrawal of Russian troops from Ukrainian soil would do—including the territories occupied since 2014. It also embittered the fighting to follow, with Ukrainian troops unwilling to give up territory, even where such a course of action would be tactically advantageous.

The battle of Kyiv did not take place in a vacuum. There was fighting along all four axes in parallel (see Map 2). The Russians had the most success in the south, moving from Crimea as per their war plan. Mystifyingly, they faced little opposition, as Ukraine had failed to put troops in their way. While eventually they ran out of steam, not taking Mykolaiv and Odesa, they took large swathes of the coastline, including the cities of Kherson and Melitopol. Eventually, after a grinding siege and heavy bombardment, they also occupied Mariupol and established a land bridge between Russian-occupied Donbas and Crimea. In Donbas, meanwhile, they successfully pinned down Ukraine's best troops, who therefore could not be deployed elsewhere.

With the battle of Kyiv lost, Russia refocused its energy on the east: Donbas. By now, Ukraine had nearly used up its reserves of artillery shells. The invaders, by contrast, still had stocks, and—after attempted breakthroughs with tanks failed, due to the determination of the dug-in Ukrainians—began a slow and systematic war of attrition. At this point, in May and June 2022, Russia had a 12:1 advantage in the amount of artillery fire they could rain down on their opponents—on average, 2000 shells per kilometre of front line a day to a total of 20 000 rounds a day on the entire Donbas front, rising to 32 000 on particularly heavy days. If the hammering of Ukrainian positions with artillery did not compel the survivors to withdraw, the Russians would send in untrained conscripts from the occupied Donbas to assault Ukrainian trenches in a first wave. These would usually be repelled or killed, but in doing so the defenders revealed their positions, which would then be pounded by more artillery, followed by better trained, better motivated and better equipped assault troops,

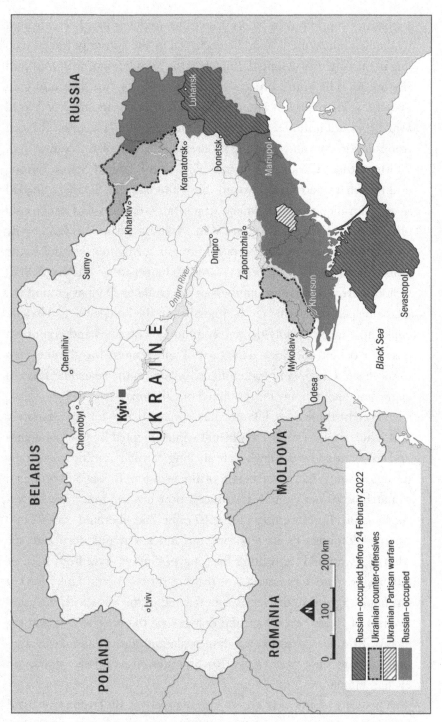

Map 3: The front line on 27 January 2023

sometimes supported by tanks. Once the trenches had been vacated by the defenders, they would be occupied by the conscript forces, who dug in overnight to defend them, while the assault teams withdrew and regrouped. The entire process would take one or two days and gain only a few kilometres at best—not as bad as in the trenches of World War I, but not a modern war of movement either. Thus, the Russian troops made slow and grinding progress in the east of the country.

Meanwhile, Ukraine's reluctant allies in the United States, Europe and elsewhere had finally woken up to the fact that Ukraine needed more than nice words, helmets (which the Germans had generously offered) or anti-aircraft weapons. While Ukraine's demands for a no-fly zone fell as much on deaf ears as requests for fighter jets and battle tanks, at least NATO now began providing longer-range artillery. NATO weapons arrived in larger numbers as the battle of Donbas ground on. These helped rob Russia of the initiative on the battlefield, as Ukraine could now target supply depots, communication lines and command posts far behind the lines. This turn of momentum was the first step to successful Ukrainian counteroffensives later in the year. The Russian aggression had not only been stopped but also reversed.

As I write these lines, Ukraine has won the battles for Kyiv, Kharkiv and Kherson, and survived a brutal winter defined by power outages and cold caused by the deliberate shelling of civilian infrastructure by the aggressor. While at the height of the invasion, Russia had occupied as much as 20 per cent of Ukraine, it now has lost much of this territory again. By November 2022, Ukraine had liberated over 74 000 square kilometres of its territory, but much remains occupied (see Map 3). Everybody is waiting for a new offensive now, from both or either side. And Ukrainians are waiting for the battle tanks NATO has finally agreed to deliver. Russia reacted to the news with the usual reversal of cause and effect: the delivery of the means of defending against Russia's aggression was 'an escalation'. Providing an exclamation mark to these statements, Russia renewed its missile attacks on civilian targets.

The costs of this war are already staggering. By December 2022, Ukraine had lost up to 13 000 soldiers, not counting the wounded, according to official statistics. American estimates were closer to 100 000 killed and wounded, with a similar number on the Russian side, but Ukraine insisted that the enemy had lost seven times more men than the defenders.[8] Maybe 40 000 civilians were dead as a result of the conflict, and there were at least fifteen million refugees: 7.8 million of them abroad, the rest displaced in Ukraine itself.[9]

This book tells the prehistory of this war—the story of how Russia, Ukraine and the world got into this mess. It has been written in Australia, where mainstream opinion, after some initial wobbles, has swung decisively behind Ukraine's war effort. Australia, a country surprisingly tough on immigration for a nation of immigrants, has, uncharacteristically, provided shelter to some 5000 Ukrainian refugees from this war, with just as many additional visas issued by early 2023. They have been actively supported by the community of Australian Ukrainians, about 53 000 strong, who live in Melbourne, Sydney and elsewhere. Australia, a nation of just above twenty-six million people, has provided $475 million in military aid and $65 million in humanitarian aid, including the gifting of sixty Australia-made Bushmaster armoured personnel carriers (with thirty more pledged recently) and the delivery of 70 000 tonnes of thermal coal to heat Ukraine's cities. Australia has provided duty-free access for Ukrainian imports and participated in the international sanctions regime against Russia, including travel bans on individuals, and import bans on Russian oil, gold, petroleum, coal and gas, as well as export bans on alumina, bauxite and luxury goods. In January 2023, Australia sent military trainers to help prepare Ukrainian troops for combat and announced a collaboration with France to produce artillery shells for the war zone. While imposing considerable costs on the Australian economy and the Australian taxpayer at a time of high inflation and a rising cost of living, thus far this support has been bipartisan.[10] The only really controversial issue on the Australian front line of this globalised conflict is whether or not Australian citizens should go fight and die defending Ukraine, a choice that might be illegal under Australian law. Several hundred have done so nevertheless, and despite government advice not to travel to Ukraine. A handful have thus far died.[11]

Much of this will sound familiar to readers from other countries: the United States is the most important supporter of Ukraine's war effort, with 47.8 billion euros of bilateral aid committed. Institutions of the European Union are second with 35 billion euros. Within Europe, the strongest political backing comes from 'New Eastern Europe', especially Poland and the three Baltic republics. 'Old Europe' is more divided internally, especially Germany and France, and was originally more inclined to see Russia's assertions of its special interests in its former colonies as reasonable, or at least understandable. However, with 5.5 billion euros of aid committed, Germany is fourth in financial terms after the United States, the European Union and the United Kingdom (7 billion euros). It is followed by Canada (3.8 billion euros), Poland (3 billion euros) and France (1.4 billion euros).[12]

Weakest is the support in the 'global south', where the conflict is not seen as a post-imperial struggle but as a continuation of the Cold War. This also seems to be the understanding in China, although here, the simple fact that support for Ukraine distracts the United States also plays a role. More generally, critics of America, including from both the global old left and the younger 'anti-imperialist left', tend to think of this conflict as a proxy war between Russia and the United States. They tend to side with Russia or at least explain away its aggression and atrocities, because anybody who is against the United States must be on the right side of history.

History

The inevitable polemics about whom to support in this war, and why, are often underwritten by consequential misunderstandings of the histories of Ukraine and Russia. This book tries to correct the record, in order to enable a somewhat better-informed debate. Chapter 1 excavates the history of Ukraine from the distortions of the Russian imperial narrative, from the nineteenth-century classics to Vladimir Putin's polemic of 2021. But it also remains sceptical of those Ukrainian national narratives which see a unified history all the way back to the medieval Rus. Instead, I follow mainstream historiography on the making of modern nations, which sees them as the product of the late eighteenth and nineteenth centuries. Ukraine's formation as a nation is a phenomenon of modern times, but despite what Putin maintains, this formation was well underway by the time the Romanov Empire collapsed during World War I.

The central moment in this formation of contemporary Ukraine is the Ukrainian Revolution of 1917 and the resulting revolutionary state of 1918–20, as Chapter 1 shows. It was the very strength of Ukraine's national revolutionary movement which drove Lenin and Stalin to the compromise of integrating it into the new Soviet state as a formally independent 'union republic'. And it was this union republic which would become independent in 1991. The history of its troubled democracy since 1991 is recounted in Chapter 3. It demonstrates that Ukraine is far from a model democracy, but it is certainly not 'fascist' as Russian propaganda would have it. It has made immense strides towards democracy and has worked hard to rein in the corruption which plagues most of the successor states of the Soviet Empire. And, again contrary to the claims of Russia's supporters, the ethnically exclusive national consciousness of some is countered by a rising ethnically inclusive civic nationalism based on pride in Ukraine's independence and its democratic institutions.

If modern Ukraine was born in 1917–20, modern Russia only came into being in 1991, as chapters 2 and 4 argue. This might seem a startling proposition. Does 'Russian history' not go back hundreds of years? To be precise, does Russia not have, according to its constitution of 2020, a 'thousand-year history' of 'continuity in the development of the Russian state'? Chapters 2 and 4 argue that we should not confuse the history of the Russian nation-state with the history of the Russian Empire. Moreover, the narrative inscribed in Russia's constitution artificially extends this imperial history further back in time than would be reasonable. If Russia had a 'thousand-year history', it would have been founded in 1020, a year when nothing particularly spectacular happened to the East Slavs, as far as we know from the available sources. But this might be taking the constitution too literally. The point of constructing this Russian 'thousand-year Reich' is to lay claim on the medieval realm of the Rus, a historically shaky proposition, as we shall see in Chapter 1. Maybe more concerningly, however, the Russian Federation today also appropriates the entire history of the Russian and then Soviet empires as its heritage—with imperialist results.[13]

The current Russian Constitution, then, along with much of the Russian public and still many outside the country, ignores the fact that this imperial history had come to an end in 1991, when the Soviet Union broke apart. 'With nearly nine-tenths of its population consisting of ethnic Russians,' wrote Richard Pipes, a historian of Russia, a few years later, 'Russia is for the first time since the sixteenth century a truly national state rather than an empire.' He declared 'the end of the imperial era of European history'.[14] In a similarly optimistic vein, one of the most eminent English-language historians of Ukraine, Serhii Plokhy, wrote, in the year before Russia would invade Crimea: 'The Soviet collapse simply concluded a process that had begun in earnest at the dawn of the century and was accelerated by the two world wars: the disintegration of world empires and their disappearance from the political map.'[15] We now know that Pipes and Plokhy were too optimistic: Russia might no longer be an empire, but large sectors of both its ruling class and the population at large remain imperialists: they never overcame a fundamentally imperial consciousness. Over the decades since 1991, this state and this society failed to decolonise both politically and, crucially, culturally. Today, we see a concerted attempt to resurrect Russia's empire. The war against Ukraine is one of the results of this legacy of imperialism.[16]

Academics can tie themselves into all kinds of terminological knots when trying to define 'empire' and delineate its borders to 'nation-states' and other political formations. This book simply insists that the chief characteristic of an empire is imperialism: the wish to extend one's territory and one's power onto the territory of others. Once the wish to expand subsides, a state begins to act like a nation-state. Conversely, if a nation-state adopts a policy of expansion, it becomes, de facto, imperial.

The history of Russia's expansion is the topic of Chapter 2. The Russian Empire was built by the princes of Moscow, later the tsars of Russia, in a continuous and bloody process before it was taken over by the Bolsheviks in no more peaceful fashion. The pre-revolutionary empire reached its height in the early nineteenth century, when it was instrumental in defeating Napoleonic France and hence bringing peace to Europe. It then entered a period of crisis at just the time when the modern notion of Ukraine as a nation solidified. The empire's auto-cratic political system and early modern political economy struggled to adapt to the modern world of transoceanic empires, industrialisation and mass politics (including liberalism, nationalism and socialism). It never came to terms with these challenges and entered World War I in a state of unsettlement. It then broke apart in an entangled web of wars, revolutions and civil wars through the years 1916–22. From this cauldron of violence emerged successor states: Finland, Estonia, Latvia, Lithuania, Poland and the Soviet Union. In terms of real estate, the latter was the largest, and geographically near-identical to the old Romanov Empire. Ideologically, politically and economically, however, it was a completely different structure.

For reasons which are explored in Chapter 1, this new empire was consolidated as a union of republics, each with a national identity. The largest of them was the Russian Soviet Federal Socialist Republic (RSFSR). This was the Russian core of the avowedly anti-imperial, anti-nationalist empire of nations that was the Soviet Union. Russians made up the largest ethnicity within this empire, roughly half of the population. When the Soviet Union imploded in 1991, the RSFSR became the Russian Federation—like Ukraine, one of the postcolonial successor states of the Soviet Union. Chapter 2 tells the prehistory of this genesis of modern Russia, while Chapter 4 deals with the history after 1991 and the reasons why this post-imperial country failed to develop a postcolonial identity.[17]

This failure to decolonise explains why many in Russia perceived as a threat the legitimate wishes of independent neighbouring states to orient themselves towards Europe. It also explains why these same states scrambled to join NATO: they (correctly, it turns out) perceived Russia as an ongoing security threat in Eastern Europe, a country with a continuing sense of its imperial mission and status as a great power.

At its centre, then, Russia's war against Ukraine is a contest between decolonisation and its discontents. It is driven not by deep-seated or centuries-old hostilities but by a divergence of the paths Russia and Ukraine took since 1991. Russia never came to terms—either as a society or as a polity—with its transformation from a continental empire with global reach into a nation-state and a regional power. Domestically, attempts at democratisation soon gave way to autocracy. In Ukraine, by contrast, strong currents in society actively pushed against similar anti-democratic tendencies. These social and cultural forces repeatedly corrected the country's political trajectory. As a result, Ukraine at several crucial junctures—2004, 2008, 2014—oriented itself away from the old hegemon, Russia, and sought alignment with Europe and NATO. It did so in a bid to cement its post-imperial independence and deepen economic development and democratic governance.

Those divergent paths are thus at the heart of this war: Russia invaded to stop, once and for all, Ukraine's drift out of its orbit. It was an open bid to make the region 'safe for empire'.[18] However, while this divergence explains the underlying reasons for the invasion, it does not explain the timing. To understand the latter, we need to come to grips with the decision-maker—Vladimir Putin. Chapter 5 argues that the Russian president is obsessed with history. He has rightly been described as a 'history man'.[19] Not only does he read Russia's current situation in the context of the long sweep of the history of the Russian and Soviet empires, not only does he routinely reach for historical analogies to make sense of the present, he is also concerned with his own role in, and impact on, Russian and world history. This obsession deepened in the years running up to his seventieth birthday, which he spent reading history books in splendid isolation from the menace of the COVID-19 virus.[20]

This individual aspect, the role of Putin's personality and his decision-making power, in part explains the timing of the invasion.[21] Having relatively little to show for nearly a quarter of a century in power, Putin entered his seventieth year in 2021. What would he celebrate at his next birthday? Russia's increased isolation? The botched COVID-19 response? The ailing economy? The sanctions on Russia? His personal wealth and power? He had failed to make Russia into a 'normal' country, as he had pledged at the beginning of his presidency—a country prosperous and free, a beacon to the world. While he had presided over economic growth, it had come at the cost of the enrichment of the few and the immiseration of the many. The opposition had built an unflattering picture of him as a thief of Russia's riches. This much Putin knew, and he did not like it. He repeatedly asked others how they thought the history books would remember him.

The invasion, then, was a bid by an ageing man to establish a legacy. But there were also wider strategic considerations: the window of opportunity seemed wide open but would possibly close soon. Opponents currently seemed weak but might soon recover. And, of course, Putin himself was no spring chicken.

Like many turning points in history, Putin's decision to launch a full-scale invasion of Ukraine was thus both structured by larger underlying forces and essentially contingent: nothing forced Russia to go to war in 2022. In fact, as one political scientist rightly argued shortly before the invasion, it was fundamentally against Russia's national interest to do so.[22] But the decision itself was far-reaching. '24/2' will be a fundamental discontinuity in European history, the European equivalent of the America's 9/11.[23] The likely consequences of this war—for Ukraine, for Russia, for the post-Soviet region, for Europe, and for the world—are sketched in Chapter 6.

'Realism'

This book, then, locates the origins of Russia's aggression squarely within post-Soviet, Soviet and imperial Russian history. Ultimately, it sees one man as being responsible for the outbreak: Vladimir Putin, dictator of Russia. This runs counter to a prominent approach to analysing not only this war but wider conflicts in the region of the imploded Soviet Empire. Such analyses focus on a global conflict between 'Russia' and 'the West' as the origin of the crisis. The latter (rendered as the United States, NATO, the European Union or all of the above) had 'encroached' on 'Russia's backyard' by expanding its reach into the lands formerly controlled by Moscow. Russia's aggression—in 2008 in Georgia, in 2014 and 2022 in Ukraine—was the inevitable result.

Displaying an excellent sense of public relations and self-promotion, this school of thought calls itself the 'realist' school of international relations. There are many sub-streams of 'realism', but the basic premise for the case at hand is that Russia's aggression is perfectly understandable, maybe even natural. Great powers will behave that way if others encroach on their territory. That 'their territory' is made up of independent states and nations who might not want to live under the hegemony of the 'great power' is shrugged away as irrelevant: such are the ways of the world. The international system is anarchic. What counts is the power of individual states, which will maximise their freedom of movement as much as they can. If Russia is a great power, a former empire, then it has certain privileges other successor states of the Soviet Union do not have. And outside powers are well advised to keep this in mind in their dealings with the region—otherwise, war is the inevitable result. Because it is a great power, Russia should have been accommodated in its quest for local hegemony, such critics imply.

What is indisputable is that Russia's annexation of Crimea in 2014 and all that followed—war in Donbas and all-out war with Ukraine since February 2022—was an attempted assertion of Russia's status as a great power. What Putin tried to demonstrate was that Russia was still the hegemon in the region and that the other successor states of the Soviet Union did not have the same rights to sovereignty and decision-making in the international sphere as Russia. And other imperial powers—NATO, the European Union—had no right to interfere in the internal affairs of Russia's post-imperial sphere of influence. (Of course, neither NATO nor the EU is an empire or even a great power. The first is a military alliance of sovereign states; the second an economic confederation of a different, if overlapping, group of sovereign states. But that's not how they were seen in Moscow.) This raises a fundamental question: is Putin right? Is Russia a great power?

How would one measure great power status? Objectively speaking, it could be either size of country, size of its population, size of its economy, wealth per capita, or size of its military, or a combination of them. If we look at these, Russia appears much more like a middling power nowhere near the two really great powers of today: China and the United States. US president Barack Obama's dictum, that

'Russia is a regional power', might have been an 'unnecessarily cutting remark'.[24] But it was factually correct.

It is true that Russia is big. With 17.1 million square kilometres, it is by far the largest country in the world, nearly twice the size of the runners-up: Canada (9.9 million), China (9.6 million) and the United States (9.5 million). But if size is a good measure for great power status, then Brazil should be in that league, too (fifth place with 8.5 million), as should Australia (sixth place, 7.7 million).[25] Sheer landmass is clearly not a compelling criterion for great power status.

Population might be more compelling. If a country has more citizens, one might well argue, it should get more power in international relations, because it represents a larger share of the world's humanity. Russia would do well in this respect, but not spectacularly so, ranking ninth in the world in 2021 with an estimated 145 102 755 inhabitants. But if this fact endowed Russia with the right to dominate its neighbours, then the same should be afforded to Bangladesh (169 356 251 people), Brazil (214 326 223), Nigeria (213 401 323), Pakistan (231 402 117), Indonesia (273 753 191) and the United States (336 997 624). But the real superpowers everybody should make special arrangements with would of course be India (1 407 563 842) and China (1 425 893 465).[26]

In terms of economic might, Russia was number eleven in the world in 2021, with a GDP of US$1 775 799.92 million. That could further bolster the argument for great power status. Let's look at the list ahead of it, though: first comes South Korea (US$1 798 533.92 million), then, after a significant gap in output, Canada (US$1 990 761.61 million), Italy, France, India and the United Kingdom. Then come Germany (US$4 223 116.21 million) and Japan (US$4 937 421.88 million). In a league of their own are China (US$17 734 062.65 million) and the United States (US$22 996 100.00 million). So if Russia is a great power, so are these others. But neither South Korea nor Canada, neither Italy nor France, neither India nor the United Kingdom, to say nothing of Germany or Japan, demand a sphere of influence in the world, or are afforded such a right by scholars. Moreover, if Russia should be regarded as a great power, so should Brazil or Australia, in positions twelve and thirteen on this list and very much in the same league as

Russia (US$1 608 981.22 million and US$1 542 659.90 million, respectively), with Spain (US$1 425 276.59 million) not far behind.[27]

Military might could be a more realistic indicator than economic strength. After all, it's the ability to coerce others to do as you please which makes you a great power. And while coercion can be economic and diplomatic, in the end, military force is a necessary last resort. With about 1 per cent of its population being active armed forces personnel in 2018, Russia was a more militarised society than, say, Germany (0.2 per cent) or the United States (0.4 per cent), but not much more so than Ukraine (0.7 per cent) and nowhere near Belarus (1.6 per cent), to say nothing of Israel (2.1 per cent) or North Korea (5.7 per cent).[28] Russia does have a large military—the sixth largest in the world in 2022, with nearly 3.6 million personnel, if we take soldiers on active duty, reservists and paramilitary members into account. This number puts Russia ahead of the United States (2.1 million) and behind China (4 million). But if the simple size of the army were a measure of great power status, Vietnam, at the top of the list with 10.5 million, should be conceded this status also, as should North Korea (second place, 7.8 million). South Korea has an army significantly bigger than Russia's (6.7 million) as does India (5.1 million). If we look only at active duty members of the armed forces, Russia moves to fifth place, with China in first, India in second and the United States in third. Again, North Korea would be a great power in this accounting, as it has a larger force than Russia (1.3 million as opposed to 1 million).[29]

In reality, of course, military power has to be demonstrated in practice—and that is not going so well for Russia at the moment. Thus, the current war has demonstrated that, militarily, Russia is *not* a great power: it has been unable to subdue a much smaller but better organised and more motivated neighbour.[30]

Militarily, the only fact that makes Russia stand out, other than the sheer size of its dysfunctional army, is nuclear capability. Russia is one of nine countries in the world with nuclear weapons, and one of the two largest stockpilers: the United State and Russia together account for about 90 per cent of all nuclear weapons in the world. The other nuclear powers are France, China, the United Kingdom, Pakistan,

India, Israel and North Korea.[31] Do they all get to have their sphere of influence? Or is it just the United States and Russia? And would that not be an incentive for everybody else to build up their own arsenals?

Historians might also point out that one of the reasons why only Russia has a nuclear arsenal in the post-Soviet space is a concerted effort by US diplomacy, backed with lots of dollars as incentives, to concentrate the nuclear weapons of the former Soviet Union on Russia's soil. The goal was not to build a stronger Russia, of course, but to prevent nuclear proliferation. The alternative model—to leave the smaller successor states with their own arsenals—was considered at the time but eventually rejected. Thus, if the nuclear arsenal is what makes Russia a great power, then its great power status is to a significant extent a result of US collusion with the Russian quest to monopolise these weapons in the former Soviet space.[32]

Within the region of the successor states, then, Russia is the only nuclear power. It is also the largest, most populous and economically strongest country. It took over 77 per cent of the Soviet Union's land-mass, 51 per cent of its population, 70 per cent of its manufacturing (however decrepit and unproductive) and 91 per cent of the actively exploited oil reserves.[33] It is also the Soviet Union's legal successor in the international arena and as such continues to occupy a permanent seat on the United Nations (UN) Security Council, which gives it veto powers in that crucial arena of international relations—a result of its past strength, not its present global power.

Russia is thus a country to be reckoned with in its part of the world—a strong regional power (if 'the region' is the former Soviet Union; if it's Eurasia, the great powers are in fact China in the east and Europe in the west—and Russia, as a middling power, would need to arrange itself with these giants). Should its relative strength compel its neighbours to accept it as the regional hegemon? Might they not, equally realistically, try to evade its strength and find allies elsewhere? And might that 'elsewhere' not logically be the strongest security pact in the world: NATO? That Russia would try to assert itself might well be understandable, but equally understandable is Ukraine's struggle to preserve its independence and its democracy.

On the global stage, why should China, the United States or the European Union, all much heavier hitters than Russia in any indicator other than sheer size of territory or stockpile of nuclear weapons, grant Russia a different status than any other middling country like, say, Australia? On objective measures, the answer is not clear at all. We quickly go in logical circles: Russia 'always was' a great power, hence it should be one now. But as we shall see in Chapter 2, that is an illusion: it was not contemporary 'Russia' but the Russian Empire, with its changing borders, which was a great power at certain moments in time. Certainly in 1918, Bolshevik Russia was no great power; nor was its successor state, the Soviet Union, in, say 1923, when the country produced a mere 100 cars and eleven tractors.[34] It regained great power, even 'superpower', status by 1945, but it lost it in 1991. Currently, it has no more entitlement to be regarded as a great power than, say, Pakistan or, again, Australia.

The Long Wars of Soviet Succession

The only reason why Russia claims great power status is because its political elite, a large share of its intelligentsia and a good part of the population as a whole have not come to terms with the fact that it is a different country now from both the Soviet Union and, going further back, the Romanov Empire. Its sense of entitlement to be treated differently from any other middling power is thus based on its failure to accept its decolonisation. And the scholars and politicians abroad who keep insisting that Russia should be treated like the great power it no longer is have likewise missed the fundamental transformation of Russia from an empire to a middling nation.

Such transformations often have violent phases until expectations have been recalibrated to the new realities of power for the post-imperial former metropole. What we witness in Ukraine today is one such violent recalibration. It is questionable if it could have been avoided, given the deeply ingrained imperialist culture in Russia. Those who argue that 'the West is principally responsible' for the war imply that had Russia been accommodated in the post–Cold War settlement in Europe, peace would reign on earth.[35] What they usually do not spell out, however, is what such an accommodation would have entailed. Sure, US politicians in particular often ran roughshod over Russia's concerns, in particular during the war in Kosovo (1998–99), when NATO intervened with air strikes and eventually ground troops, without receiving UN Security Council approval to do so. More generally, as former British ambassador to Moscow and historian of Russia Sir Rodric Braithwaite noted in 2022, 'the Americans acted as if Russia's foreign and domestic policy was theirs to shape.' Diplomacy 'has been by turns arrogant and incompetent'. Awareness of this hubris 'seeped into the Russian public consciousness and aroused an overwhelming sense of humiliation and resentment'.[36] Putin expressed these sentiments succinctly in a 2007 interview with *Time* magazine, which had just made him 'person of the year'. In the view of the Americans, he said, the Russians 'are a little bit savage still or they just climbed down from the trees, you know, and probably need to have their hair brushed and their beards trimmed. And have the dirt washed out of their beards and hair.'[37]

But, like many of his compatriots, Putin held openly imperialist views ever since the early 1990s; that is, well before NATO expansion became an issue or a decade and a half of American arrogance could seep in.[38] His turn to imperialism was not a reaction to NATO expansion or US arrogance. It preceded it. And he was not alone. Given the Russian elites' 'post-imperial phantom pains' for their lost status, what could possibly have made a real difference?[39] Accepting that Russia continued to be a great power and the hegemon over the former Soviet lands as well as Eastern Europe? Declaring Eastern Europe Russia's 'sphere of influence', without asking the Europeans if they desired to be part of it? It is hard to see retrospective calls for 'a genuine and inclusive partnership' between Russia and 'the West' as anything other than nostalgia for the utopian time of 1989–91, when everything suddenly seemed possible. Including Russia in NATO, or disbanding NATO and replacing it with an entirely different security structure in Europe, would have resulted in a different history from the one which actually emerged. But whether that history would have been better, less violent or more just is another matter. It is 'clear that the West should have dealt with post–Cold War Russia better than it did', writes a prominent historian, only to add: 'It is hard, however, to specify what alternative paths would have looked like.'[40]

'Concerns about NATO's paralysis in case of Russia's entry were not unfounded,' writes another historian who genuinely wishes that history would have turned out better. He also points out that Russian and Eastern and Central European visions of what an alternative security structure would look like were 'basically irreconcilable'.[41] And it is not clear at all why Russia's concerns should necessarily trump those of newly democratic nations in its immediate neighbourhood. As a careful counterfactual analysis has it, the rift between NATO and Russia was overdetermined: 'Russia mourned its lost status more than it feared a new security danger, and no realistic alternative to NATO's geographic enlargement would have restored Russia's status in the system.'[42]

Some analysts have gone further. It was not NATO enlargement, they argue, which pushed Russia into war in Ukraine. It was the opposite: the attempt somehow to accommodate Russia's demands in 2008, when Ukraine and Georgia were told that they would not be admitted anytime soon, but that the door would remain open in principle. In the same year, Russia invaded Georgia and recognised two breakaway republics. It was condemned by NATO for this assault on a sovereign nation's territorial integrity but essentially got away with it. Then came 2014 and the annexation of Crimea, followed by support for insurgents in Donbas. Again, Russia got away with it, suffering only verbal condemnation and relatively mild sanctions. NATO's posture, in this reading, was simply 'not strong enough to deter Russia'.[43]

If we zoom out from the immediate context of the first quarter of the twenty-first century and put the war in Ukraine into a wider chronological frame, we see some other patterns. This war is one moment in a larger conflict over empire and decolonisation in the lands once dominated by the Muscovite state and then the Russian Empire. This conflict reaches back to the period 1916–22, broke open again in 1989–91, and has simmered since the breakdown of the Soviet Union into fifteen successor states in 1991. What we are witnessing, in effect, is one battle in a potentially much more regional set of conflicts: the (civil) wars of the Soviet succession, combining domestic and international aspects, struggles over independence and empire with contests between dictatorship and democracy.

Ukraine is only one theatre of these contemporary conflicts. Mass protests in Belarus against the dictatorship of Alexander Lukashenko in 2020–21 were subdued with utter brutality. Russian support for the dictator kept his regime going despite crippling sanctions, effectively turning him into a client of Moscow. While in Belarus the violence was administered by domestic forces, similar anti-regime protests in Kazakhstan in January 2022 prompted the intervention of Russian, Belarusian, Armenian, Tajik and Kyrgyz troops to help prop up the government. Most recently, on 12 September 2022, the conflict over Nagorno-Karabakh returned from a frozen conflict between (Russian-backed) Armenia and (Turkish-supported) Azerbaijan to a shooting war, when the latter, exploiting Russia's distraction elsewhere, attacked Armenian positions. What all of these conflicts have in common is that they are rooted in unresolved problems stemming from the breakdown of the Soviet empire in 1989–91.

Civil wars and other conflicts are not untypical when empires break apart: boundaries between possible successors are not clear, loyalties fragile, legitimacies tenuous. When the Romanov Empire imploded in 1917–18, its lands were enmeshed in years of horrible fighting lasting in some regions to early 1920, in others into early 1921, and in Central Asia until 1923. The result, however, was the re-establishment of a new empire—the Union of Soviet Socialist Republics (USSR). Only Estonia, Finland, Latvia, Lithuania and Poland remained independent, at least until World War II. Thereafter, the three Baltic states were annexed, Poland was made a satellite, and Finland forced into neutrality.[44]

What is unique about the current conflicts of the Soviet succession is that they took so long to gestate. The breakdown of the Soviet empire was largely peaceful. This point can be overstressed: there was violence in Georgia in 1989 and in Lithuania in 1991; wars for and against independence in South Ossetia in 1991–92, Transnistria in 1992 and Abkhazia in 1992–93; a civil war in Tajikistan and a war-turned-frozen conflict in Nagorno-Karabakh from 1992; and two wars to prevent Chechnya from breaking away from Russia in 1994–96 and 1999–2000. Nevertheless, overall, the Soviet lands were spared the horrors of the wars of the Yugoslav succession nearby.[45]

One reason for this relative lack of violence was that the Soviet Union broke apart, not through acrimony but from exhaustion. Anti-imperial feelings were rife not only in the non-Russian periphery of the empire but also in the Russian heartland. Many thought their economic woes were caused by the drain the empire imposed on the state's coffers. Better to let the non-Russians go and build a Russian national homeland. Borders, too, were relatively well defined, as the Soviet Union's republics provided ready-made territories for succes-sor regimes. Again, there were exceptions (South Ossetia, Abkhazia, Nagorno-Karabakh and Transnistria) but by and large the boundaries of Soviet times held firm, until recently.

While in the broadest terms and longest time frame, the Russia–Ukraine war is not extraordinary in comparative context, it did not have to happen when it did, or even at all, as this book makes clear. It is certainly not the necessary culmination of a thousand years of Ukrainian–Russian relations, entangled as they are, as the historical chapters demonstrate. Even the increasingly divergent developmental paths the two countries have embarked on since 1991 do not inevitably lead to war. And while this divergence, the continuing imperial culture of much of Russia's society and the increasing orientation of much of Ukraine's society towards Europe and NATO certainly have had a lot of potential for conflict, this potential had not come to a head recently. None of the grand structural forces social scientists like to employ to explain the genesis of wars explain why war broke out the moment it did. Instead, the invasion was very much Putin's initiative.

In this respect, it is right to call this 'Putin's war'. Events in the past, and their outcomes, did not determine this war. They merely made it possible. Part of this past is in Putin himself: his biography and his result-ing personality, and his obsession with history and his own place within it. Other events are on the level of Russia's state and society. Russia's move towards a harder dictatorship was not preordained by its history. But it was not an unlikely outcome of the post-Soviet transformation.

And certain events did push the country more and more down that path: Boris Yeltsin's violent victory over the parliamentary opposition in 1993; his appointment of Putin as his successor; Russia's wars against Chechnya; the failure of the democratic movement of 2011–13; the constitutional reform of 2020 and Putin's decision to stay on as president. All of these events could have resulted in a different outcome, but they did not. Each step was a step towards dictatorship. And dictatorship within was linked to dreams of past empire abroad. And Ukraine, seen by many in Russia as central to its imperial past, was a logical target for this imperialism. From this perspective, then, Putin's war is also Russia's war—a war to restore empire and with it glory.

CHAPTER 1

UKRAINE: A SHORT HISTORY TO 1991

Precursors

As a political reality, modern Ukraine was born between March 1917, when the Central Rada, the Ukrainian revolutionary government, was formed, and January 1918, when it declared in its Fourth Universal:

> In order for neither the Russian government nor any other to stand in the way of Ukraine establishing the desired peace and lead our country to order, to creative work, and to a consolidation of the revolution we, the Ukrainian Central Rada, announce to all citizens of Ukraine: effective immediately, the Ukrainian People's Republic becomes an independent, free, sovereign state of the Ukrainian people. We want to live in harmony and friendship with all neighbouring states, including Russia, Poland, Austria, Romania, Turkey, and others, but none of them will be allowed to interfere in the life of the Independent Ukrainian Republic. Power in it will belong only to the People of Ukraine, in whose name we, the Ukrainian Central Rada, will govern until the Ukrainian Constituent Assembly convenes as the representative of the working people of peasants, workers and soldiers.[1]

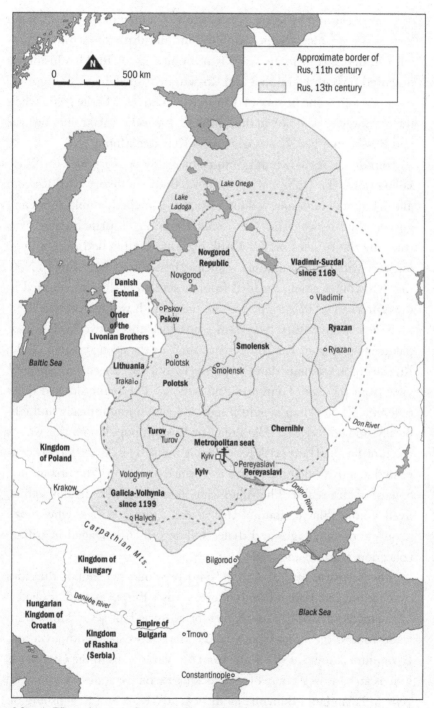

Map 4: The realm of the Rus, eleventh and thirteenth centuries

This declaration was the culmination of a long history of national formation, a process which would continue throughout the twentieth century and in many ways is still ongoing today. This history is obscured by both Ukrainian and Russian myth-making.[2]

Some follow the history of Ukraine back to the Middle Ages, when the first large-scale polity in the lands of what today is Ukraine, Belarus and Russia emerged. It was centred in Kyiv (see Map 4).

Founded in the late ninth century, probably by Norsemen (or 'Rus') sailing down the Dnipro River to Byzantium—a theory both Russian and Ukrainian nationalists do not like, lest somebody thinks they can't govern themselves—this loose confederation of principalities was ruled by the princes of the Rurik dynasty. It stretched over a huge territory with shifting and often unclear boundaries (see Map 4). Note that Moscow, a small, fortified frontier settlement first mentioned in the sources in c.1147, is not even on this map. It was too provincial.[3]

Nineteenth-century historians would call this network of principalities the 'Kievan Rus' or 'Kyivan Rus', as the alleged origin of the Russian or Ukrainian state, respectively. But this was a retrospective view from the age of empires and nations. The reality looked quite different. Rather than a centralised state with a linguistically and ethnically unified 'original' Ukrainian or Russian population, this was 'a chain of fortified outposts', Kyiv among them. They were 'loosely connected in a dynastic union' with the prince of Kyiv as 'the first among equals' of this realm. The ruling elite, descendants of the Norsemen, lived among Slavic, Baltic, Turkic and Finnish tribes, who spoke a variety of languages and dialects. The princes engaged in tribute collection, warfare and trade.[4]

The latter was central both to Kyiv's pre-eminence among the cities of the realm and its wealth and culture: it was 'a European trading center' of the medieval world. Rus stood at the crossroads of several important trade routes: the north–south connection between Scandinavia and Byzantium (known as the 'route from the Varangians to the Greeks') as well as an east–west route of interlocking exchange zones which linked Kyiv to Poland and Bohemia all the way to Mainz and Regensburg on the one side and to Central Asia in the other direction. Via Novgorod, the lands of Rus were also connected to the Baltic trade zone, which 'saw Rusian merchants as far afield as England'.[5]

In an attempt at finding a unifying ideology for the patchwork of peoples and tribes he and his relatives were trying to rule, Prince Volodimer I (Ukrainian: Volodymyr; Russian: Vladimir) of Kyiv shopped around for a religion strong enough to paper over the many divisions of the realm. In a much-loved passage from the Primary Chronicle, the first written source for East Slav history, he invites representatives from all major religions to pitch their wares. Ultimately, he chose Christianity over Islam, because the latter forbade alcohol and, as the chronicle tells us, the Rus liked to drink: 'we cannot exist without it.'[6] In reality, political and dynastic considerations played a larger role in the decision. Rus was integrated through trade and politics with Christian Europe; Christianity had already taken root in the region; and Volodimer desired to marry Anna, sister of Byzantine emperor Basil II. Such a course of action was only possible if 'the barbarian chieftain … would accept Christianity'. Hence he did and thus the Rus adopted Christianity in 988. Given Kyiv's links to Byzantium, the flavour of this Christianity was what would become the eastern or 'Orthodox' branch.[7]

Christianity gave the Rus more than a unifying ideology. The church provided a ready-made hierarchy and an institutional network aside from dynastic family ties. And it gave the Rus a written language, or indeed two: Church Slavonic was based on South Slavic dialects and had been 'devised specifically for the purpose of translating the Scriptures from Greek'. It 'brought a mass of concepts which were alien to the pagans north of the steppes, and it often expressed them in elaborately structured sentences brimming with participles and subordinate clauses'. This was not how ordinary East Slavs spoke, but it was 'probably perceived as a functional variant of the native tongue, at some level accessible, though with an aura of solemnity'. Secular texts, from notes on 'mustard' or 'oil' to law codes, were instead written in the vernacular, using the Cyrillic alphabet introduced by Church Slavonic but reflecting the spoken languages of the Rus realm. There is considerable scholarly debate about whether there was one unified language in the lands of Rus, with a variety of local dialects, or if there had been separate if related (and mutually comprehensible) languages in the first place. What is clear from the surviving sources is that there was significant linguistic variety in the written discourse of different parts of the realm. The peoples of Rus both spoke and wrote in different ways.[8]

These, then, were the three elements which drew the loose federation of Rus principalities into a shared sociocultural orbit: the dynasty of the Rurikids, the religion of Eastern Christianity complete with a church organisation and Church Slavonic, and Cyrillic for secular use in the various vernaculars of the realm. While the languages of the Rus would evolve into three distinct linguistic systems—Ukrainian, Belarusian and Russian—in the centuries to come, Eastern Christianity and the Cyrillic script (with minor variations among the three languages) would form a lasting heritage the Rus bequeathed to today's Ukraine, Belarus and Russia.

Disintegration

The traditional way to tell the story of the Rus is to begin with an initial period of expansion, economic boom and cultural bloom from the 980s to the early twelfth century, followed by internal crisis and civil war: the princes of the realm competed for power over Kyiv or unlinked their own principality altogether. This disintegration was completed by the Mongol invasion of the 1220s and 1230s. More recently, historians have stressed that the period of 'decline' was indeed a continuing expansion of the realm of the Rurikids, with new principalities formed, some rising in status, others declining. As in the earlier period, the various branches of the dynasty vied for power over Kyiv and the period of alleged decline instead 'witnessed the flowering of culture, especially in ambitious building projects'. The story of the 'rise and fall' of Kyiv now appears much more like a later projection of the history of a unified 'state', which did not exist in this form at the time. What existed were changing lands dominated by a dynasty, united by an evolving culture strongly influenced by Orthodox Christianity.[9]

In either case, the Mongol invasion was a rift: there was no continuity of statehood or territory between the Rus federation and any of the states which claimed its legacy later (today's Russia, Belarus and Ukraine all claim Kyivan ancestry but none of them can show continuity of governance or polity). Kyiv was sacked by the invaders. Most of the lands of Rus were integrated into the Mongol empire and the local princes became tax collectors.

Two new political centres emerged under Mongol domination: in the north-east was Vladimir-Suzdal in what today is Russia, and in the south-west was Galicia-Volhynia in what today is Ukraine. They can serve as convenient starting points for a Ukrainian and a Russian historical narrative: both inherited their dynasties, their law and literary traditions, and their religion from the pre-Mongol realm of the Rus. They also each received their own church as the once united metropolitanate of the Rus was divided into two: one for Vladimir-Suzdal and one for Galicia-Volhynia. After its move to Moscow, the former eventually became autocephalous in 1589 (that is, had its own patriarch), while the latter remained accountable to the patriarch of Constantinople. As a result of these developments, 'the political and ecclesiastical unity of the Kyiv-centred Rus' Land had disintegrated'.[10]

However, Galicia-Volhynia and Vladimir-Suzdal were not the only pre-eminent principalities in the old Rus lands. A third centre, without a twentieth-century nation-state claiming its heritage, escaped direct submission to the Mongols: Novgorod in the north, located west of Vladimir-Suzdal. Its annexation by its aggressive Moscow neighbour would play an important role in the history of Muscovy, as we shall see in Chapter 2. Novgorod's fate also points to a serious problem with a narrative of continuity, be it Ukrainian or Russian: neither Vladimir-Suzdal nor Galicia-Volhynia survived. Its ruling house extinct, Galicia-Volhynia would, in the second half of the fourteenth century, split. Galicia and western Podolia would be swallowed up by Poland, and Volhynia by the Grand Duchy of Lithuania. Meanwhile, the first century of Mongol rule over the lands of the Rus saw not only the separation of the north-east from the south-west (or 'Russia' from 'Ukraine') but also the fragmentation of Vladimir-Suzdal 'into numerous, smaller principalities'. Moscow was one of these. Its rise, discussed in Chapter 2, was yet another discontinuity in the history of the Rus.[11]

Meanwhile, the Grand Duchy of Lithuania as well as Poland took control of the west. If one wanted to play the game of historical continuities with 'Kyivan Rus', so popular in the national historiographies of both Russia and Ukraine, Lithuania would be a good candidate. Not only did it acquire Kyiv in 1362, in contrast to Poland, Lithuania also preserved 'the local elites' political influence, social status, and cultural traditions'. The Lithuanian rulers 'went native', married into Rus families, 'gladly accepting Orthodoxy and Slavic Christian names' along with the law code and chancery language of Galicia-Volhynia (written in Cyrillic). As a result, 'the grand duchy effectively became an heir' to medieval Rus 'in every respect but dynastic continuity'.[12]

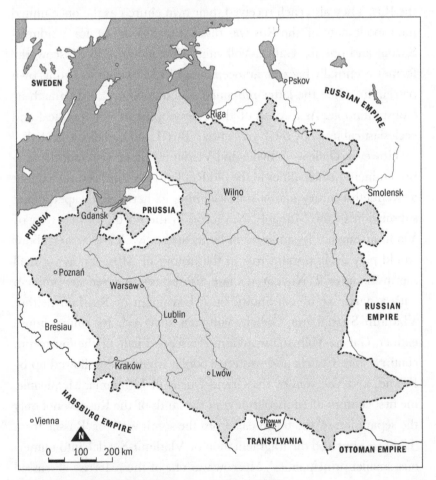

Map 5: The Polish-Lithuanian Commonwealth in 1772

Cultural Separation

This continuity did not last. Between the late fourteenth and late six-teenth centuries, the polity which ruled over the south-western Rus changed dramatically, culminating in 1569 in the Union of Lublin, which united Lithuania and Poland into the Polish-Lithuanian Commonwealth. This was yet another discontinuity: the Union of Lublin redrew the borders between the two member societies. One part of the western Rus thus joined Poland, the rest Lithuania—a borderline which corresponds roughly to today's demarcation between Ukraine (Polish) and Belarus (Lithuanian). What would become Ukraine then went from essentially taking over Lithuania's political culture to being subsumed into a Polish state.

Paradoxically, this integration into Poland enhanced rather than limited the power of the Rus princes within the Polish lands, as they received the privileges of the Polish nobility. Searching for an ideological underpinning of their new powers, the Orthodox rulers looked to the past—to Kyiv and Galicia-Volhynia. 'For all their attention to the past,' writes Serhii Plokhy in his masterful history of Ukraine, 'they were actually creating something new'—an imagined polity which aligned the political space created by the Union of Lublin with the culture and history of Rus. 'Their invention would eventually become "Ukraine".'[13]

That it did so was a result of long-term historical changes during the 300 years the south-western Rus remained first under Lithuanian then Polish rule (see Map 5). These three centuries separated the cul-ture and politics of the south-western Rus from that of Muscovy further east. Throughout the period from the fourteenth through the sixteenth centuries, for example, the cities and towns of Polish Rus acquired the rights of self-government, patterned on German examples; and the local elites (including, as we shall see, the Cossacks) got used to the political rights and freedoms of the Polish nobility—traditions absent further east.

In the late sixteenth and seventeenth centuries, other far-reaching cultural changes occurred. The Orthodox Church in the Polish lands was exposed to the influences of the Reformation and Counter-Reformation. They left their mark in the creation, at the Union of

Brest in 1596, of the Uniate Church (today known in Ukraine as the Ukrainian Greek Catholic Church), a 'hybrid church that combines elements of Eastern and Western Christianity'. They also led to the reform, along Catholic models, of the Orthodox Church itself. Once the 'texts, practices, and ideas' of this westernised, Kyiv-based orthodoxy were exported to Muscovy later in the seventeenth century, they, in turn, caused a split in the Russian church between the Kyiv-inspired modernisers and the 'Old Believers'—an important moment of entanglement of Ukrainian and Russian political and cultural histories.[14]

What would become Ukraine, then, are the lands and peoples of the medieval realm of the Rus, who subsequently lived under Polish influence and domination until the middle of the seventeenth century. 'It was this period,' write the authors of a Ukrainian grammar, 'that resulted in the formation of a Ukrainian language essentially as we know it today'—an evolution of East Slavonic dialects under the influence 'of thousands of Polish lexical items'.[15] By 1700, writes a cultural historian, 'a distinct linguistic, cultural, and … political entity' had thus emerged in the territory which today is Ukraine.[16] Only in 1654, in the Treaty of Pereiaslav, were large numbers of these Ukrainian speakers incorporated into the growing Muscovite state, now called the Tsardom of Russia—the precursor of the Russian Empire (from 1721).

The Formation of Ukraine

The integration into Russia in 1654 was most likely a great historical misunderstanding. The contracting parties were Russia and an independent Cossack state, the Hetmanate, led by Bohdan Khmelnytsky (b. 1595, ruled 1648–57). He had rebelled against Polish rule in an anti-urban, anti-Polish, anti-Jewish and anti-Catholic, pro-Orthodox bloodbath starting in 1648. The Cossacks were seeking military support against the commonwealth and thought of this treaty as 'a contract with binding obligations on both sides', while the tsar's emissaries insisted it was a subjugation to autocratic rule.[17] The Cossacks saw the treaty as 'a kind of military convention' which retained the Hetmanate's independence; Moscow, by contrast, saw it as the first step to integration into its own empire.[18] More fighting and switching of sides followed until, in the Truce of Andrusovo (1667), the Hetmanate was divided along the Dnipro River: the lands to the east ('left bank') went to Russia, and those to the west ('right bank') were returned to Poland where they remained until the end of the eighteenth century. This division established a boundary still relevant today: between left-bank and right-bank Ukraine.

In the standard Ukrainian national narrative, the 400 years between the Mongol invasion and Russia's annexation of some of the Cossack lands are crucial. The decline of Kyivan Rus, the Mongol invasion and the existence of the southern lands under the Polish-Lithuanian Commonwealth are stressed as having a deep effect on the people living there. They transformed from Rus into Ukrainians—a more European and more democratically minded East Slavic people than their brethren under the iron fist of the Muscovite princes and later tsars further east. As the father of modern Ukrainian historiography Mykhailo Hrushevsky argued in a short history of his country, published in exile in 1920: 'The modern Ukrainian people ... emerged, through a continuous evolution.'[19] This social and cultural process was advanced enough by the seventeenth century that 'the Ukrainian nationality was decidedly manifest'.[20] What once had been the East Slavic peoples of the Rurikid realm had now become 'the three nationalities of the East Slavs'—Ukrainians, Belarusians and Russians—and 'even their living together under the same sceptre' later in history would not 'erase this separation'.[21]

Whether we can follow a Ukrainian identity as far back as Hrushevsky did is a matter of historical debate. One way to approach this question is to investigate the history of the term 'Ukraine'. It appeared first in sources in the twelfth and thirteenth centuries (the first documented use dates from 1187) to describe borderlands of the Rus, and continued to be in use in Lithuania and later Poland, albeit referring to different (and evolving) geographical locations. By the seventeenth century, it described the area ruled over by the Cossack Hetmanate. The term 'Ukrainian' also began to describe the people living within the Hetmanate and to replace the older term 'Rus', which had been circulating since Kyivan times (where it first described the Viking conquerors, then their retinue, and eventually the lands and peoples they ruled). This use of 'Ukraine' and the beginning of the linguistic shift from 'Rus' to 'Ukrainian' is one of the arguments for seeing the Hetmanate as a 'Ukrainian' rather than a 'Cossack' state. After Andrusovo, 'Ukraine' was also circulating in the Polish-Lithuanian Commonwealth, where it referred to the palatinates along the Dnipro's right bank, which once had been part of the Hetmanate as well. The notion that both sides of the Dnipro were 'Ukraine' and that 'Ukraine' was a Cossack fatherland animated the Cossack uprising, led by Hetman Ivan Mazepa (1639–1709, ruled 1687–1708). 'Ukraine' was one of the names used to describe this state and it appears twice in the Constitution of Pylyp Orlyk (1710), which attempted to regulate the powers of the Hetman and Cossack parliament within the Cossack state in exile after Mazepa's death. Thus, there certainly was a 'Ukraine' (or, indeed, several 'Ukraines') between the twelfth and seventeenth centuries, but people did not always agree where it was located and who belonged to it.[22]

When did the descendants of the Rus in any of these 'Ukraines' begin to think of themselves as 'Ukrainians'? This is a difficult question to answer, in particular as far as the peasant majority is concerned. They surely knew 'that they were not Jews, not Muslims, not Catholics'. They also knew that they were Orthodox, like their Muscovite brethren further east, or Uniates, unlike the Muscovites. And they knew that they were not 'Muscovites' (*moskali*) in the first place. Whether they thought that they were part of one unified 'Ukrainian' people is a different matter. 'Ukrainian' began to spread as a term of self-identification only in the nineteenth and twentieth centuries, at first among educated city dwellers, later among the rural population as well. By the revolutionary year of 1917, however, the vast majority of rural Ukrainians voted for distinctly Ukrainian parties, indicating a strong sense of national identification, alongside social, regional and other politically significant identities. Even then, the notion of being Ukrainian did not necessarily replace other forms of self-understanding, such as 'Orthodox', 'local' or 'peasant'.[23]

Uncontroversial is the assertion that 400 years is a long time. Cultural, linguistic and political differences between the descendants of the south-western Rus and the Muscovites existed as a result of this long separation. The following 300 years under Russian dominance also left their imprint on the Ukrainian language and identity. But they impacted on a linguistic and cultural system already differentiated from Russian. 'Judging by written poetic records,' notes one specialist, 'the vernacular spoken in the last quarter of the sixteenth century ... was practically identical in form with the Ukrainian spoken today.'[24] From the late eighteenth century through the nineteenth century, these differences could be distilled into a sense of Ukrainian national identity.

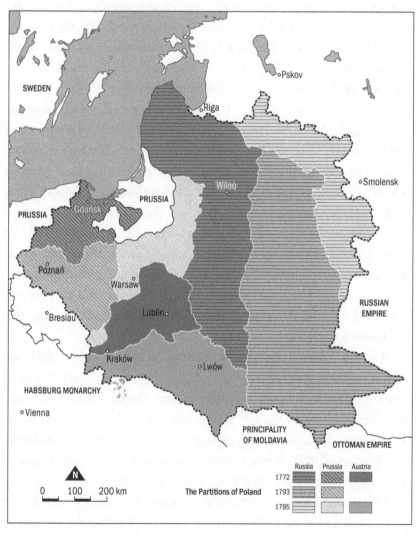

Map 6: Partitions of Poland

Initially, much of this work was done by intellectuals hailing from the former Hetmanate, then part of Russia. It was 'the only region of nineteenth-century Ukraine where the landowning elites shared the culture of the local population', a circumstance which helps to explain why the Ukrainian national movement emanated from here. The Hetmanate also 'provided a key historical myth, a cultural tradition, and a language as building blocks of the modern Ukrainian nation'. Like elsewhere, then, one particular dialect—here, the one from the Poltava region— was elevated, through the work of literati and grammarians, to become the literary language of Ukrainians (just as in Germany, for example, the dialect of Martin Luther's Leipzig home, rather than the poetic language of, say, the Allgäu, became 'German'). Finally, the Hetmanate also supplied the name for the new nation: Ukraine.[25]

The intellectuals from the Hetmanate were soon joined by others from Galicia, which had become part of Austria after the partitions of Poland had replaced the Russia–Poland border with the Russia–Austria border as the main political division within Ukraine (see Map 6). Ukraine's national awakening was thus trans-imperial: both ideas and people moved between the empires. Galicia became particularly important, as the Austro-Hungarian government, in an attempt to play one minority against others, allowed publications in Ukrainian. In the Russian Empire, almost all publication in this language was prohibited in 1863 and, with additional restrictions, in 1876. Galicia now became a hotbed for Ukrainian publications, which then could be smuggled back across the border.

The Ukrainian national movement of the nineteenth century was transnational in another sense as well: it was part of a larger European intellectual fashion of nation-making, kicked off by the French Revolution and fuelled by the aesthetics of romanticism. Sicilians, Sardinians and Piedmontese began to think of themselves as Italians, and an Italian state was formed in 1861. Further north, Austrians, Bavarians and Prussians began inventing a German nation, which only came into being in 1871, and then only in part of what was seen as the German lands by the intellectual dreamers, many of whom were, like Hrushevsky, historians.

All of these new nations invented primordial roots in states and traditions of earlier times, when the unchanging Italian, German or French
nation was allegedly born, just as Hrushevsky did for the Ukrainians.
All of them were wrong, of course. While there always was some kind
of ethnic belonging, these ethnicities did not conform to the cultural
forms, let alone have the political aspirations, of the modern nations as
they were imagined in the nineteenth century: as culturally homogenous
communities of equals with a right to political self-determination. First-
year undergraduate students sometimes mistake the notion that nations
are 'constructed' to mean that they are unreal—which then makes the
nationalist fervour with which many of these constructed people went
to war in 1914 rather hard to explain. That something has a history
(that is, is 'constructed'), it turns out, does not make it imaginary. It just
makes it historically contingent and subject to change.

The Ukrainian Revolution

The revolution of 1905 was a major event in this history of an evolving Ukrainian nation. This was not just a social and political revolution
in Russia but also a 'springtime of the peoples' in the multinational
Romanov Empire. And it gave the growing national movement
renewed impetus, not least as the ban on publications in Ukrainian
was lifted. By the time the empire collapsed under the weight of World
War I and its own incompetence, there were enough people in Kyiv
who thought of themselves as Ukrainians that they could unleash not
a Russian but a Ukrainian revolution.[26]

This revolution was not, initially, anti-Russian. At first, Kyiv was in
lockstep with Petrograd, where the tsar had just been toppled. Like the
Russian liberals who came to power in early 1917, Ukraine's revolutionaries, led by Hrushevsky, the historian we've already encountered,
were intent on keeping the empire together in a new, democratic
polity. What the Central Rada, formed in early March 1917 in reaction to the events in Petrograd, asked in its First Universal (June 1917)
was not independence but autonomy within a democratic, federal
Russia—a reformed empire. This autonomous government, which

combined liberal nationalism with socialist ideas, 'claimed jurisdiction over a good part of today's Ukraine', essentially creating Ukraine as a political reality. Unable to stop this usurpation of power, the Russian Provisional Government in Petrograd soon recognised the Rada as 'the regional government of Ukraine'.[27]

Not even the October coup in Russia, which replaced the Provisional Government in Petrograd with a Bolshevik dictatorship, dampened the determination of Kyiv's leaders to remain in the Russian orbit. The Third Universal did proclaim the Ukrainian People's Republic but insisted that it was not 'separating from the Russian Republic' and was indeed 'maintaining its unity'.[28] Only when direct confrontation with Bolshevik Petrograd had become the order of the day, with Bolshevik troops on Ukrainian soil marching on Kyiv, did the Rada finally proclaim, in the Fourth Universal, an independent Ukrainian state. This moment, not medieval Kyiv or the early modern Cossack state, is the real origin of modern Ukraine as a nation-state.

In a diplomatic emergency measure, this new state then made peace with Germany in the First Treaty of Brest-Litovsk (9 February 1918) before Bolshevik Russia could do the same. Facing German troops on Ukrainian soil, Lenin's fledgling state had to accept, in the Second Treaty of Brest-Litovsk, that Ukraine was an independent state. This state did not encompass all lands the nationalists imagined were theirs—the Ukrainian regions of Austro-Hungary, an ally of Germany, were excluded, as was Crimea. Moreover, the young nation was subjected to German occupation, a puppet regime under 'Hetman' Pavlo Skoropadsky (1873–1945, ruled 1918), fairly severe repression, and forced extraction of grain to feed hungry Germans suffering from the naval blockade of their country.[29]

While Skoropadsky came into power through a German-backed coup, relied on German bayonets to secure his dictatorial power, and collaborated with the occupiers in grain extractions, his regime also had a positive impact on Ukraine's state- and nation-building. In particular, he founded two universities as well as the Academy of Sciences. He was a more diligent institution builder and took more care in establishing a functioning administration than the intellectuals who had led the Rada.

Wars of the Romanov Succession, 1917–21

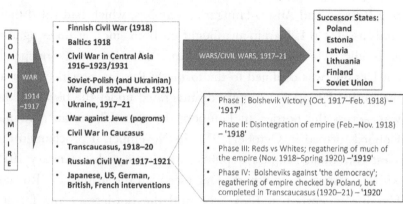

Figure 1: The 'Russian Civil War' as part of the wars of the Romanov succession

These legacies were passed on to his successors after they had removed him from power once the Germans left at the end of the year.[30]

In November 1918, then, the Germans were defeated at the Western Front and they began pulling out of Ukraine. Power in Kyiv passed from the hands of Skoropadsky back to the Ukrainian People's Republic, now ruled by a provisional government, the Directorate. Ukraine now became embroiled in the wars of the Romanov succession, a bloodbath readers might know under a somewhat misleading term: 'the Russian Civil War'. This moniker is wrong-headed because this civil war entailed Polish, Finnish, Ukrainian, Estonian and Central Asian elements (see Figure 1), and it was fought not only on internal fronts but also on external borders between states or proto-states. It thus combined a conglomeration of civil wars with interstate warfare between a bewildering number of new polities. Ukraine and Bolshevik Russia were by no means the only new political entities which initially emerged from the breakdown of the Romanov Empire in 1917–18. By the middle of 1918, no fewer than thirty governments were in existence on the territory of the shattered Russian Empire. Soon, they started fighting each other as well as parts of their respective populations. In Ukraine, this period is known as 'the liberation struggle' or the 'wars of independence'. [31]

Ukraine became a major front line in these complex struggles—and those of the neighbouring and equally crumbling empire. Already during the world war, Ukrainians had been caught between the warring Russian and Austro-Hungarian empires, which had ruled their lands as of 1914. Ukrainians fought on both sides, at times against each other. This split was continued in 1918, when newly independent Ukraine was confined to the formerly Russian provinces. But as the Austro-Hungarian Empire disintegrated under the blows of the war, across the border, in Lemberg (Lviv), a Ukrainian National Council formed in October 1918. In November, it proclaimed the West Ukrainian People's Republic, which merged in January 1919 with its eastern counterpart. This extended the history of 'Russian Ukraine'—centred in Kyiv—'beyond the borders of the former Russian empire' and 'into the world of the east-central European wars of imperial succession'.[32]

By now, these were in full swing, as were the wars of the Romanov succession. In this environment, the united Ukrainian state lived on borrowed time. Weakened by social revolution and internal rebellions, and left with barely an army after the recruits melted away to participate in revolutionary land distribution in the villages, the new state was eliminated and its lands divided, in 1921, between two of the more successful successor states of the Romanov Empire: Poland and Bolshevik Russia.[33]

The victory of the Russian and Polish revolutions over Ukraine's had far-reaching consequences for the political history of Central and Eastern Europe, as historian Mark von Hagen wrote in 2017: 'The Bolshevik revolution and its rapid evolution toward single-party dictatorship quite consciously repudiated the Central European Social-Democratic outcome of the revolution, but the Ukrainian revolutions, both in Kyiv and in Lviv, aspired to the more western alternative.'[34] Meanwhile, Poland, confronted with the threat of Bolshevik and then Stalinist Russia, moved further and further to the right. It never became 'fascist', as its Bolshevik opponents claimed, but by the 1930s it was a dictatorship of the right.[35] Across the border, the Bolsheviks resurrected a severely repressive empire which was in many ways a transfiguration of the old Russian Empire of the Romanovs, albeit one devoid of tsars, landlords or capitalists. Their main opponents in the interwar years, in

Ukraine as elsewhere, came from the ranks of ultranationalists, either inspired by fascism or outright fascists. In Ukraine, these challengers converged in the Organization of Ukrainian Nationalists (OUN), a party founded in Galicia (still Polish) in 1929 and imported into the Soviet Union along with the rest of eastern Poland in the opening stages of World War II.

Soviet Ukraine: The Catastrophic Years

Ukraine's democratic revolution was thus quashed by the emerging red empire and the resurrected Polish state. However, Ukraine continued to exist as an organised polity—an important continuity from 1917 through 1991. The Ukrainians had fought so hard, and their national consciousness seemed so strong, that Lenin—a Marxist enemy of nationalism but also a pragmatic politician able to see political realities—insisted it be integrated as a national unit: the Ukrainian Soviet Socialist Republic. This model of a nominally independent national territory was then applied to other non-Russian regions of the growing Soviet empire.[36]

This new empire of nations was a contradictory structure. On the one hand, it had regathered much of the lands of the Romanovs under the red flag and thus seemed to be a successor of the old empire. On the other hand, its leaders tried to avoid the appearance of 'Great Russian chauvinism' in a state dominated by Russians and Russian speakers. Two historians summarise the confusing situation as follows: 'The language of national liberation and anti-imperialism remained a potent discursive cloak under which an empire of subordinated nations was gradually built.' That this 'self-denying empire' remained ideologically devoted to anti-imperialism and decolonisation would lead to endless squabbles among historians about whether it was, indeed, an empire.[37]

The role of the imperial breakdown of World War I and the following wars of the Romanov succession is crucial for understanding the reasons for the establishment of the Ukrainian SSR. Developments in this period link the national movement of the nineteenth century with the first Ukrainian state of 1917–20, which in turn inspired the creation of the Ukrainian republic within the Soviet Union. The latter, then, became

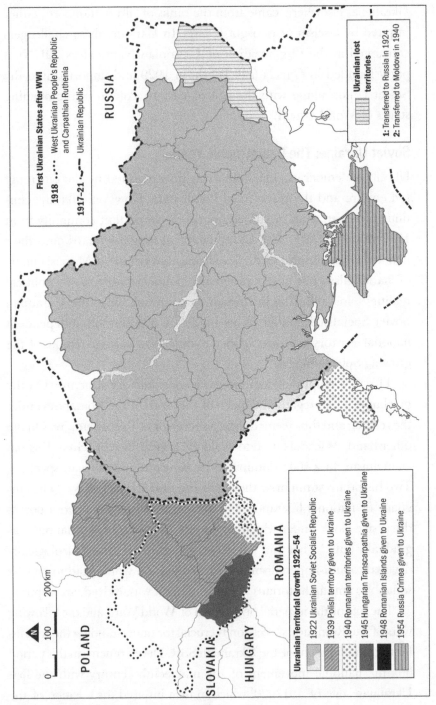

Map 7: Territorial evolution of Soviet Ukraine

the entity which would emerge as an independent state from the rubble of the Soviet Union in 1991. Of course, they were not all the same, and what it meant to be Ukrainian continued to change over time. Ukraine, like all other nation-states, has a history. That does not mean that it is an artificial creation, as Vladimir Putin wants us to believe. It was the result of a historical process, not the wilful invention of the Bolsheviks.[38]

The Ukrainian Republic, as it formed in 1917–20 and was then incorporated into the Soviet Union in 1922, was not territorially identical with today's Ukraine. Over the seven long decades of Soviet power, a variety of border changes took place. Some territories were transferred to Russia in 1924 and to Moldova in 1940. In the west, the annexation of parts of eastern Poland, Romania and Czechoslovakia during World War II moved the territory further west. And in the south, Crimea was transferred from the Russian Republic in 1954. It was this Ukraine which became independent in 1991 (see Map 7).

When Russia illegally occupied Crimea in 2014, its propagandists claimed that it had 'always been Russian' until Nikita Khrushchev, unfairly, gave it away. This is a historical nonsense. Nothing was 'always' Russian except maybe the Moscow region. Conquered by Kyiv's princes in the tenth century, in the thirteenth to fifteenth centuries the peninsula was part of the Mongol's Golden Horde before becoming a virtually independent polity of the Crimean Tatars—the Crimean Khanate, an Ottoman vassal. It was conquered by Russia even later than Ukraine: in 1783. Less than a century and a half later, it first became a revolutionary People's Republic of the Crimean Tatars (in late 1917), then a stronghold of anti-Bolshevik Russian forces during the wars of the Romanov succession. The Bolsheviks occupied it in 1920, as part of their generalised reconquest of much of the Romanov lands. In 1954, it then became Ukrainian, which it remained until the Russian invasion of 2014.

From the 1920s onwards, then, the history of Ukrainian statehood merged with the history of the Soviet Union. The 1920s saw the promotion of Ukrainian cadres, Ukrainian culture, Ukrainian language and a Ukrainian intelligentsia. This was part of the Leninist project of disarming nationalism all over the red empire by granting a national form, while the content—power—was to be Soviet. This project was constantly fraught with danger, as form and content could not always be separated, a problem which would become acute once the suspicious Stalin had won the succession struggle after Lenin's death in 1924. Under Stalin, who had secured his power by 1928, the centre in Moscow increasingly perceived Ukrainian national cadres as a threat—as 'bourgeois nationalists' rather than Soviet Ukrainians.[39]

Ominous signs began to appear in the second half of the 1920s with the increasing repression of and discrimination against the Ukrainian Autocephalous Orthodox Church, independent from Moscow since its foundation in 1921. It was dissolved in 1930 and many of its clergy arrested. While this was part of the generally Soviet anti-religious drive of these years (Moscow-loyal Orthodox clergy were also repressed, as were Jewish religious leaders), it set the scene for a broader onslaught on Ukrainian intellectuals as part of the 'cultural revolution' of the early Stalin years: an attack on intellectuals trained under the old regime, who could not be trusted. In Ukraine, this class war had a distinctly national inflection. It began earlier here than elsewhere, with the 1927 dismissal of the critic of Moscow centralism, Ukraine's commissar for education, Oleksandr Shumsky. His 'nationalist bias' was blown up by Moscow into a fully-fledged ideological deviation from the Bolshevik party line, which allegedly suffused Ukrainian party cadres: 'Shumskysm'.[40]

Stalin's suspicions were further fuelled by the fact that in Ukraine, resistance against his signature policy of collectivisation was particularly fierce in the early 1930s. It 'reminded the Soviet leadership of the civil and national wars' after 1917, the wars of the Romanov succession, writes George Liber, 'and convinced them that the party had to introduce extraordinary measures to break the peasants, who in Stalin's mind waged a "war by starvation" against Soviet power'. Thus, he instrumentalised the famine of 1932–33 in order to break this resistance—among the reasons why the famine was worse only in Kazakhstan.[41]

By the mid-1930s the Ukrainian countryside was licking its wounds, traumatised by the aftermath of the famine, which continued to structure everyday life long after starvation had ended. Families had lost sons, daughters, fathers and mothers, and sometimes broke apart due to the strains imposed by starvation, death and the struggle for survival. Meanwhile, arrests of participants in imaginary Ukrainian opposition groups continued in the background. In 1935, there were 24 934 arrests in Soviet Ukraine, and in 1936 there were 15 718. These were not of the level of the Great Terror, when 159 573 arrests were recorded in 1937 and 108 006 in 1938, but still, these were not quiet years. In 1934, in an attempt to scapegoat 'national communists', the Kremlin organised show trials, including of Andrii Richytsky, a former member of the Central Committee of the Ukrainian Bolshevik Party, who had faithfully implemented Moscow's policies, deepening the famine. Now, he was accused of 'Ukrainian nationalism' and sentenced to death in a public trial. In addition to arrests, deportations engulfed national minorities. In 1934 and 1935, well over 50 000 Soviet Poles and Germans were either arrested in Ukraine or deported within or from the republic.[42]

The Great Terror was devastating everywhere in the Soviet Union, and Ukraine was no exception. The years 1937 and 1938 saw in excess of 122 000 executions in Soviet Ukraine. They witnessed the destruction of nearly the entire political elite of the republic. Stalin's executioners 'liquidated the overwhelming majority of the leaders' of the Communist Party of Ukraine. 'The Central Committee could not hold meetings because it lacked the required quorum.' But, as elsewhere, the bloodletting of these terrible years was by no means restricted to the communist elite. On the contrary, the terror really became 'great' only with the so-called 'kulak operation' of 1937–38, which saw close to 70 000 executions of ordinary people in Ukraine.[43]

Soon after this mass murder ended, Ukraine became the tip of the spear of 'revolution from abroad'—the acquisition of Polish territories and their forceful sovietisation. After the division of Ukraine between Poland and Russia in 1921, the largest part of the country had fallen to the Bolsheviks. But western Volhynia and Galicia were now Polish (and other Ukrainian lands were included in Romania and Czechoslovakia). The Polish state became increasingly discriminatory vis-a-vis both Ukrainians and Jews in its eastern borderlands. This unfriendly treatment gave Stalin a ready-made excuse for his invasion of Poland on 17 September 1939 (a bit over two weeks after the Germans had marched in from the west). The Red Army, Soviet propaganda claimed, was 'liberating' its Ukrainian brethren from the Polish lords. In reality, of course, Stalin was conquering lands for military reasons. And he acquired not just fraternal peoples but also the new and bitter enemies of the OUN.[44]

While in 1939 life thus began to normalise somewhat in the Russian heartland of the Soviet Union, Stalinist terror focused on these new, formerly Polish, territories. In the period between the arrival of Soviet troops in Poland and the German attack on the Soviets in June 1941, 52 per cent of all arrests in the Soviet Union took place in what was now western Ukraine and western Belarus: over 107 000 people. Their families were deported, along with an array of others considered 'potentially dangerous' and 'class enemies', altogether over 330 000 people.[45]

And, of course, the defensive war against Germany of 1941–45 had its specific inflection in Ukraine: while only parts of Russia were occupied by the German Nazis, all of Ukraine was. War-related destruction, German armies living off the land and economic exploitation of the occupied territories were only the tip of an iceberg of suffering. Ethnic cleansing (of Poles by Ukrainian nationalists, of Ukrainians by Poles), the Nazi genocide of the Jews (implemented with the assistance of Ukrainian collaborators), and a multilevel civil war behind the front lines between German counterinsurgency troops (often staffed by Russian, Cossack or Ukrainian collaborators), the nationalist insurgents of the OUN, the Polish Home Army, a few Jewish resistance groups, Soviet special forces and Soviet partisans, devastated Ukraine to an extent historians are only beginning to understand.[46]

To render this war as 'Russia's war' is a serious misrepresentation. It is true that Russians bore the brunt of the fighting. They were over-represented among Soviet military losses. However, with 36 per cent of civilian losses, Ukrainians (who had made up around 18 per cent of the 1941 population) 'suffered disproportionately'. And while the war ended in Soviet Russia in 1945, it continued in Ukraine (as in the Baltics) as a fierce counterinsurgency campaign, entangled with collectivisation and mass deportations. The earliest end date of the war in the western borderlands is 1949.[47]

Soviet Ukraine after Stalin

The entire period from 1927 through 1949, then, was a relentless onslaught of revolution from above, famine, terror, repression, arrest, deportation, war and genocide. The impact of these two decades of relentless violence and traumatisation cannot be overstated.[48]

It would be wrong, however, to stop the history of Soviet Ukraine here, or to construct a straight line from this catastrophic period to the breakdown of the Soviet empire and the re-establishment of Ukrainian statehood. The decades after Stalin's death in fact saw the integration of Ukraine further and further into the Soviet whole. We might remember here that Khrushchev, first secretary of the Communist Party of the Soviet Union from 1953 to 1964, promoted Ukrainian cadres as part of cementing his own power base. We might also remember that, in 1954, he 'gifted' Crimea to Ukraine, to the continuing annoyance of Russian nationalists, who took it back in 2014 by force of arms. Under Khrushchev, as Plokhy writes, Ukraine rose 'to honorary second place in the hierarchy of Soviet republics and nationalities'. Khrushchev 'relied heavily on his Ukrainian clients to gain and strengthen his position in Moscow'.[49]

At the same time, the policies of Russification, initiated under Stalin, were deepened under Khrushchev, when a 'rapid Russification of the Soviet educational system' took place.[50] This trend accelerated under Khrushchev's successor, Leonid Brezhnev (in power from 1964 to his death in 1982), when 'the concept of the Soviet nation' became the 'centrepiece' of nationality policy, and cultural Russification became 'official policy'.[51] As a result, the share of Ukrainians who thought of Russian as their mother tongue rose from 6 to 16 per cent between 1959 and 1989. By the end of the Soviet experience, the formation of 'a big Russian nation out of the Eastern Slavs' was 'clearly under way'.[52]

And when the prospect of national independence became more and more thinkable after the breakdown of the wider Soviet empire in 1989, the majority of residents of Ukraine wanted to stay Soviet, albeit in a more federalist and democratic union. We might hear echoes here of the first, second and third universals of 1917, which claimed Ukrainian nationhood, democracy *and* unity with Russia.

Again, it was Russia that pushed away Ukraine, not the other way round. In the March 1991 referendum, 71 per cent of respondents in Ukraine wanted to remain in the USSR, although as a sovereign part of it. It was only after the failed coup in Moscow later in the year that public opinion shifted decisively: if the choice was between hardliner repression and independence, Ukrainians preferred the latter. And, of course, independence was attractive to the political elite of the country, who could now run their own affairs rather than play second fiddle to Moscow. Hence, on 24 August, the Ukrainian Parliament declared independence; on 2 December this declaration was approved in a referendum by over 90 per cent of the votes cast.[53]

We should not read the current rift between Ukraine and Russia backwards into history. Instead, we should remember that the most important reason for the fall of the Soviet Union was not a rebellion of the non-Russian republics, but the fact that Russia had, for a moment, abandoned the Soviet imperial project: it was Russian president Boris Yeltsin who put his cards on a Russian national state rather than competing for rule over the Soviet Union. Hence, the Soviet Union imploded at the end of 1991. It has been in the three decades since then that Russia and Ukraine have drifted apart. We will explore this process in later chapters. But first we need to have a closer look at Russia's history.

CHAPTER 2

RUSSIA: A SHORT HISTORY TO 1991

The Rise of Muscovy

In 1300, Moscow was a provincial outpost of the disintegrated principality of Vladimir-Suzdal, its prince serving as a tax collector to the Mongol overlords. From the 1330s, it became a new centre of gravity in the north-east of the old realm of the Rurikids. This rise to predominance was aided by the move of the northern metropolitanate of the Orthodox Church from Vladimir to Moscow in 1325. By the 1470s, the principality had challenged the Mongols under whose suzerainty it had become dominant in the region. Ivan III (b. 1440, ruled 1462–1505) required an ideological foundation for his conquests of neighbouring polities. He found it in the claim that what he was doing was not military expansion but simply the regathering of the land of the Rus; that is, a resurrection of the Rus federation, but as a much more tightly integrated state.[1]

While the claim to the succession to the Rus was ideological, the Moscow princes did benefit from the civilisational achievements of the Rus. Literacy (of a few) and Orthodox Christianity were among the cultural legacies left to Moscow as much as to the peoples of the lands under Polish and Lithuanian rule which would become Ukraine and Belarus. Architecture, 'the fortified kremlins, domed churches, and bell

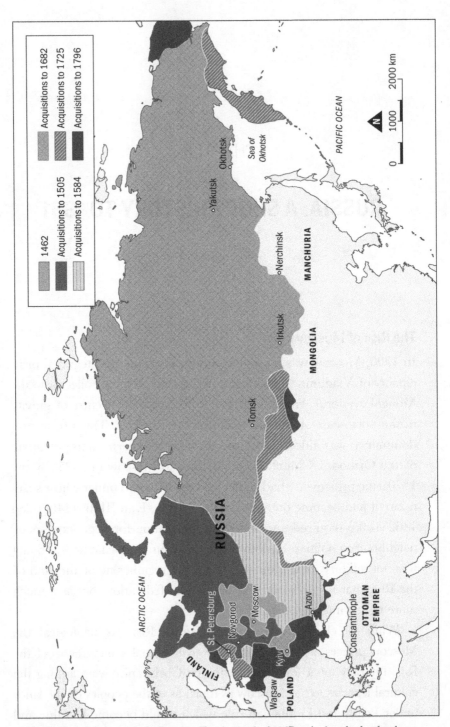

Map 8: From Muscovy to the Russian Empire: gathering 'Russian' and other lands

towers', as well as law codes and chronicles left over from the times of the Rus federation and copied in the new Muscovite environment, were other 'markers of continuity'. And, until the dynastic crisis of the Time of Troubles (1598–1613), the rulers of Moscow came from the old Rurik dynasty which collectively had ruled over the realm of the Rus.[2]

The 'gathering of the Russian lands' and its extension into the building of the empire was a violent process (see Map 8). Between the 1470s and the early nineteenth century, Moscovy-Russia was nearly constantly at war. Novgorod, the third major successor besides Vladimir-Suzdal and Galicia-Volhynia, was defeated in 1471 and annexed in 1478. In 1480, the 'Mongol yoke' came to an end with the 'standing at the Ugra river', more a facing off between the Muscovites and their former masters than a battle. Five years later, Tver was captured. The fall of Kazan, one of the successors of the now fractured Mongol Empire, in 1552 marked the moment when Muscovy moved into non-European territory. This annexation opened the path to Siberia, which would be conquered between 1580 and 1762, adding more non-Slavic peoples to Russia's realm. The Khanate of Astrakhan was conquered in 1556 and the Crimean Khanate—one of the successors of the old Mongol overlords—was defeated in 1572, after its troops had sacked Moscow the year before. It became a vassal of Moscow in 1774 and was fully annexed in 1783. From the eighteenth century onwards, Russia began to encroach on Central Asia and the Caucasus as well, regions it would incorporate in the nineteenth century.

While eying the vast expanses of the east and the south, Moscow had to contend with competition from the west and the north. It fought a series of wars against Lithuania (1492–94, 1500–03, 1507–08, 1512–22, 1534–37), Sweden (1495–97, 1554–57, 1590–95), a coalition of Poland-Lithuania, Sweden, Denmark-Norway and the Livonian Confederation in the Livonian War of 1558–83, as well as a changing constellation of Sweden, Poland-Lithuania and others in the Northern Wars of 1654–67, 1656–58 and 1700–21. Recurrent internal rebellions added to the bloodshed—of Bashkirs, of Cossacks, of peasants.

How terribly things could go when Russia was weak was driven home in 1610, when, during the Time of Troubles, Poland-Lithuania drove deep into Russia, occupying Moscow itself. Eventually, however, Moscow established itself as the ruler not only of the north (where it cemented its power with the building of St Petersburg in the early eighteenth century and the acquisition of Finland from Sweden a century later) but also of the west: with the partitions of Poland (1772, 1783, 1795), it brought much of Eastern Europe under its sceptre.

Warfare State

It would be tedious to recount all these wars here—there are excellent studies which tell the history of the Romanovs and their empire. But several general points need to be made. The first is that the ambitious principality of Moscow, later the Empire of Russia, had many competitors in the region: the Lithuanians, the Crimean Tatars, the Poles, the Swedes, the Ottomans. The princes of Moscow reacted to this situation by harnessing all resources to the service of their state, which existed for the sole purpose of waging war, conquering territory, and enriching and glorifying the ruler. This warfare state was built in a series of 'service class revolutions', the most important of them instigated by Ivan III (b. 1440, ruled 1462–1505) and Peter I (b. 1672, ruled 1682–1725).[3]

Ivan III found the basic formula of how to further imperial conquest by harnessing everybody to the state. Its very existence was a novelty in the land of the Rus and part of Russia's success: the realm of medieval Rus had only had the Orthodox Church and the familial ties among the dynasty, together with trade and tribute collection, to hold together a loose federation. Politics were conducted from the princes' chambers in consultation with their retainers. Under Ivan III, by contrast, Muscovy acquired an administration. As two historians describe it, 'Official business began to be conducted by designated clerks and scribes working in particular administrative units, chancelleries, dedicated to conducting diplomatic affairs, or later, to supervising the military, land distribution, and so forth.'[4]

This state would become the centre of Muscovite society. When in 1478 Ivan annexed Novgorod, he deported the former landowners and took their land, which he parcelled out to his cavalrymen. In return, they had to provide lifelong military service. This solved the problem of the old boyars, the nobles who held land as hereditary property—they had an independent source of wealth and hence power. The new service class Ivan built, by contrast, did not own property independently—it was granted to them by Ivan. By 1556 this system had been extended to all of Moscow's lands: all landholders had to render military service; all peasants had to till the land and pay rent and taxes to provide for the upkeep of the service class and the state bureaucracy. The new burden on the peasantry caused another problem in search of a solution: how to keep the peasant on the land. After all, if their life became too miserable, they could always walk off and find a new place to live in the vast wooded lands of Eastern Europe. Hence serfdom: the state commanded the peasants stay on the land, and would hunt them down and return them if they fled. Thus the turn to full enserfment in central Russia, a process completed by 1649. By the time of Catherine II (b. 1729, ruled 1762–96) it resembled slavery: peasants could be bought and sold without the land they were formally attached to.

The annexation of Novgorod eliminated a 'boyar republic', which some historians see as 'an undoubtedly significant alternative to autocracy'. Novgorod, a city-state with extensive hinterland, which made it one of the largest polities in Europe at the time, had avoided the Mongol yoke and later fought off the Teutonic Knights and Lithuania. Its governance included an assembly of the city's boyars, the *veche*. Novgorodians elected the head of state, the head of the merchants and artisans, the head of the clergy, and eventually other officials as well. There still was a prince but his power (military as well as judicial) was circumscribed by the elected officials, and he had to live outside the city proper. The influence of the self-administrative traditions of German towns—which Novgorodians would have known from their commercial interactions with the Baltic, including eventually the Hanseatic League—is visible in these arrangements. They came to an end in 1478, when Ivan dissolved the *veche* and removed its bell, the symbol of its power.[5]

Empire

Thus, the northern Rus lands became the homeland of autocracy and the warfare state. Peter I further deepened the state's entrenchment within society. He is usually called 'the Great' but could equally be remembered as 'the Terrible', given how miserable life was for most of his subjects. Peter was a warlord par excellence. During his reign, only the years 1682, 1724 and 1725 saw no major wars. He was also a westerniser, forcing his courtiers to shave their beards and adopt European dress and manners (and if they did not, he was liable to hit them with his knout). He founded St Petersburg in the north as a 'window to the West' and moved his capital there. An autocrat, he abolished the Boyar Duma, a council of the most influential nobles, who used to run affairs in the tsar's absence (which would have been most of the time, given that Peter was constantly campaigning). Instead, he instituted the Senate, appointed by the emperor himself. That title—emperor of all Russia—he adopted in 1721. What he is probably most remembered for, however, is that he was a moderniser: he overhauled the state bureaucracy, reorganised the army along Western European lines, built a fleet, decreed compulsory schooling for the service class, and introduced the Table of Ranks, which defined a hierarchy for both civil administration and the military, and allowed able and ambitious commoners to move up into the service elite. Together, these reforms further strengthened the warfare state in what amounted to a second service-class revolution: sources of power and prestige outside the state were diminished, autocracy strengthened, and the state's power expanded for the more rational waging of war.[6]

Second, the resulting state was not a homeland for the Russians or a kingdom of the East Slavs, but a multi-ethnic and multiconfessional empire. Despite the rhetoric of the 'gathering of the lands of the Rus', this empire acquired lands and peoples which were not Rus at all, long before it conquered what used to be the heartland of the old Rus—Kyiv was only annexed in 1667 (see Map 8). From at least the conquest of Kazan (1552) and the subsequent subjugation of Siberia in the sixteenth and seventeenth centuries, the Muscovite state was not a national homeland of Russians (or Rusians, or East Slavs). It was a multinational empire, and increasingly so.

As it expanded, the share of East Slavs dropped. If, in the late sixteenth century, the Moscow prince had ruled over a population which was maybe 90 per cent Russian, by the first half of the eighteenth century that share had decreased to 71 per cent (plus Ukrainians and Belarusians to a total of 86 per cent East Slavs), with 5 per cent ethnic groups of the middle Volga (Tatars and others) and another 5 per cent peoples from the Baltic provinces. The rest were nomads of the steppes and the peoples of the north and of Siberia. By the end of that century, the proportion of Russians had dropped to 53 per cent. Ukrainians now made up 22 per cent and Belarusians 8 per cent. National minorities with no connection to the Rus at all now constituted 17 per cent. In the imperial census of 1897, only 44 per cent of the population were registered as 'Great Russian' speakers, 18 per cent as 'Little Russian' (that is, Ukrainian) and under 5 per cent as 'White Russian' (Belarusian). A third of the population were now classified as non-'Russian'.[7]

The conquest of Kazan and the subsequent subjugation of Siberia well before the lands of the old Rus exposed the 'gathering of the Russian lands' and the claims to succession to medieval Rus as what they were: ideological justifications for conquest. Kazan was central to controlling trade routes across the Euro-Asian space; Siberia was about fur, one of the most valuable commodities at the time. Of course, the quest for power and wealth was expressed through Christian language, but it was not driven by it and conquered peoples were not forced to convert.

Economically, this empire was based on the subjugation of the peasantry in the Russian heartland and the extraction of furs (in particular, sable) from the Siberian colony. The Siberian conquest was a most brutal form of settler colonialism, complete with massacres, disease, economic exploitation, and the dispossession of native lands by settlers from the Slavic heartland (first Russians, later Ukrainians). The latter were the typical mix of exploited and exploiters who drove settler colonialism elsewhere: they escaped an increasingly nasty serfdom which became hard to distinguish from slavery, but which did not exist in the Siberian frontier; they then subjected the native populations to their own (fire) power.[8]

Militarily, imperial expansion was made possible by modern European weaponry. Moscow might have been much more provincial than Kyiv had been in medieval times, but it was still a European

outpost and it partook in European military-technological innova-
tions. The gunpowder revolution came to Muscovy in the sixteenth
and seventeenth centuries, giving the colonists the guns the Siberians
did not have. The gunpowder revolution also played its role in driving
enserfment as well as the expansion of the administrative structure of
the autocratic state. Thus, imperial expansion, internal colonisation
and state-building were linked.[9]

Russia, then, never had an empire. It was one.[10] Like the Mongol,
Chinese or Austro-Hungarian empires, it was land based—the one
overseas acquisition, Alaska, turned out to be hard to supply and was
sold at a bargain price to the United States in 1867. It was also not an
empire where the Russians lorded it over the non-Russians. Instead,
among the most repressed, indeed enslaved, populations were Russians
and Ukrainians. Indigenous peoples of Siberia and the far north were
decimated in the quest for furs, but in other instances, instead, the elites
of subjugated peoples were coopted into the multinational imperial
elite. Ivan IV (b. 1530, ruled 1533–84) married a Circassian princess
in 1561, and other Circassians played major roles during his reign
of terror against the older boyar families as well as in the complex
struggles of the following Time of Trouble. They remained important
members of the 'Russian' aristocracy. One of them, prince Mikhail
Iakovlevich Cherkasskii, 'was the single richest man in late seventeenth
century Russia'.[11]

Multinationality remained a feature of the elite to the very end of
the empire. Sergei Witte, the minister of finance who masterminded
the industrialisation of Russia in the late nineteenth century, was a
Baltic German. Gustaf Mannerheim, the Finnish national hero, was,
until 1917, a loyal follower of the tsar, a career military man who
spoke Russian and had served on the imperial frontier in the East.
He only returned to Finland after he lost control over his rebellious
troops in 1917 and found no support for a counter-revolutionary force
in the capital of St Petersburg. He went to Finland, not in order to
build a Finnish state, but to use his homeland as a bridgehead for the
counter-revolution—the liberation of the Romanov Empire from
the Bolsheviks and other, as he saw it, revolutionary rabble. These were

not exceptions. The Russian Government of the nineteenth century was run by Germans ('the Benckendorffs, Lievens, Nesselrodes, Kankrins'), Ukrainians ('Kochubei, Bezborodko, Paskevich and Miloradovich'), scions of the 'Finland-Swedish nobility and the absolutely crucial and rarely mentioned Poles'. Twenty-eight per cent of the men appointed by Nicholas II to the State Council—that is, the tsar's top advisers—had non-Russian names; 13 per cent were not Orthodox Christians.[12]

The Long Nineteenth Century

In this multi-ethnic, continuous land empire, it was hard to see where the metropole ended and the periphery began. This fact caused some intellectual concerns once the French Revolution (1789–1815) promoted the notion that a modern state was the organisation of a nation on a particular territory. This newfangled idea not only inspired intellectuals in Ukraine to construct a Ukrainian identity but also infiltrated the imperial elite more generally, and convinced a section of it to treat Central Asia, acquired in the Great Game with the British Empire in the second half of the nineteenth century, as a territory apart. Rather than coopting the local elites, they were now treated as colonial peoples subjugated by Europeans. The new Russian nationalism also led to Russification policies in European parts, such as Poland, Finland and what would become Ukraine, which only served to further fuel the national movements.

It also led to intellectual efforts to reconcile the idea of empire with the idea of nation—a process in which Kyiv intellectuals played a major role. The solution—partial only, given the many other peoples of the realm—was to insist that there was one 'tribe' (later 'nation') with Kyivan ('Little Russian'; Ukrainian), Muscovite ('Great Russian'; Russian) and White Russian (Belarusian) sub-branches. Putin's contemporary claims that Ukrainians are not a separate people draws heavily on this imperial attempt to make sense of the differences within the empire's whole.[13]

How to come to terms with new ideas about the relationship between nation, empire and state was not the empire's only struggle in the nineteenth century. Its very success until that point had been underwritten by an early modern warfare state, based economically on the extraction of labour from an enserfed peasantry and waging wars with a military commanded by the service-class elite but staffed by serfs pressed into lifelong service. In the long nineteenth century, from victory over Napoleon in the Patriotic War of 1812 to the outbreak of World War I in 1914, this early modern state now confronted the industrialising overseas empires of Europe: of Russia's competitors, only Austria-Hungary and the declining Ottoman Empire were land-based empires.

The Patriotic War marked the high tide of Russia's power in Europe and the world. Napoleon, that dictatorial and imperialist offspring of the French Revolution, had invaded with 450 000 men plus some 50 000 civilian camp followers, a large army at the time. He managed to push all the way to Moscow, his army suffering from heat, fatigue, thirst and hunger. No victory awaited them. Moscow burned, it is true, but this conflagration did not force Napoleon's retreat. 'Those who were billeted in Moscow,' writes one historian, 'lived reasonably well, and enjoyed an abundance of food, at least for a while.' But supply lines were stretched and soon the surrounding villages were denuded of food and fodder. And Russia did not surrender, refused even to negotiate. The retreat that followed was catastrophic. Napoleon's army—starved, freezing and demoralised—was continuously attacked by Russian raiders. Stragglers were killed by the peasants. Only 75 000 troops managed to extricate themselves.[14]

The French defeat in Russia was a turning point in the Revolutionary and Napoleonic wars. In the following War of the Sixth Coalition (1813–14), Russia was joined by most other European powers to destroy Napoleon's empire. In March 1814, victorious Russian troops entered Paris. Napoleon abdicated and was sent into exile on Elba. At the Congress of Vienna (1814–15), the victors redrew the map of Europe. Russia gained much of what, under Napoleon, had been the Duchy of Warsaw. It became the Congress Kingdom of Poland, whose king was the Russian tsar.

Crisis

Thus things seemed to be going well for the tsars (Alexander I until 1825, Nicholas I until 1855). The empire had helped liberate Europe from Napoleonic oppression and gained significant European real estate in return. In parallel, it expanded into the Southern Caucasus (what today are Armenia, Georgia and Azerbaijan), acquired as a result of two wars with Persia (1804–13 and 1826–28). But then, imperial progress started to stutter. The military road across the mountains, which linked the imperial heartland with its new Transcaucasian acquisitions, was threatened by the mountaineers of Dagestan and Chechnya. It took decades of genocidal, scorched-earth warfare to subjugate them.

Worse was to come when confrontation moved from the 'Caucasian Imamate' in the mountains to the major European powers. Trying to project its power into the Balkans and the Near East, Russia got into strife with the Ottoman Empire, supported by Great Britain and France—both now overseas empires with growing industrial economies, especially in Britain. The resulting Crimean War (1853–56) was a disaster. It showed the organisational, military and technological inferiority of an early modern, agrarian warfare state based on serfdom, when confronted with industrialising overseas empires. Four decades after Russia's triumph over Napoleon, this was a humiliating defeat.

Defeat spurred on reforms, which 'enlightened bureaucrats' had long contemplated. But more than enlightenment was at stake. To win wars in the modern world, Russia needed a modern economy which could create modern weapons. This in turn required the emancipation of the peasantry in the East Slavic lands. Enserfment had been a central part of the first service-class revolution, the economic base of the early modern warfare state that drove imperial expansion. But in the modern world, it inhibited urbanisation, kept agriculture unproductive, and severely constrained the recruitment of a workforce for the factories necessary to equip a modern army and build modern infrastructure, such as railways. That it was possible to free the peasantry without the social structure crumbling had been demonstrated in more limited experiments on the periphery of the empire: serfdom was abolished in the Baltic provinces of Estland in 1816, in Courland in 1817 and in Livonia in 1819. All that was needed was the political impetus to break the resistance of the landowners of the old service elite, who over the centuries had privatised the old service lands and the peasants working them (in 1762, mandatory service had been abolished, and the 1785 charter of the nobility guaranteed property rights). The Crimean disaster created this necessary momentum and the serfs were freed across the entire empire in 1861.[15]

Tsar Alexander II now was on a roll with his 'Great Reforms'. In 1864, he introduced local government, law reforms, and European-style law courts, which improved the governance in his far-flung empire. The local government bodies, which were elected under an estate-based unequal vote, for the first time introduced 'an element of democracy' into the autocratic structure of the empire. And in 1874, the recruitment base of the military was fundamentally shaken up by the introduction of universal male conscription. Hitherto, soldiers had been recruited from local communities on the basis of quotas of men to be delivered for lifelong service to the tsar (later reduced to twenty-five, twenty, then twelve years). Now, all twenty-year old men were to serve six years, with nine years in the reserve. This created the basis for a much more modern force: relatively small at peacetime, but capable of quick expansion in times of war. It also allowed the army to become the school of the empire: soldiers often learned to read and write, but also to think of their own role as part of the larger imperial whole.[16]

Alexander, the 'Tsar liberator' for the peasants and the empire's most visionary reformer since Peter I, was assassinated in 1881 by members of a revolutionary group hoping to shake the peasants into a more revolutionary mood. His successor, Alexander III (b. 1845, ruled 1881–94), built one of the most repressive police states of the nineteenth century to get on top of the growing revolutionary threat. But he continued the transformation of his realm, encouraging industrial development and beginning the construction of the Trans-Siberian Railway, a crucial artery linking the far east of the empire with its European core. His son, the ill-fated Nicholas II (b. 1868, ruled 1894–1917), continued in this vein: under the guidance of Witte, industrial development took off in the 1890s and Russia became one of the fastest-growing economies of the world. Cities expanded and the working class grew by leaps and bounds. At the same time, however, Nicholas II continued the repressive policies of his father and refused, unless he had no other option, to contemplate political reforms which would limit his autocratic powers.

While trying to update the empire's economic and military base, Russia's rulers reoriented the direction of expansion. Further moves into Europe became increasingly difficult after Crimea, but there were territories ready for the taking in Asia. Russia 'acquired' the Amur region from the ailing Chinese empire in 1858, some 600 000 square kilometres in the Far East. After the Second Opium War (1856–60), the Maritime Region with Vladivostok (which translates as 'Ruler of the East') followed suit. And after helping the other European imperialists crush the Boxer Rebellion (1899–1901), the tsar kept Russian troops in Manchuria, just in case.

Russia's aggressive moves into China brought it into conflict with another rising power: Japan. Tokyo increasingly saw its role as that of the hegemon over Asia, hoping to displace the white imperialists. The ultimate result of this competition was the Russo-Japanese War of 1904–05, which Nicholas II also hoped would calm the increasingly restless realm by bringing a focus on the external threat. Instead, Russia was defeated on land and at sea. The empire exploded into revolution.

The 1905 revolution ultimately failed. But with many of his troops engaged in the Far East, and the Trans-Siberian Railway, which could have brought them back, subject to revolutionary strikes, the emperor was forced to make political concessions. The most well-known outcome was the Duma, a pseudo-parliament which would play its role in the ultimate end of Nicholas II's rule in 1917. It also introduced yet another democratic element into autocracy. While 'suffrage was not universal or equal', it was 'widespread' and elections 'were free and not notably corrupt'. The Duma was part of a growing public sphere in the final decade of the empire, now less hindered by censorship and bustling with a growing number of organisations, legal and illegal political parties, voluntary and professional societies, and a huge number of publications—from boulevard dailies telling stories of the city's dreadful delights, to serious intellectual journals debating the issues of the day. This new public sphere was not just Russian but also enabled the national self-exploration of non-Russian nationalities.[17]

Time of Troubles

Thus, the attempts to deal with the crisis of the premodern warfare state after Crimea only increased the fissures in the empire. The emancipated peasantry did help create an industrial proletariat, but the peasants were unhappy with the terms of 1861 (they had to pay for the land they acquired and did not get as much of it as they thought they should), and the newly minted proletarians were restless from the start. Their former owners were often alienated from the regime which had taken away what they thought was their rightful property. The government and law reforms improved the grip of the central government on the localities, but it also created an entire class of educated professionals—engineers, doctors, lawyers, teachers—whose political outlook was much more European and modern than the old service elite focused on duty to the emperor had been.

The military reform did increase the military capacities of the empire (as had been shown in the victorious war against the Ottoman Empire in 1877–78, which led to further expansion in the Transcaucasus) but it also brought disquiet to the villages. Previously, the village patriarchs could send young troublemakers to the army and thus keep control of rural society; now, the misfits came back after six years, often literate and equipped with new ideas and broader horizons. They were part of a growing reading public which consumed a variety of print media in the last years of the empire. The spread of higher education also had a destabilising impact. European-style universities created a new group of potentially oppositional subjects: the 'intelligentsia', alienated from the state but also from the majority of the population.[18]

Meanwhile, these new social, political and cultural forces were not effectively channelled into a reformed political system. The voting base of the Duma—a toothless tiger at the best of times—was reduced further and further as the emperor regained control after 1905. The new working class, but also the growing professional classes, were never integrated into the political system to the extent they were in other industrialising societies, like Britain or Germany. As importantly, the increasingly self-assertive non-Russian nationalities, too, were not accommodated sufficiently in this largest land empire since the Mongols.

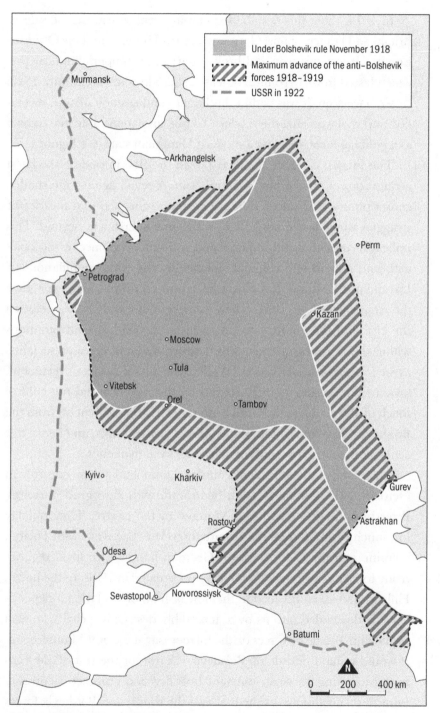

Map 9: Bolshevik Russia, 1917–19

In 1914, then, this destabilised empire went to war on the side of Britain and France against Germany, Austro-Hungary and the Ottoman Empire. It lost this war and broke apart in an 'imperial apocalypse' which lasted from 1916 until at least 1922—in some areas until 1926. As we have seen, it was within this larger conflagration of war, revolution and civil wars that the modern Ukrainian nation came into its own as a political force, forming a modern Ukrainian state (see Figure 1).[19]

The longest of these conflicts began in 1916 in one of the latest acquisitions of the empire: Central Asia. A revolt against the sudden conscription of Muslims, hitherto exempt, morphed into a series of struggles which lasted until 1926, with some aftershocks beyond. This upheaval combined anti-imperial and anti-settler violence by the locals with anti-nomad and colonial violence by the settler populations of Ukrainians, Russians and Cossacks, who had moved here ever since the emancipation of 1861. There were tensions and clashes between the city and the countryside, as well as ideological confrontations within the European populations between different types of socialists as well as anti-socialist forces. While there was a Soviet government, loyal to the Bolsheviks in Petrograd, in the region, it did not control much of the countryside. Until September 1919 it was cut off from the Bolshevik heartland by the 'White' forces further north, and hence this civil war proceeded according to its own local dynamics.[20]

Meanwhile, the Bolsheviks under Lenin had taken control, in October 1917, of the Russian heartland, with Petrograd (formerly Petersburg) in the north and Moscow in the centre. They quickly lost much of the rest of the empire, however. The west, with Poland, Ukraine and the Baltics, was in German hands, with local regimes ready to take power once the Germans retreated in 1918. In the north, Finland had taken the lead in the new fashion of declaring independence. It descended into its own, incredibly destructive, civil war, won by the anti-Bolshevik forces of the former tsarist general Mannerheim. It would remain outside of Bolshevik control for the rest of the century, oscillating between outright hostility and enforced neutrality towards its neighbour. In the east and the south, anti-Bolshevik forces established competing governments in Siberia, on the Don and in the

Transcaucasus. By the end of 1918, Bolshevik Russia had contracted to about the area from which the Muscovite princes had started their expansion five centuries earlier (see Map 9).

From this low point, the Bolsheviks then reconquered much of the empire (see Figure 1). First came many of the areas controlled by non-Bolshevik and anti-Bolshevik forces, all lumped together as 'Whites' by the Bolshevik 'Reds', a colour coding re-enacting memories of the French Revolution (November 1918 through the spring of 1920). As we saw in Chapter 1, in Ukraine this phase dragged on until the end of the Polish-Ukrainian-Russian war of 1920–21, which brought much of Ukraine into Bolshevik hands but also checked further westward expansion. In the same period, however, the Transcaucasus was re-annexed, while internally, the Bolsheviks were kept busy suppressing peasant uprisings, labour unrest, and a major rebellion by revolutionary sailors in Kronstadt. In Central Asia, no longer cut off from the heartland after the Whites had been defeated in Siberia, the fighting continued until 1926.

The Birth of Red Imperialism

The Bolsheviks—anti-Imperial Marxists—thus rebuilt an empire which was geographically nearly identical to the old Romanov realm, an imperialist force they detested. True, there were some territories beyond their control—Poland, the new Baltic countries of Latvia, Lithuania and Estonia, as well as Finland. But the rest was the old empire which had become Bolshevik. That raises two questions: how did they manage to rebuild this empire and why did they do it?

There is a large scholarly literature on the 'how'. The short answer is that the Bolsheviks had a combination of good luck and good sense. They were lucky, because they had taken over the heartland of the old empire rather than, as their competitors had, parts of the periphery. That had several advantages. Internal lines of communication made moving troops from one front to the other easier, particularly as they controlled the regions with the densest network of train lines. The weapons industry and much of the old regime's stockpiles were also located here, giving the Bolsheviks a material advantage.[21]

Equally important, however, was that the Bolsheviks were much more successful than many of their competitors in rebuilding a new warfare state, which again, like its imperial predecessor, geared everything towards fighting. Meanwhile, many of the White forces essentially functioned as warlords without an administration. Ukraine did build a state but focused on cultural institutions (universities, academies of science and so on) rather than the means of destruction and defence. The Bolshevik state had a core personnel of highly motivated, ideologically united political warriors (the communists) and ensured the compliance of others by a combination of skilful agitation and propaganda, material inducements, and the ruthless application of repression and terror.[22]

The Bolsheviks proved pragmatic when it came to making sure they had the personnel to fight their wars. They recruited 'military specialists' from the old regime to command their army and made sure the rank and file stayed in line with a mixture of carrot and stick: persecution of deserters on the one hand and material benefits to soldiers and their families on the other. The same pragmatism extended to the nationality policy discussed in Chapter 1. In order to disarm national movements, they granted them cultural, linguistic, territorial and personnel rights, while making sure that political power remained concentrated in Moscow. Likewise, the New Economic Policy (NEP) of the 1920s was a pragmatic accommodation of the economic demands of the peasantry, a liberalisation which flanked the brutal repression of their uprisings.

More difficult to answer is another question: why did a bunch of anti-imperial Marxists, whose goal was to liberate humanity from oppression, rebuild an empire? More than that: they built one of the most repressive imperial edifices the world has seen. The answer is convoluted.[23]

One factor was ideology. Bolsheviks were no nationalists; they were internationalist revolutionaries. When they found themselves contained to the old Russian heartland in 1918, only nationalists could have embraced this state of affairs. The goal was world revolution, not a national homeland for Russians, even proletarian ones. Russia, the Russian Empire, was meant to be the weakest link in the chain of imperialist forces. Once it broke, others would follow. But to break the link completely meant to get rid of the counter-revolutionary forces surrounding the Bolshevik heartland. They were located on other territories of the disintegrated empire. Defeating them meant reconquering these territories, all the more because bringing revolution to, say, Central Asia could maybe encourage anti-imperial revolution in nearby territories, thus further helping along world revolution. 'The idea of social and political freedom for the long-suffering working masses of the East,' wrote one Bolshevik imperialist in 1919, 'must be transfused through Turkestan to Asia.' Thus, anti-imperialism required imperial reconquest.[24]

This reconquest had been made easier by some of the remnants from the old empire. For one thing, there was infrastructure, in particular the railway network, which made moving back into Siberia or Turkestan relatively easy—easier, certainly, than moving further into, say, Chinese Central Asia, where no rail links existed. Second, there were frames of reference and the more general imperial culture. The Bolsheviks were children of the empire. This was the space they had grown up in. They had crisscrossed it while still in opposition. Their networks extended through the empire's breadth, including its cities, its prisons and its far-flung places. This was the space of their experience of politics; the empire was inscribed in their mental maps. When they thought of 'Russia' and 'the Russian revolution', they thought of a revolution in the Russian Empire, not in a Russian national space.

Another reason for the resurgence of empire was strategic. The Bolshevik state was surrounded by enemies. The territories which had broken away, even when not outrightly hostile in the first place, might well become staging grounds for 'imperialist' forces. The enemy—'international imperialism'—needed to be denied such potential bridgeheads. Hence, it was better to occupy them. This logic applied in part in Central Asia as well as in the Transcaucasus, where it was also reinforced by the existence of Bolshevik forces and regimes which asked Moscow for help against their local competitors.

Economics exerted its own force field on the new rulers. Before its fall, the Russian Empire had been an integrated economic whole. The main industrial centres—Petrograd, Moscow—were under Bolshevik control early on, but they needed raw materials produced elsewhere. Ukraine, Europe's breadbasket, was needed to feed the proletarians in the cities; its Donbas region had produced more than 85 per cent of the coal used in the empire's industry in 1913 and provided much of its steel. 'Russia could not survive' without the Donbas coal, noted one Bolshevik in 1917. Others concurred: 'Ukrainian sugar, coal and pig-iron were vital for Russia, and thus Ukraine's independence [was] impossible.' The Caucasus and Transcaucasus were required for their oil. 'We desperately need oil,' wrote Lenin in 1920. 'Issue a manifesto to the population that we will slaughter everyone if they burn and ruin oil and oil fields, while we will grant life to everyone if Maykop and especially Grozny are handed over intact.' Central Asia was needed for its cotton, and so on. Thus, if the Russian revolutionary republic was to survive, if it was to become a bridgehead for the world revolution, if it was to defend itself against counter-revolutionaries and 'imperialists', it needed to reconquer the empire.[25]

Hence, red imperialism was born from the spirit of anti-imperialism. That the latter was deeply held was shown in cases where the red imperialists sent from Moscow made common cause not with the Slavic settler populations but with the indigenous peoples the latter were exterminating in their own civil war, as happened in Central Asia.[26]

The Bolsheviks, then, were no Russian nationalists (at least not yet), and neither were their predecessors, the provisional government which had taken over from the tsar in early 1917. Neither regime constituted, unlike Ukraine in the same period, a precursor to the post-1991 nation-state. Instead, these were imperial governments. The provisional government tried to hold together the empire and indeed continue to prosecute the imperialist war aims (one of the reasons for its downfall). It was an imperial edifice, not a nation-state. Bolshevik Russia, likewise, was not a Russian national homeland but the bridgehead of the world revolution. With this revolution taking its time, Bolshevik Russia was always destined to become an empire, and it became an empire of nations only because it needed to deal with the competition from nationalism within its own borders.

Map 10: Soviet Empire in the west after 1945

Red Empire Victorious

The economic and political settlement of the 1920s had been a compromise: nationalists got national cultures, national cadres and national spaces; the peasants were freed from grain requisitions and allowed to enrich themselves in a semi-market economy so they could pay taxes; the working class often grumbled because of high unemployment and continuously bad living conditions; and many in the Bolshevik party also complained: this was not what they had shed blood for after 1917.

Their moment came when Stalin secured power in the succession struggles after Lenin's death in 1924. In 1928 he launched his first revolution from above: the NEP's mixed economy was replaced by the command structure of the First Five-Year Plan. The goal was to expand at breakneck speed the empire's heavy industry to get ready for the next major war. To pay for this industrial revolution, grain needed to be extracted from the peasantry for export. As the peasants resisted this new attempt to confiscate the fruits of their labour, they were forced into collective farms ('collectivisation'), their leaders deported or shot ('dekulakisation', or 'dekurkulisation' in the Ukrainian variant).

The result was a new, much more modern, but all the more repressive and destructive warfare state—a new 'service-class revolution', if you will. Again, the entire social structure was geared towards the state, civilian consumption was subordinated to arming the country, and few spaces of independent interaction remained. It was this Stalinist warfare state which proved itself, with some modifications, in World War II: first, it expanded into Eastern Europe, taking over parts of Poland, Romania, Finland and all of the Baltic States; then, in alliance with Britain, China and the United States, it defeated the Nazis and won the war in Europe, adding some German real estate (Königsberg/Kaliningrad) to its inner empire and obtaining an outer empire of satellites protecting its western flank (see Map 10). Victory convinced not just Stalin but also the leadership more generally that the basic policy line of the 1930s had been correct. Victory thus 'locked in' the basic institutional arrangements of Stalinism as the backbone of the Soviet Empire.[27]

The Soviet imperial economy was an updated version of the old tsarist division of labour. Moscow (rather than Petersburg-Petrograd-Leningrad) now formed the administrative and political centre, while Leningrad was an important node of the Soviet defence and other industries. Within the inner empire, Central Asia was a supplier of raw materials (especially cotton) and used as the Soviet equivalent of the Bikini Atoll: as a nuclear bomb test site. Siberia was both a raw material supplier (oil, gas, coal, wood) and a dumping ground for unwanted populations, who could then be put to use in mining or logging, which struggled to attract free labour. Ukraine was 'the backbone of the Soviet industrial empire'. Like other colonies, it did supply raw materials: iron ore and coal as well as food (about one-quarter of Soviet food production on the eve of independence), but the Donbas and Dnipro regions were also major industrial centres where such raw materials were transformed into machinery and weapons. Ukraine was, moreover, a major source of hydroelectric and nuclear power, some of it exported to the outer empire or other Soviet republics. By 1991, Ukraine produced about one-fifth of Soviet industrial output.[28]

Stalin's successors left intact the basic structure they had inherited: an empire of nations bolstered by an outer empire of satellite states, kept in line, if necessary, with military force (as happened in Germany in 1953, in Hungary in 1956, and in Czechoslovakia in 1968). The command economy and the secret police remained pillars of the empire as well. The former was redirected in parts from warfare to welfare in the 1950s, 1960s and 1970s, and the latter changed its modus operandi from mass repression to mass surveillance and the intimidation of potential dissidents. In fact, the two were intertwined: one of the major sectors of KGB work was repressing the underground economy.[29]

The 'National Problem'

The process of transforming the warfare state into a welfare state took place in a settled empire. Its borders, fluid ever since the start of Muscovy's expansion, were now stable. No further expansion took place after World War II. Internally, there were some developments towards cultural unification of the three East Slavic nations. In the 1930s the Russians had been elevated to the status of leading Soviet nation. The fear of war and the example of National Socialism convinced Joseph

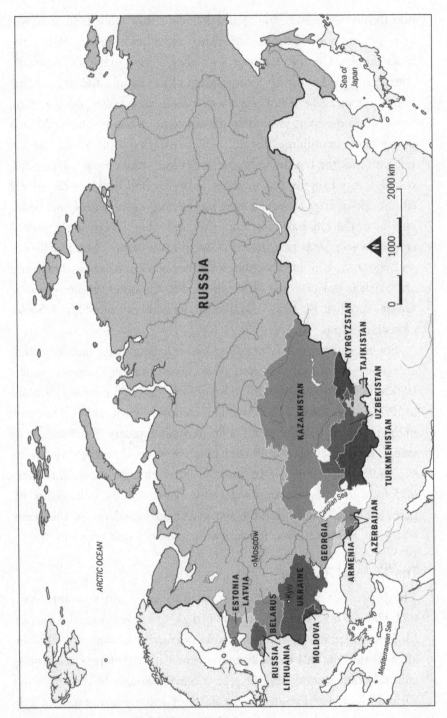

Map 11: Successor states of the Soviet Union

Stalin to wager on Russian patriotism. Ironically, once war actually came in 1939, a partial retreat from this Russification was necessary. The expansion into Poland in 1939—legitimised as it was by concern with saving Ukrainians and Belarusians—elevated the status of these 'lesser' nations. 'From then on,' writes historian Serhii Plokhy, 'Stalin would have to balance the interests of the newly empowered Russian nation with the demands and expectations of the minorities.' The war effort against Germany, too, relied on the loyalty of Ukrainians, Belarusians, Jews and Central Asians. Hence, wartime patriotism was more multifaceted than is sometimes remembered.[30]

After a return to Great Russian chauvinism in the final years of Stalin's life, another subtle change took place after his death. Instead of promoting the Russians as first among the peoples of the Soviet nations, the regime began to push the idea of an all-Soviet nation. This Soviet nation, however, spoke Russian, read the Russian classics and was steeped in Russian history. Careers in the apparatus of power depended on such Russification, and it was this Russified multinational elite the young Vladimir Putin (b. 1952) encountered while working his way up in the KGB. This experience, together with longstanding prejudice and deep cultural currents within his society, would form the basis for his later conviction that Ukrainians and Russians were one and the same people.

Thus, by the 1980s, the Soviet Union was well on its way to transforming from an empire into a nation-state. Again, since the end of World War II, its borders had been stable, and internally the population began to be integrated via equal rights within the Soviet welfare state (rather than the steeply stratified structure of entitlements of the earlier period), and via an all-Soviet national identity, beginning to supplement, if not replace, the national self-identifications. This process was not complete, which is why the Soviet Union presents itself to historians in its final decade as 'a pseudo-federal unitary state with both imperial and national aspects and practices'.[31]

For many Russians, however, this transformation had an additional twist: it led to a conflation of Russian national identity with the imperial space of the Soviet Union. This imperial-national consciousness was aided both by the existence of the many Russian diasporas in non-Soviet republics of the union and by the institutional structure of the Russian Federation within the Soviet Union: because Lenin had wanted to decrease 'Russian chauvinism', the RSFSR did not receive, like the other union republics, its own Communist Party, secret police or Academy of Sciences. This state of affairs irked many Russians, but it also had the unintended effect that the union-level institutions—the Communist Party of the Soviet Union, the USSR KGB, the USSR Academy of Sciences, all headquartered in Moscow—became understood as Russian institutions. 'The result,' writes a specialist on Russian nationalism, was that many 'viewed the USSR as essentially a Russian nation-state rather than an empire'.[32]

Gorbachev and Breakdown

And then, in 1991, just when the new imperial nation of Russian-speaking Soviets finally took shape, the empire collapsed. The reason for this collapse was an attempt to reform the empire—to finally transform it from the warfare state Stalin had built into a prosperous, democratic welfare state (or 'socialism', to use the language of the actors at the time). The man who headed this transformation was the new general secretary, Mikhail Gorbachev (b. 1931, ruled 1985–91).

Gorbachev inherited an empire in crisis. The attempts, after Stalin's death in 1953, to re-gear the warfare state in parts to also deliver welfare for the population had been hampered both by the inherent unresponsiveness and wastefulness of the command economy, and the arms race with the much richer and more productive United States. By the time Gorbachev became general secretary in 1985, the economy was in deep crisis, the society riven by despair and alcoholism. The outer empire was increasingly seen as an economic liability.

Nevertheless, it could have rumbled on, like many other dysfunctional states, societies and social institutions do all the time. Part of Gorbachev's problem was that he was no imperialist: he actually believed in the rhetoric of the 'friendship of the peoples', was hesitant to use force to keep the empire together, and was too fixated on making 'socialism' both more democratic and more prosperous. The results of his attempts to do so weakened what held the empire together (the command economy, the secret police and the Communist Party) and it imploded in 1991, leaving behind fifteen successor states—Ukraine and Russia among them (see Map 11).

CHAPTER 3

UKRAINE SINCE 1991: THE STRUGGLE FOR DEMOCRACY

Birth Pangs

When Ukraine emerged as an independent nation from the rubble of the Soviet empire, it was riven with problems. The economy was in a shambles and would continue on a downward slide until the early 2000s. The political structure was left over from Soviet times—a partially reformed system which, moreover, had been built to rule a union republic, not an independent nation. The population was ethnically mixed but with a strong dominance of Ukrainians, who made up 73 per cent of the people. Russians constituted a significant minority of 22 per cent, followed by Jews, Belarusians and Moldavians, all with just under one in 100. Other nationalities of the Soviet empire, from Bulgarians and Poles to Azeri, Koreans, Germans, Kyrgyz and Lithuanians, made up the remaining 3 per cent.[1]

There were strong regional differences in political outlook. In the December 1991 referendum, all regions voted for independence but some were more enthusiastic than others. In Lviv in the west of the country, 95 per cent of the people voted and 97 per cent of them approved the declaration of independence, which had been made in late August in response to the coup attempt in Moscow. In Crimea, an ethnically strongly Russian region at the other extreme, only

68 per cent of eligible voters went to the polls, with 54 per cent of them voting in favour. Donetsk, an industrial region in the east of the country with strong economic ties to Russia, stood somewhat between these extremes. Here, 77 per cent registered their vote and 84 per cent of those people voted for independence.[2]

The Economy

With the partial exception of the three Baltic republics, all post-Soviet nations struggle with three interrelated crises: a crisis of democracy, an economic crisis and corruption. A persistent problem is the continued low level of wealth of the population overall (see Figure 2). Outside the three outliers in the Baltic (Estonia, Latvia and Lithuania), the relatively well-performing Russia, Kazakhstan and Turkmenistan are all resource-exporting economies. Everybody else is struggling. In terms of wealth per person (measured here in GDP per capita), Russia is about at the level of China (US$10 500), while even the rich Baltic countries are nowhere near the United States (US$63 500) or Australia (US$51 800).

This comparative poverty of the region is in part a legacy of the poor performance of the Soviet economy, and in part a continuing hangover from the economic catastrophe of the 1990s. In Ukraine, agriculture continued to be run by the disastrously unproductive

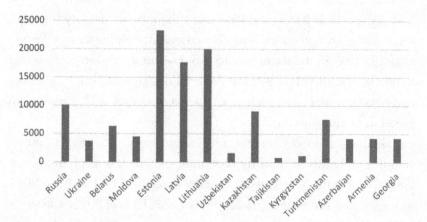

Figure 2: GDP per capita (US$), 2020
Source: World Bank

collective and state farms until the year 2000![3] Other economic reforms were also slow in coming. Meanwhile, the unravelling of the integrated Soviet imperial economy, the economic burden of the 1986 Chornobyl nuclear catastrophe, ageing and inefficient equipment, and dependence on Russian oil and gas constituted problematic legacies. Moreover, Ukraine's state apparatus had controlled no more than 5 per cent of Ukraine's GDP before 1990 (the rest was under the direct control of Moscow). Officials thus 'lacked the experience necessary to take quick and effective control' of Ukraine's economy, and the quick expansion of the share of the economy Ukraine's officials controlled in 1990 and 1991—to 40 per cent on the eve of independence—only added to the problems.[4]

Together, all these issues combined to create disaster: between 1991 and 1996, Ukraine's economy contracted every year by at least 10 per cent and as much as 23 per cent.[5] Overall, by 1996 it had contracted to 43 per cent of its 1990 level—a decline worse than what the United States experienced during the Great Depression of the 1930s. It was Ukraine's 'worst experience since the Second World War, when gross domestic product was reduced to a quarter of its pre-war size'.[6]

The main reason why nobody starved after 1991 was similar to Russia's: the existence of private gardening, a legacy of the Soviet period. 'The overwhelming majority of workers have out of town kitchen gardens,' wrote a worker from the Dnipro region in 1996. These were 'little patches of land given them by the factory management under an agreement with the agricultural authorities ... People work five days in the factories and two days on their plots'. According to official statistics, by 1996 some 80–95 per cent of fruit, vegetables and potatoes came from such plots. Even a quarter of all livestock were raised in private gardens.[7]

Ukraine's economy has not recovered nearly as much as that of resource-rich Russia, and its economic growth has stagnated since 2009 (see Figure 3.2). Russia's war by proxy in Donbas since 2014 again stunted economic growth. Between 2013 and 2015, Ukraine's GDP halved.[8] The current war will have catastrophic consequences for this overall picture. In early 2022, the World Bank predicted a contraction of the economy by 45 per cent.[9] In the same year, 47 per cent of Ukrainians surveyed responded that they did not have 'enough money even for food' or had money sufficient 'only for the most basic items'.[10]

Corruption

The post-Soviet space is not only poor, it is also among the world's most corrupt regions. Among European countries, Ukraine, Belarus and Russia are all known as deeply corrupt societies. Of the 336 politicians whose secret offshore financial accounts were leaked in the so-called 'Pandora Papers' of 2021, thirty-eight came from Ukraine, including President Volodymyr Zelensky. This was the largest number of any country in the world, followed by Russia with nineteen.[11]

Over time, however, Ukraine has improved its record in this regard. In Transparency International's Corruption Perceptions Index, a higher score means less corruption. Figure 4 shows the scores for both Russia and Ukraine from 1998 to 2021. In Ukraine, we see a significant improvement in the situation after 2004. While this progress was undone after a few years, there was steady improvement from 2009. Meanwhile, Russia has stagnated since 2012 and is classified today as more corrupt than its neighbour.

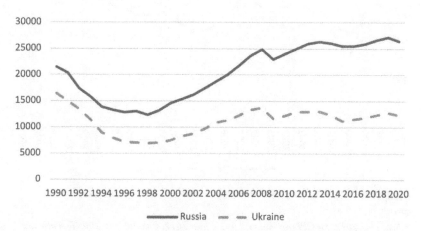

Figure 3: Wealth creation by head of population, Russia and Ukraine, 1990–2020
Source: Our World in Data, 'GDP Per Capita', 2020

Democracy

Corruption and economic crisis tend to do little to embed democracy. Maybe unsurprisingly, then, the majority of the societies which succeeded the Soviet Union are ruled by authoritarian regimes (nine out of fifteen, or 60 per cent, according to the 2021 classification by Freedom House, an organisation that measures democratic performance). Only the three Baltic States, which are members of both NATO and the European Union, are classified as consolidated democracies. Three others, Ukraine among them, are hybrid regimes, where authoritarian elements compete with democratic ones (20 per cent).[12]

Within this general context, then, Ukraine is doing relatively well. Between 2017 and 2022, Ukraine was classified as 'partly free' by Freedom House, the score oscillating between 60 and 62 on a scale out of 100, where the higher number indicates a higher level of civic and political liberty. Such numbers do not indicate that Ukraine is a beacon of democracy, either in the region (where Latvia, Lithuania and Estonia stand out as the freest countries, with scores of between 89 and 90) or around the world (the troubled United States scored 83 in 2021, while Australia stood at 97). But it contrasts positively with

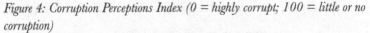

Figure 4: Corruption Perceptions Index (0 = highly corrupt; 100 = little or no corruption)

* *Note: until 2012, the CPI was measured 0–10; from 2012, it shifted to 0–100. To enable long-term comparisons, we scaled the data for 1998–2011 up by a factor of 10.*

Source: Transparency International, 'Corruption Perceptions Index', 2022

Russia, which has been categorised as 'not free' with a score of 20, falling to 19 in 2022. And Vladimir Putin's state, in turn, still compares favourably with other dictatorships in the region, which are even more repressive: Belarus with 11 and Tajikistan with 8. For comparison, China scored 9 in 2021 and North Korea 3.

To a significant extent, the predominance of authoritarian regimes in the post-Soviet space is a Soviet legacy. 'In all parts of the former Soviet empire,' write two legal scholars who studied this problem in detail, 'the socialist party-state structure left a shared legacy of an executive-dominated state.' Change depended on whether a postcolonial or neocolonial mindset won the day. In other words: did people want to stay in the Russian orbit or not? If not, the obvious choice was an orientation towards Europe, which came with mixed constitutions stressing checks and balances, weakening the executive; if yes, the constitution would be modelled much more closely on the Russian model of 'crown presidentialism', further entrenching the centrality of the executive. In Ukraine, the former tendency won out, but not without political struggles.[13]

One rather basic aspect of democracy is that governments are changed peacefully by elections. Ukraine is doing quite well in this regard, particularly if compared with its two autocratic neighbours. In Belarus, Alexander Lukashenko has been in power since 1994; in Russia, Putin since 1999. Ukraine, meanwhile, has seen seven presidencies since 1991: of Leonid Kravchuk (1991–94), Leonid Kuchma (1994–2005), Viktor Yushchenko (2005–10), Viktor Yanukovych (2010–14), Oleksandr Turchynov (2014), Petro Poroshenko (2014–19) and now Volodymyr Zelensky (since 2019). The majority of these presidents were elected into office and left when they lost elections or decided not to contest them. Two were removed through revolutions, one peaceful (the Orange Revolution of 2004–05), one violent (the Revolution of Dignity or Euromaidan of 2013–14). But both revolutions resulted in elected governments again, not the imposition of revolutionary dictatorships.

The presidents ruled in competition with parliament, at first the one elected still under Soviet conditions in 1990, then, since 1994, a post-Soviet one. This competition was formalised in the 1996 constitution, which put the directly elected president next to a one-chamber parliament that limited his powers to a much larger extent than in Russia.[14] Its 'for the post-Soviet space unusually strong parliament' became an issue because of the fragmented party system, however. First, there were too many parties; second, the existing parties were not based around major ideological positions or clearly elaborated political philosophies; third, there were many socially influential groups competing for power. This system was based 'not on ideological factors, but on the competition of financial and industrial groups and regional elites' interested 'in dispersing power in order to control at least a small segment of it'. The result was 'political instability'.[15]

Ukraine's political system, then, constituted something of a unique case, both within the post-Soviet space and in the world at large. There was a huge number of parties—more than 120 were officially registered in 2002—that were often internally divided as well. This fragmentation was 'unprecedented for a modern democratic republic'.[16] It 'hindered democratization' because it 'made it difficult for the population to orient itself politically'.[17] But it also made it more difficult for would-be autocrats and their networks of clients to consolidate power.

The same can be said for the much-quoted regional fragmentation of Ukraine. On the one hand, regionalism has defined voting behaviour and hence fragmented the political system. In both parliamentary and presidential elections until 2019, voters in the more Russian and Russian-speaking regions of eastern Ukraine and Crimea 'voted for one set of parties', while those in the more Ukrainian-speaking western Ukraine preferred a different set. 'No party managed to elect candidates across Ukraine.' Presidential elections show a similar regional pattern. At their extreme, regional divisions can define conflict lines within Ukraine, including the threat of secessionism and ethno-political conflict.[18]

On the other hand, regional identities and political networks also help balance power within the broader political system and prevent any one group of elites from monopolising power. Ukraine's regional, cultural, religious and economic diversity can be seen as an asset as much as a liability. It is 'one of the main reasons for Ukraine's success as a democracy'.[19]

There were three main regional power groups: one based in Kharkiv in the north-east; the second from the industrial heartland around Donetsk in the east; and the third from Dnipro in central Ukraine, the heart of the Soviet Union's defence and space industries. These had already been part of the political structure of late Soviet times; after 1991 they developed into a 'multi-pyramid system of competing patronal networks'. This structure led to a specific form of 'patronal democracy' where clans competed for political power within a republican set-up.[20]

At the same time, winners often tried to replace this competitive structure with a single hierarchy of power. The first attempt came under Leonid Kuchma, who built a 'patronal autocracy'—until the Orange Revolution of 2004 destroyed this system and reverted to the status quo ante; that is, a dual competition between president and parliament on the one hand and multiple power networks on the other. Yanukovych then tried again. He successfully neutralised competing clans—until ordinary citizens intervened to stop this usurpation of power. The 2013–14 Revolution of Dignity not only undid Yanukovych's dictatorial slide but also led to an election 'that was probably the fairest one in the country's history'. However, this transformation of the political system was one-sided: while it did constitute a re-democratisation, it did not eliminate regional and patronal politics.[21]

It was only with Zelensky's election in 2019 that things began to change in this regard. Zelensky 'is no chief patron and has no patronal pyramid' but instead gathered strong support from the new middle and creative classes. He campaigned on an anti-corruption platform. During his campaign, he mostly spoke Russian, which helped overcome regional differences between Russian speakers in the east and Ukrainian speakers in the west. And he achieved what many thought impossible: his election was the first in Ukraine's post-Soviet history where voting did not follow regional patterns.[22]

The Orange Revolution

Ukraine's democratic development after 1991, then, was defined by the push and pull between president and parliament, between multiple power networks, between the ruling elite and society at large, and between democratic and autocratic tendencies. Thus, 'democratisation' was not a linear process (see Figure 5). After the revolutionary 1990s, there was a sharp decline in the level of democratic performance, followed by a spike after 2004, triggered by the Orange Revolution. However, as the post-revolutionary regime consolidated, the gains were again undone. This new downward slide was arrested in 2013–14 by Euromaidan.

The Orange Revolution was initiated when the scandal-plagued outgoing president Kuchma, supported by Russia, tried to help one of his clients into power by falsifying the election. The fraud was of a relatively sophisticated variety, returning a relatively believable narrow victory for Yanukovych with just under 50 per cent of the votes. Yushchenko had allegedly garnered just under 47 per cent. Unfortunately for the falsifiers, however, an independent exit poll showed a completely different result: 53 per cent for Yushchenko and 44 per cent for Yanukovych. Moreover, the opposition also benefited from competition within the power structure of the state itself: the Ukrainian Security Service (SBU) had tapped the phones of the falsifiers and passed the recordings on to Yushchenko's team. They proved that the discrepancy between the exit poll and the official result had been caused by vote rigging.[23]

Like the later Revolution of Dignity, the Orange Revolution had two major sites: the streets, in particular of Kyiv, where mass protests took place, and the corridors of power, where the transition of power was negotiated with assistance from the European Union. The resulting compromise was a rerun of the election, won by Yushchenko, and a constitutional reform which rebalanced power away from the presidency and towards parliament. In Moscow, the reaction was 'horror, indignation, anger'. Putin was convinced, remembered an insider, 'that this was the direct result of meddling from the West'. The nefarious forces of Washington were trying 'to turn Ukraine into an anti-Russia'.[24]

Putin need not have worried, however. The renewed democratisation was not here to stay either (see Figure 5). In 2010, the loser of the 2004 revolution, Yanukovych, won the presidential elections, this

Figure 5: The development of Ukraine's democracy, 1984–2021
* *Chart shows central estimate of V-Dem index, which captures the extent to which political leaders are elected under comprehensive voting rights in free and fair elections, as well as the level to which freedom of association and expression are guaranteed.*
Source: Our World in Data, 'Electoral Democracy, Ukraine, 1984 to 2021', 2023

time in a fair contest. Within months of his victory he had gathered unprecedented powers, which he increasingly used to build an 'autocratic kleptocracy'. Opposition politicians, journalists and historians were intimidated, arrested and censored. Yanukovych and his circle of family and business partners exploited his developing dictatorship for personal gain. In short: Ukraine began to resemble Russia.[25]

The Revolution of Dignity

Hence, the second, much more violent, revolution of late 2013 to early 2014. The protests began in late November 2013, touched off by the announcement that the government had decided not to sign an association agreement with the European Union. This decision indicated that Ukraine would turn back to the old imperial centre of Russia. It also signalled the further entrenchment of autocratic tendencies along Russian lines rather than European-style democracy. The antidemocratic signalling was probably as important, maybe more important, than the anti-European gesture. Large sectors of society were unhappy with the renewed autocratic turn under Yanukovych and the open corruption of his regime. Police brutality against the at first small group of protesters further galvanised society and the protests quickly grew.

The demonstrations turned violent, first because the police tried to destroy the protest encampment on Independence Square (30 November, 11 December), second because a radical minority of violent protesters tried to break through police lines to reach the Presidential Administration building (1 December) and parliament (19 January). The government also mobilised thugs to attack the protesters, who in turn reacted with the organisation of 'Self-Defense Forces'. On 18 December, police began shooting live rounds at the protesters.[26]

The action then moved from the streets into the halls of parliament and government. On 21 February 2014, the foreign ministers of Poland, France and Germany arrived in Ukraine to help negotiate a peaceful settlement—an attempted rerun of the 2004 solution. The result of their intervention was an agreement between Yanukovych and the parliamentary opposition, signed on the same day. It called for an interim government, a renewed rebalancing of the political system in favour of parliament, and presidential and parliamentary elections before the year was over. Until then, Yanukovych would remain in power.

Only he did not. On the evening of the same day, with violence continuing in the streets, he left Kyiv for exile in Russia. 'I never imagined that he was such a cowardly piece of shit,' fumed his patron in the Kremlin, who had shouted at him over the phone to 'sit still' and take control of the situation. This time, Putin was right to panic: he had lost Ukraine.[27]

After Yanukovych left, parliament implemented the agreement insofar as it restored the 2004 constitution on 22 February, removing much of the president's powers and returning Ukraine to a parliamentary republic. Parliamentarians also selected a new government, as planned. But instead of leaving Yanukovych in power until a new election could be held, parliament voted to remove him from office immediately. There was no mechanism to do so in the current constitution, except to impeach him for high treason. This procedure was not followed either, however, hence the move was, technically, illegal.[28]

The move to oust Yanukovych was thus an 'extra-constitutional act'.[29] It was an insurrection by one democratically elected part of the political system (the parliament) against another (the president) against a backdrop of street violence embedded in peaceful mass protest. This description is probably as close to the definition of 'revolution' as one gets. The resulting interim government thus had dubious legitimacy and Russian propaganda was basically correct in asserting that 'the decision of the Rada [parliament] has no legal basis since the impeachment procedure was not followed'. As historian David Marples has pointed out, the Russian account, discussed in more detail in Chapter 5, is thus partially true. The original compromise solution would have offered 'a more democratic path to unseat him [Yanukovych] through elections, as the European leaders had advocated'.[30] However, legitimacy was restored in new elections soon thereafter. The Revolution of Dignity did not result in a revolutionary dictatorship. It embedded democracy.

Right Sector

A particularly controversial aspect of Euromaidan was the participation of militant far-right groups, which was also exploited by Russian propaganda in an attempt to classify the Revolution of Dignity as a fascist coup. 'The main perpetrators of the coup,' claimed Putin in a speech trying to justify the annexation of Crimea in March 2014, 'were nationalists, neo-Nazis, Russophobes, and antisemites.' These dark fascist forces, he continued, 'determine life in Ukraine to this day'.[31] This narrative has also gotten some traction outside the region, in particular on the political left. How serious is the charge?

First, there were right-wing radicals on Maidan—which refers to Maidan Nezalezhnosti, or Independence Square, in Kyiv. These were people with anti-Semitic, anti-Russian, generally xenophobic but also anti-feminist and homophobic views who not only advocated for but also used physical violence as a means of political struggle. Members of such groups 'had been the first to begin scuffles with the police' on 1 December 2013. They became known as 'Right Sector', after the part of Independence Square where they first went into action against police. At first they included 'several dozen people' from a variety of

far-right, neo-Nazi, football hooligan and other groups prone to violence. After the police violence on 30 November, Right Sector grew as
ideologically diverse people, indignant at police brutality, joined forces,
ready to defend the revolution. Hence, Right Sector 'became the core
of paramilitary mobilization, and more and more people were becoming active participants'. This increased Right Sector played a central
role in the escalation of violence on 1 December. But it remained
a minority among protesters: 300 to 500 people among the several
thousand who ended up participating in anti-police violence as well as
hundreds of thousands of mostly peaceful protesters.[32]

It is thus clear from journalistic and participant accounts as well as the
investigations of scholars that the far right did play a role in Euromaidan,
from the very beginning to the very end. Evaluations of exactly what that
role was, however, differ. Analysts from the left of the political spectrum
tend to stress the role of fascists on Maidan. According to one such
analysis, 'the Right Sector was the most active group in Maidan confrontation and violence.' Far-right groups played a part in 20 per cent of
confrontations and 29 per cent of 'specifically violent events'.[33]

These data imply, of course, that 80 per cent of confrontations and
71 per cent of 'specifically violent events' were driven by other political
actors. Right-wing militants thus neither initiated the protests nor dominated the majority of confrontations. Neo-Fascists continued to form
a minority. Most protesters on Independence Square were not part of
any organised party, social organisation or political movement.[34] The
violent turn was initiated as much by the police and militant supporters
of the regime and the subsequent radicalisation of sectors of the protest
movement. Protesters all over the country numbered maybe two million,
and organised Self-Defense Forces included some 12 000 in Kyiv alone.
Among the latter, there were two radical right 'hundreds', one with 300
members, the other 150. 'Most of the participants of these radical right
groups can be rightly called neo-Nazis,' writes Vyacheslav Likhachev, a
graduate of the Jewish University in Moscow and head of the National
Minority Rights Monitoring Group of Ukraine. By the same token,
however, 'this does not give any grounds to characterize the entire protest
movement as a "neo-Nazi" movement'.[35]

Democracy in a Time of War

Euromaidan was a major discontinuity in Ukrainian politics, a political revolution arresting a continuing slide towards dictatorship. However, as Figure 5 illustrates, the following years of the Poroshenko presidency only saw stagnation in democratic development. These were years of war, of course: the Revolution of Dignity, misunderstood in Moscow as a plot by 'the West' to take Ukraine away from Russia, triggered the occupation and annexation of Crimea in 2014 as well as Russian sponsorship of war in Donbas. It was only after 2018 that a new upward movement commenced in the context of the presidential election of 2019.

That Ukraine saw a democratic surge during times of war is remarkable: wars usually have the opposite effect. Moreover, this tendency has continued after 2019. 'Instead of losing confidence in democracy as the best form of government,' writes political scientist Olga Onuch, 'Ukrainians have rallied around democracy.' Seventy-six per cent of those surveyed in May 2022 agreed that 'democracy is preferable to any other kind of government'. These returns constitute 'a sharp rise from the 41 per cent who agreed with this proposition only three years earlier, in April 2019'. More Ukrainians today support democracy than ever before.[36]

Moreover, both opinion polls and the standard scores used to measure democratic performance obscure the high level of social self-organisation evident in Ukraine. Particularly since the 2013–14 revolution, Ukrainian society has been mobilised in a thick web of volunteer and voluntary organisations, informal networks and self-help groups peculiar to the specific social and political formation of modern Ukraine. This grassroots movement goes across the political spectrum—from fascists on the right to anarchists on the left and mainstream society in between. Thus, Ukraine is a remarkable case of democratisation, as Onuch stresses: 'More than is typical in a democratizing context, its people in recent years have backed democracy, expressed rising satisfaction with government and key institutions, and embraced civic life as something they feel requires their personal engagement.'[37]

There are, however, also countervailing trends. The authors of a different opinion survey, held in July 2022, note that their data suggests there are reasons to believe 'that the demand for a "strong hand" is growing against the background of the war'. Fifty-eight per cent of respondents thought that 'a strong leader is more important for Ukraine' than democracy and 79 per cent thought that presidential interference with parliament was 'justified to strengthen defense'.[38]

The Role of Fascism

The perceived need for a strong hand might be explained by the contingencies of war. Ukrainian politics have been developing under conditions of war, foreign threat and a certain siege mentality ever since 2014; that is, for nearly a decade. To some critics, however, the support for strong leadership reflects an underlying authoritarian streak in Ukraine's society. According to some depictions, in fact, the country is either ruled or dominated by fascists. This is a central claim of Russian anti-Ukrainian propaganda, of course, and is eagerly embraced by Russian fellow travellers abroad. But it also has adherents among Ukraine's left and their international allies. What are the realities behind these claims? How important is fascism in contemporary Ukraine?

'There is no doubt that right-wing nationalism and extremism in modern-day Ukraine poses a threat to the democratic development of society,' one expert warned in 2018. Right-wing extremists try to intimidate ideological opponents through the use of exemplary violence, an attempt at silencing those they do not agree with. This threat makes it more difficult to speak out in public, to attend street protests or demonstrations.[39] Such violence is concerning, but it is also an expression of the political weakness of the far right in Ukraine. Ultranationalists tried to compete at the ballot box in the 2014 parliamentary elections, but failed. If in the 2012 elections, for example, the Svoboda party received over 10 per cent of the vote, in the post-Maidan parliamentary elections of 26 October 2014, its vote was down to just under 5 per cent, with Right Sector (organised as a party now) garnering another 1.8 per cent. Their influence continued to decline both in opinion polls and in election results. In the 2019 elections, the combined far-right parties won a total of 2.3 per cent of the vote.[40]

Meanwhile, over 73 per cent of participating voters elected a Jewish president, Zelensky, in the same year.[41] As the former chief rabbi of Moscow Pinchas Goldschmidt noted in December 2022, this fact alone 'made a nonsense' of the claim that Ukraine was dominated by fascists. 'Show me another country that is in the grip of Nazis where the Jewish community is thriving.' Instead, the rabbi, who resigned from his position and left Russia in July 2022 because he refused to support the Russian aggression against Ukraine, called on Russian Jews to leave their own country 'before they are made scapegoats for the hardship caused by the war'.[42]

There are other concerning developments, in particular a rapprochement between far-right groups and sections of the state structure, especially in the context of the war in Donbas. Most famous in this regard is the Azov Battalion, one of the many volunteer military units which emerged from early 2014 to help fight the war against Russian proxies (and, indeed, at times Russian regular troops). By September of that year, some 7000 volunteers were fighting alongside 50 000 regular soldiers in Ukraine's east. A month later, a total of thirty-eight volunteer units existed, organising some 13 500 armed men. They constituted a militarised version of the larger civil society mobilisation in the context of Euromaidan and war. A minority are better understood as parts of an 'uncivil society', however, hindering rather than helping Ukraine's democratisation. The Azov Battalion was, initially, among the latter.[43]

With around 500 members by June 2014, the battalion was one of the larger volunteer units. It was soon discovered by Russian propaganda and exploited in the attempt to paint a picture of Ukraine's defence effort as fascist (just as Euromaidan was portrayed as a fascist coup). And there were indeed Neo-Fascist tendencies in the battalion, particularly in the leadership. As two well-informed analysts write, the most influential Azov commanders espoused 'openly fascist opinions'. The unit also used clearly fascist symbols to represent its cause.[44]

The democratic Ukrainian state dealt with the existence of a militarily highly successful volunteer unit with Neo-Fascist leadership—by coopting it into the official structure! The commander of the Azov Battalion, Andriy Biletsky, was promoted to lieutenant colonel and awarded a bravery medal for his military record, while his battalion was integrated into a larger regiment of the same name under the command of the ministry of the interior. This 'Azov Regiment' was then, in late 2014, integrated into Ukraine's National Guard. The tactic was to dilute the far right by growing the unit and subsuming it into a state-controlled military structure. Biletsky was removed from his command position in 2016. Under President Zelensky, a crackdown on the wider far-right 'uncivil society' movement followed. Nevertheless, the 'case Azov', highly untypical as it was, played into the hands of Russian propaganda. It falsely came to represent to many outside observers the essence of the volunteer movement: a Ukrainian version of fascism.

The Politics of Memory

Outsiders' perceptions about the prevalence of fascism in Ukraine were also fuelled by the sometimes clumsy politics of memory which past Ukrainian governments pursued. Nations need to construct a useful past which shows where the nation came from and what its past achievements, and maybe failures, are. These official histories hardly ever accord with the critical and evidentiary standards of academic history writing. They usually exist in some tension with professional historiography. Ukraine was no exception here, but the authorities did make a few peculiar choices.

There were several obvious choices for a positive backstory for contemporary Ukraine. One was a celebration of the medieval Rus as the ultimate ancestor, maybe flanked by the Galician-Volhynian successor. A second choice was the Cossack state of the early modern period, a polity which could be celebrated for its democratic traditions and fight for freedom (if one forgot its anti-Jewish and anti-Polish violence). Third was the first Ukrainian republic of 1917–20, which had several attractive features, including its initial social democracy, multi-ethnic tolerance, and the role it played in building Ukrainian cultural institutions. But it also lived for some of its existence under German occupation and ultimately failed to survive. And during the final stages of the wars of the Romanov succession, their troops, too, killed Jews (as did the Whites and Bolshevik forces).

To some extent, Ukraine chose all of these, but the centre of gravity of memory politics was a fourth choice: to celebrate the suffering Ukraine was subjected to under the Soviets. Central to this memory is the great famine of 1932–33, known in Ukraine as 'Holodomor'. It was central to Ukraine's official memory.

Finally, there was the national resistance against both Nazi and German occupation during World War II. This was maybe the most problematic past, as the wartime ultranationalists had at times collaborated with the Germans and were entangled in the implementation of the Holocaust as well as in ethnic violence against Poles. In sharp contrast to the Ukrainian revolutionaries of 1917, the ultranationalists of the 1930s and 1940s were not in favour of a multinational Ukrainian state but instead were ethnically exclusive: anti-Semitic, anti-Polish and anti-Russian. Their embrace as heroes of liberation was maybe the most unhelpful decision by the post-1991 nation-builders: it alienated Poland, raised alarm bells in Germany and Israel, and gave Russian propaganda grist to its mill. It made the job of anti-Ukrainian propaganda rather easy: at times, Ukraine did celebrate fascists from World War II as positive role models and ancestors.[45]

Ironically, by the time Russian troops invaded in 2022, allegedly in order to 'denazify' Ukraine, President Zelensky had already begun steering public discourse away from hagiographic accounts of yesteryear's ultranationalists. No wonder: Zelensky had family who were killed in the Holocaust; four of his ancestors fought in the Red Army during World War II.[46] Ukraine's desperate fight for survival as an independent nation will further lessen the reliance on the resistance from World War II as embodying the Ukrainian nation. The war produces democratic Ukrainian heroes on a daily basis, whose feats can be commemorated and celebrated with much less ambiguity.

Rather than a fascistisation of democratic Ukraine, then, we can observe a process of appropriation and democratisation of sometimes ambiguous pasts. The phrase *Slava Ukraini!* (Glory to Ukraine!) is a case in point. It is often cited by anti-Ukraine propaganda as evidence of the fascist nature of Ukraine's war effort, because of its assumed World War II origin. In fact, it originated in the nineteenth century's national awakening. Later, it was popularised in the Ukrainian revolution and wars of independence of 1917–20. Only much later was it adopted by the ultranationalists, who added the ritualistic reply *Heróyam sláva!* (Glory to the heroes!). Introduced into Euromaidan by far-right forces, it soon began to lose its original connotations and was interpreted as 'Glory to the fallen heroes of the Maidan!'. By 2022, both phrases had become central slogans of Ukraine's current war effort. They will remind generations to come of Ukraine's just war of defence against Russia from 2022, not of the national resistance's problematic wartime record of the 1940s.[47]

From Ethnic to Civic Nationalism

The trajectory of Ukraine, then, has not been towards fascism but towards a civic form of nationalism which allows multi-ethnic belonging. Ukraine continues to be a multi-ethnic nation, albeit one with a strong dominance by the titular nationality. The 2001 census showed an increase in the share of Ukrainians in the population (from 73 per cent in 1989 to 78 per cent in 2001) and a decline in the share of Russians (from 22 to 17 per cent). Other minorities grew from 3 to 5 per cent, however. In particular, the return of Crimean Tatars (deported by Stalin) and migration by Armenians, Azerbaijanis, Georgians and Romanians grew these minorities significantly.[48] This multi-ethnicity poses some challenges for nation-building along nineteenth- and early twentieth-century lines. But these are obstacles which can be overcome, as there have long been two competing models for a modern nation: an exclusionary ethnic and an inclusive civic identity. In the former, ethnic belonging defines the state; in the latter, the state's territory and civic institutions define citizenship.

Since independence in 1991, Ukraine defined its polity and citizenship around a civic form of nationalism. True, like elsewhere, the ethnic variant was present as an alternative model, advocated by some in the political class and embraced by sectors of the population. In this alternative model, only people who speak Ukrainian as their first language and consider themselves shaped by a wider Ukrainian culture are seen as Ukrainians. At the fascist fringe, this ethnic nation is defined in racist terms by 'blood' or 'race'. But this variant never became dominant. Instead, what was institutionalised was civic nationalism, in which anybody who is a citizen of the democratic polity built within the borders of Ukraine is a 'Ukrainian', no matter if that person speaks Russian, is of Jewish heritage, or is a descendant of the Crimean Tatars or other groups.

It is this sense of civic nationalism which is inscribed in the Ukrainian Constitution: it defines the 'Ukrainian people' as 'the citizens of Ukraine of all nationalities'.[49] 'Ukrainian' was not described with reference to language or ancestry but simply according to where people lived at the time Ukraine became independent. Thus, Russians felt much less disenfranchised than in Latvia or Estonia, which adopted different policies. The civic form of nationalism enshrined in the constitution helped lessen pressures on national minorities to emigrate, assimilate or secede. Civic nationalism was one of the main reasons why Ukraine did not experience major ethnic conflict before the Russian invasion of Crimea.[50]

Remarkably, over the course of the tumultuous history of Ukraine since 1991—the Orange Revolution of 2004–05, the Revolution of Dignity or Euromaidan of 2013–14, the Russian annexation of Crimea and the Russian-sponsored war in Donbas since 2014—it was the civic version of Ukrainian national consciousness that triumphed, not the ethnic one. In 2019, in the middle of a war against Russian-backed rebels in Donbas, Ukraine opted against ethnic nationalism and for its civic sibling. It elected not the Ukrainian ethno-nationalist, Poroshenko, but the Russian-speaking Jewish Ukrainian, Zelensky, as its president.[51]

And in the current war in Ukraine, this multi-ethnic and civil nationalism—this is our country and we defend our freedoms—has played an enormous role in mobilising the citizens of the state of Ukraine to fight and die for their country.[52] It is noteworthy, for example, that one of the most famous slogans emerging from this war—*Russkii voennyi korabl: idi nakhui!*, or *Russian military vessel—Fuck off!*—was uttered in Russian, not Ukrainian, and is promoted as such. And in what other country would a video of the president as a younger man, clad in skin-tight leather and dancing in high heels while poking fun at national icons—the Cossacks—increase his popularity?[53] The contrast with the earnest, unironic, homophobic and masculinist nationalism of Putin's Russia could not be more extreme.

CHAPTER 4

RUSSIA SINCE 1991: FAILED DECOLONISATION

The Problem of Metropolitan Decolonisation

That Russia and Ukraine have diverged politically so radically since 1991 is partially due to their position vis-a-vis the imploded empire they emerged from. Ukrainians could make sense of the breakdown of the Soviet empire as a moment of liberation from foreign oppression; Russians, as the inhabitants and 'owners' of the metropole, could not. The resulting phantom pains for a lost imperial status are familiar from other contexts: all metropoles struggle with the loss of empire. Imperial nostalgia is a fact of life in many of them. But an additional peculiarity made the transition particularly fraught in Russia. Here, the empire came historically first, and the nation second.

There is a fundamental distinction between the experience of 'having an empire' (like Britain) and 'being one' (like Russia or China). In the first instance, empire is 'a distant and profitable appendage'; in the latter case, the empire 'was part of the homeland' itself.[1] Decolonisation plays out differently in the two types, as a historian of China explained succinctly: 'If you *have* an empire, you can shed your colonies and preserve the metropolitan core … If you *are* an empire, losing the periphery means total transformation of the state and society.'[2] The decolonisation of a continuous land empire with no clear line of demarcation between the metropole and the periphery had unsettling geopolitical implications for the former colonial centre, unless it fundamentally re-thought its place in the world and its neighbourhood.[3]

1991 as a Decolonial Moment

Decolonisation would thus always be difficult for Russia and Russians, and maybe we should not be surprised that it failed. However, the failure was not preordained. The year 1991 was a time of great anti-imperial dreaming in Russia as well. The damn colonies, many thought, could fend for themselves. Once liberated from the economic burden to prop up 'the nationals', Russia could reach standards of living like Sweden or Switzerland. This thought was particularly enticing as 'the Union's greatest riches, especially its vast mineral resources, were on the territory of the Russian Federation'. As a result, 'Russia stood to benefit from the loss of its imperial possessions more than any other empire of the past.'[4]

Such views indeed persisted in some quarters of the intelligentsia well after they had been discarded by most state actors. As late as 2011, Dmitri Trenin, an influential Moscow think-tanker, tried to convince both himself and the outside world that Russia was a post-imperial state. 'The dismantlement of the USSR,' he wrote, was a good thing: 'It relieved Moscow from the need to keep the Balts and Moldovans under control. It released Russia from quasi-colonial responsibilities in Central Asia and the South Caucasus.' He concluded optimistically: 'The Russian empire is over, never to return.'[5]

Others were more pessimistic but still argued against the imperial nostalgia of their compatriots. Yegor Gaidar, minister of finance under Russia's first post-Soviet president, Boris Yeltsin, in a book first published in Russia in 2006, noted that his country suffered from the 'post-empire nostalgia' typical of post-imperial metropoles. This post-imperial syndrome was 'a disease' which was, however, 'curable'. In fact, it had to be overcome if Russia wanted to become a normal country. 'Dreams of returning to another era are illusory. Attempts to do so end in defeat.'[6]

These were throwbacks to the anti-imperial moment of 1991, when the question of what it would cost Russia to maintain the empire was on the actors' minds, particularly as it became clear that Ukraine would not help share the burden after the failed coup of August.[7] Once the union was dissolved, Yeltsin 'attempted to build something like a territorially bounded nation', pushing 'for the creation of a civic patriotism within Russia, reviving the old term *rossiyanin(a)* to refer to a citizen of the state irrespective of ethnicity, while downplaying responsibility for ethnic Russians (*russkie*) living outside the Russian Federation's borders'.[8]

This was a 'liberal Russian nationalism', opposed to both the 'small' ethnic nationalism of Russian racists and the 'big Russian nation of imperial times'. Like Ukraine's civic nationalism, it instead focused on the extant post-Soviet state and tried to forge a nation out of its multi-ethnic inhabitants.[9] This *rossiiskaia* (rather than the narrowly ethnically *russkaia*) nation was to be 'united across ethnic and cultural lines by a commitment to common values and institutions'.[10] This anti-colonial sentiment found its expression in the constitution of 1993, which embraced democratic constitutionalism, subordinated the country to international law, and did 'not reflect imperial nostalgia'.[11] The citizenship law of 1991, like its Ukrainian equivalent, focused on residence at the time of independence rather than language, culture or ethnicity.[12]

Imperialism

What followed was a rude shock. Some of the 'colonies' did remarkably well once the original economic crisis of the breakdown was over. The three Baltic republics soared in terms of living conditions and economic growth, enabled not least by their acceptance into the exclusive club of the rich European Union in 2004. Russia's economy continued its crash. Decolonisation, it turned out, did not increase the former metropole's wealth. Sweden and Switzerland remained pipedreams—except for the new rich, who could travel there.

While the economic catastrophe was universal across the former Soviet space, and had begun well before the dissolution of the Soviet Union, such complexities were not necessarily understood. What Russians saw was that decolonisation coincided with economic catastrophe and political instability. The years of the Yeltsin presidency (1991–99) were humiliating to many. As the state disintegrated, violence became widespread, crime endemic. Loss of security, loss of job, loss of income, loss of savings, loss of political stability and loss of empire were experienced as a package. And the perceived arrogance towards Russia of the old enemy, the West—NATO, the United States, the European Union and all the rest—only added to the humiliation.

Soon, therefore, the tide turned. Decolonising rhetoric was edged out by imperial nostalgia. Already in 1994 a veteran US analyst warned that 'the imperial impulse remains strong and even appears to be strengthening'.[13] The old hawk was right. The first Chechen War (1994–96) drew a line in the sand: if Chechnya, one of the acquisitions of the empire in the nineteenth century, would break away, where would things end? Where was the natural border of Russia once the disintegration continued? Would Siberia be next?

Vladimir Putin expressed these anxieties of many of his compatriots when he proclaimed that the anti-colonial resistance in Chechnya was 'a continuation of the collapse of the USSR ... If we don't put an immediate end to this, Russia will cease to exist'.[14] That he cut his teeth as prime minister and then acting president in the second Chechen war (1999–2000) was symbolic: his would be an imperial presidency. Under his leadership, Russia would be at war frequently: the Chechen adventure turned into a long-term insurgency which lasted to 2009, in 2008 Russia fought a war with Georgia, from 2014 it was engaged in Ukraine and from 2015 in Syria.

Externally, many Russians continued to see the post-imperial periphery of the old Soviet empire 'as their patrimony', a '"near abroad" lacking the full complement of sovereignty reserved for Russia and states in the "far abroad"'. Moscow's ambassador to Washington noted in a 1993 conversation 'that relations between Russia and Ukraine were to be "identical to those between New York and New Jersey"'. In the same year, President Yeltsin demanded the international community recognise Russia's 'special authority as guarantor of peace and stability on the territory of the former USSR'. Such notions were enshrined in a presidential decree of September 1995, still in force today, which declared that the region covered by the Commonwealth of Independent States (CIS), a relatively loose intergovernmental organisation of nine of the fifteen successor states of the Soviet Union, was 'first of all Russia's zone of influence'. Institutionalisation soon followed. By 1998, the Russian *internal* security service, the Federal Security Service of the Russian Federation (FSB) had a special department for intelligence activities specifically in the former Soviet republics.[15]

After Putin assumed office in 2000, this nearly reflexive imperialism of Russia's political elite was given a more carefully worked-out ideological structure. History became a major battlefield in this culture war, with the president actively engaged in the discussion. His positions, while raising alarm bells among professional historians both at home and abroad, were often much less radical than those held in society at large.[16] The rehabilitation of Russia's imperial record, including and in particular victory in World War II, was quite popular, as was the embrace of the Russian Orthodox Church as a guarantor of conservatism and the unity of 'Russia's world'. This was, indeed, 'a turn to populism', an appeal to 'the less educated, more nationalistic, more religious and less affluent'.[17]

Think tanks close to the Kremlin saw their staffing changed. 'New people started appearing at the institute,' remembered a veteran of the Russian Institute for Strategic Studies (RISI), a once 'sleepy research arm' of Russia's foreign intelligence and 'something of an old spooks' home'. Rather than featuring retiring spies, younger men started to take over. They were

> growing long beards and imitating the manners and dress of [anti-Bolshevik] White Guard officers [of the Civil War years], or how they imagined White Guard officers to look like, based on Soviet films ... They would hang icons over their workstations and would cross themselves fervently over the soup served in the institute's cafeteria.[18]

These new analysts, whose treatises now made it all the way to Putin's desk, began to promote openly imperialist policies. They had two arms. One was cultural imperialism, expressed in the notion of the 'Russian world'. The idea was that Soviet and post-Soviet migrations of Russians both within the Soviet space and beyond had created 'a transnational *oikumene* of Russian language and Russian culture'. It was destined to be led by Moscow as the Third Rome, which would 'unite Russians, Slavs or Orthodox believers around the world'. The second arm of this new imperialism was political: the notion that 'former Soviet republics should not be considered to have full sovereignty and were thus not entirely the subject of international law.'[19]

The Yeltsin Years: Democracy, Privatisation and Chaos

Why this transformation? To understand how the Russian state ended up embracing imperialism and an aggressive form of Russian imperial nationalism, we need to understand internal developments in Russia since 1991—the task of this chapter—as well as Putin's thinking on his position in both Russian and world history—the task of Chapter 5. Putin, the dictator of Russia, is certainly important in what transpired, but in a way he and his position are expressions of a larger malaise in Russian politics and society since 1991. The turn to neo-imperialism, which resulted, first, in the illegal annexation of Crimea and support for the anti-Kyiv insurgents in Donbas in 2014, and eventually the full-scale invasion of Ukraine in 2022, was the long-term result of the failure of the post-1991 settlement to create a vibrant democracy and economic prosperity for the majority of the population.

Part of the reason, in other words, why decolonisation of the metropole failed was that the hopes of 1991 were disappointed: that Russia would become both free and prosperous. Instead, Russia became chaotic, divided, unequal. Outside of a small, westernised middle class in the big cities, who lived 'in a happy little bubble where people ate and drank well, dressed even better, worked in well-designed centrally located offices doing something at least vaguely creative',[20] the present and the imaginable future did not seem to hold a positive alternative for large numbers of Russians. Instead, they clung to an imagined past of stability (nostalgia for the Brezhnev years) and relevance (nostalgia for empire).

Economically, the 1990s were horrendous for most Russians as much as for their Ukrainian neighbours. Like Ukraine's, Russia's GDP declined by 43 per cent between 1991 and 1998, an economic catastrophe worse than what the Soviets had experienced in World War II (when GDP fell by 24 per cent) or the Great Depression in the United States (when GDP dropped by 31 per cent). Particularly hard hit was industrial production, which contracted by 56 per cent. The average real incomes of working Russians fell 46 per cent in 1992 alone, and later, in 1998–99, by another third.[21]

Politically, too, these were years of upheaval. Yeltsin faced increased opposition from the resurgent communists, a phenomenon which worried many both inside and outside the country and made them tolerant of his drift towards authoritarianism. A turning point came in 1993, when the president ordered the shelling of parliament. It was the culmination of a constitutional crisis and has been retold as a tragic necessity or as a betrayal of democratic hopes. It led to the resolution of a structural crisis—through violence.

Not unlike Ukraine, Russia had entered the post-Soviet world with a political system which combined both a strong parliament and a strong president, thus embracing '"two models" of the political system whose relations became progressively conflictual'. This situation was the result of the historical evolution of the Russian Constitution. It had been created by adding new elements to reformed parts of the Soviet constitution, with 'a presidency badly grafted onto a cumbersome parliamentary system, both institutions in their pure, ideal-type and unworkable forms'. The two parts of the system were 'incompatible' even without the personal and ideological conflicts between parliament and presidency. While Ukraine oscillated between periods of stronger presidencies, at times with autocratic tendencies, and resurgencies of parliamentary power, in Russia the conflict was resolved, once and for all, in favour of the former. In 1993, Russia took a one-way path to an ever stronger executive presidency.[22]

The 1993 confrontation between president and parliament was also a moment of contestation over the post-imperial order. Part of the stand-off was over the Belovezha Accords, the 1991 agreement which had disbanded the Soviet Union. Many parliamentarians—communists and nationalists alike—were opposed to its terms; Yeltsin, who was one of the signatories, wanted to save it. It came down to a bare-knuckle fight. In the end it was tanks which decided the stand-off—the original sin of post-1991 Russian democracy.[23] After his successful coup and under the new constitution, Yeltsin had 'powers well in excess of those held by his French and American peers'.[24]

The violent confrontation also had an unintended consequence: it seriously imperilled the project of liberal nationalism Yeltsin had originally promoted. If citizenship in Russia was a function of loyalty to institutions, how could such loyalty develop if the president shelled parliament? Clearly, those in power, those with the beautiful words about democracy and prosperity, just cared about their own power and enrichment—or so many ordinary Russians thought.

Meanwhile, the president's actual hold over the largest country in the world became more and more tenuous. Post-1991, Russia had retained a plethora of territorial units inherited from Soviet nationality policy, which extended not only to the national forms of the union republics but also to cultural autonomy for minorities within union republics themselves. These regions became stronger as the centre became weaker. Eventually, the entire federal edifice was held together only by 'a hodgepodge of bilateral arrangements between Moscow and the different provincial authorities'.[25]

The Putin Years: Economic Recovery and Political Retrenchment

Putin would re-centre power away from provincial overlords and back towards Moscow; in the capital itself, he would build on the strong presidency Yeltsin had bequeathed; and he would eventually discard liberal nationalism as useless. As Figure 6 illustrates, democratic governance took a nosedive the moment Putin got into power, first as acting president at the end of 1999, then as elected leader from May 2000 through 2008 and again from 2012, after having switched places with his prime minister, Dmitry Medvedev, from 2008 through 2012.

The takeover was swift, as journalist and opposition activist Masha Gessen remembered: 'The political system changed so quickly that even political activists and political analysts needed time to get their bearings.' Only six days after his inauguration, Putin signed the first

Figure 6: *The development of Russia's democracy, 1984–2021*
* *Chart shows central estimate of V-Dem index, which captures the extent to which political leaders are elected under comprehensive voting rights in free and fair elections, as well as the level to which freedom of association and expression are guaranteed.*
Source: Our World in Data, 'Electoral Democracy, Russia, 1984 to 2021', 2023

of many decrees which would dismantle democratic structures and strengthen 'vertical power'.[26]

The ongoing insurgency in Chechnya provided further opportunities, showing the close relationship between imperialism and authoritarian retrenchment. Chechnya was a nineteenth-century acquisition of the Russian Empire; Chechens fought against Russian domination then as well as subsequently, in the twentieth century. After 1991, many again thought the time was ripe to shake off the Russian yoke. In 2004, Putin used a Chechen terrorist attack on a school in Beslan to further strengthen his imperial presidency. Elections for provincial governors were suspended and replaced by direct appointment by the president, and elections to the Lower House became indirect, via voting for political parties, 'which would then fill their seats with ranking members'. These and some associated changes amounted to a quantum change in the political process: 'there remained only one federal-level public official who was directly elected: the president himself.'[27] Russia had returned to 'pseudo-federalism not unlike what had been the pattern in the USSR'.[28]

Another set of constitutional revisions pushed this presidential system further away from the de-colonial thrust of the 1993 (Yeltsin) constitution. If the former had stressed Russia's integration into the system of international law, now the primacy of the Russian Constitution over international law was asserted. If Yeltsin's constitution remained expressly silent on the relationship between Russia and the other Soviet successors, the 2020 version expressly claimed succession to the Soviet Union along with the assertion of continuity of the Russian state all the way to the medieval Rus. The powers of the president were further strengthened and the Russians declared to be the country's 'state creating people' (*gosudarstvoobrazuiushchii narod*), both asserting the population's multi-ethnicity and imposing the Russians as first among equals. This is an imperial constitution which defines Russia as the heir of the Russian Empire, not as a constitutional state among others linked by universal values and international law.[29]

As liberal nationalism thus receded more and more into the background, two alternatives were left: an ethnic nationalism ('Russia for *russkie*') and an imperial nationalism. The former was potentially problematic, given that Russia had, not unlike Ukraine, 20 per cent national minorities among its population.[30] The notion that Russians were the 'state creating people' has thus some serious potential for internal conflict. Hence, Putin also repeatedly stressed the experience of hundreds of years of multinational empire, which led to 'tolerance, as is now fashionable to say'. Such tolerance, he continued, was 'in our blood'.[31] At the same time, the ethnic nationalism of the 'state building people' could come in handy: to lay claim to the 'near abroad' as part of Russian civilisation and to instrumentalise Russian minorities to destabilise neighbouring polities. And there were Russians minorities in all fourteen non-Russian successor states, the result of decades of internal migration during Soviet times.[32]

Protecting Russians abroad was a powerfully mobilising notion domestically also. The idea that Russians in non-Russian states were 'a societal problem of nearly civilizational proportions' was shared across the political spectrum. Russian liberals embraced it as much as Russian fascists. Of course, living 'abroad' is only a problem if you indeed are discriminated against (as Russians are under certain circumstances in some, but by no means all, successor states), or if you think that the normal state of affairs is for Russians to live in 'Russia'. In other words, the very notion that this is a 'problem' unveils you as either an ethno-nationalist or an imperialist (liberal or otherwise).[33]

As imperial nationalism became more and more dominant in Russian public discourse, the political system continuously drifted towards dictatorship. Opposition to Putin became more dangerous. A string of political murders took place, most famously of journalist Anna Politkovskaia in 2006 and opposition activist Boris Nemtsov in 2015. In 2020, anti-corruption activist Alexei Navalny escaped a poisoning attempt only by the skin of his teeth. All the while, media freedoms and civil society's ability to organise have been eroded continuously. An important turning point came in July 2012, when a law on 'foreign agents' was passed. It required all organisations which accepted foreign money to register with the authorities, mark their public utterances with a special warning, and undergo an arduous auditing regime. It served to name and shame anybody with foreign contacts (a lot of non-governmental organisations got grant money from abroad), and those who refused to budge could be prosecuted or shut down.

Overall, then, with a Freedom House score of 20, Russia has long been classified as a 'consolidated authoritarian regime'. While it is not as grim a dictatorship as Belarus (11) or Tajikistan (8), it is way more autocratic than the country its state media love to depict as 'fascist': Ukraine, a hybrid regime with a score of 60. In the run-up to the war of 2022, things were further tightened, and since the start of the war the situation has gotten dramatically worse. Before the invasion, writes a veteran journalist, 'there was a space in Russia's political ecosystem for political opposition and for free speech. The space was narrow, but it was defined by a series of unspoken rules that were observed by the authorities more often than they were broken.' After 24 February, by contrast, says the journalist, 'many of my sources insisted that we sit metres away from our smartphones, or leave them behind when coming to a meeting'. Even 'pro-Putin people suddenly discovered fear'.[34]

Paradoxically, fear and terror were never really necessary, as Putin's rule was hardly ever under serious pressure from the majority of the population. Putin has approval ratings most other politicians could only dream of (see Figure 7). Anything less than 70 per cent is seen as a crisis of confidence in the president. And this crisis has been brewing from 2008 onwards, as his approval ratings have steadily declined, although they did get a boost from both of his imperial adventures—the annexation of Crimea in 2014 and the invasion of Ukraine in 2022. It might be noteworthy that, in late 2021, Putin's approval ratings were at—for him—a crisis low: 63 per cent in November of that year, just when he was pondering whether or not he should invade.

The Economy

Why was Putin so popular? Part of the answer is his ability to express what ordinary Russians feel—his views on history, his nostalgia for imperial greatness, his sense of having been wronged by the West,

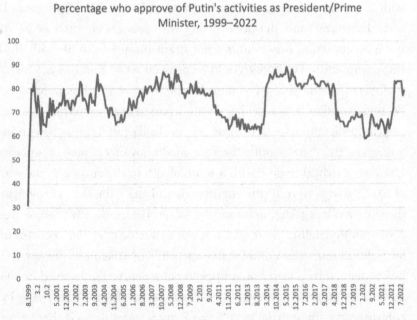

Percentage who approve of Putin's activities as President/Prime Minister, 1999–2022

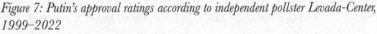

Figure 7: Putin's approval ratings according to independent pollster Levada-Center, 1999–2022
Source: Levada Center, 'Indicators', 2023

all are quite common sentiments in the society he rules over. Putin is 'in many crucial ways the Russian everyman'. Not unlike Helmut Kohl, the endlessly boring chancellor of Germany from 1982 to 1998, or John Howard, the equally banal prime minister of Australia from 1996 to 2007, Putin embodies the hopes, dreams, prejudices and resentments of many of his compatriots.[35]

It doubtlessly helped, too, that, for a long time, as the civil and political rights were contracting, the economy was expanding. This expansion had, in fact, been one of Putin's original aspirations: he wanted to be remembered as the president who, after a decade of chaos, humiliation and poverty, brought prosperity to his country. He was lucky in this regard: Russia is a major exporter of oil—the second-largest in the world in 2021 with 13 per cent of the total global production of crude oil, just ahead of Saudi Arabia (12 per cent) and trailing the leader, the United States (14.5 per cent), only slightly.[36] And oil prices, which had crashed just as Gorbachev became

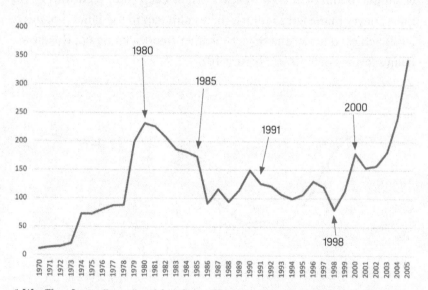

* West Texas Intermediate, adjusted for inflation. The arrows point out the following landmarks in this history: 1980—high point of oil boom; 1985—Gorbachev becomes general secretary; 1991—breakdown of the Soviet Union; 1998—all-time low point of oil price. Putin becomes acting president a year later, on 31 December 1999; May 2000—Putin elected president

Figure 8: Oil prices and Russia's political history, 1970–2005
Source: Our World in Data, 'Crude Oil Prices', 2023

general secretary, saw a spectacular recovery just when Putin became president (see Figure 8). Russia could exploit this recovery by massively expanding oil production after 1999 (see Figure 9). Together, the rising prices and increased production refloated the economy. The average Russian became better off, and increased prosperity nearly always helps approval ratings.

However, Putin's economic miracle, while remarkable if compared with Ukraine at the same time, was neither floating all the boats nor lifting Russia into the league of rich nations. For one, it was accompanied by a dizzying polarisation of wealth. By 2017, Russia had become 'the most unequal of all the world's major economies'. The top 10 per cent of the population owned 87 per cent of all the wealth. Even in the remarkably unequal United States, the equivalent figure was 76 per cent; in China, certainly not a haven of social equality, it was only 66 per cent. The conspicuous consumption of the political elite became a major avenue of attack for the anti-Putin opposition.[37] Moreover, the economic boom of the Putin years, while steep compared with Soviet times, never managed to return the wealth gap to the United States to levels achieved under the Soviets. Rather than catching up, Russia was falling further behind (see Figure 10).

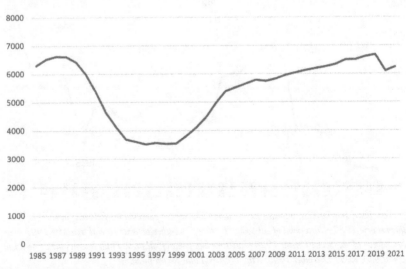

Figure 9: Russia's oil boom, 1985–2021
Source: Our World in Data, 'Oil Production', 2023

Increased prosperity and increased approval ratings of the president did not translate into increased democracy or transparent governance, moreover. Corruption ebbed a little during the first few years after Putin took the helm, as Figure 4 shows. But any progress made on this front was undone by the time he switched to become prime minister in 2008. When he returned to the presidency in 2012, things had again improved somewhat, returning to levels of corruption similar to 2004. Ever since then, Russia has stagnated in this respect.

Increasingly, then, economic and social development and political development were out of sync. As Russia became more prosperous, a cosmopolitan middle class developed in the big cities, and it demanded a say. However, the political system became less open, more dictatorial, more corrupt, and less responsive to input from below. This contradiction exploded in the 2012 protests against Putin's re-election as president, seen as rigged by the opposition. Putin let the protests run for a while but then ordered a crackdown—a deepening of the 'preventive counter-revolution' the regime had been engaged in ever since Ukraine's Orange Revolution. In effect, it ended Putin's attempts to come to terms with the more liberal parts of society: often young, well educated and urban—a new middle class Putin's petrodollar-driven

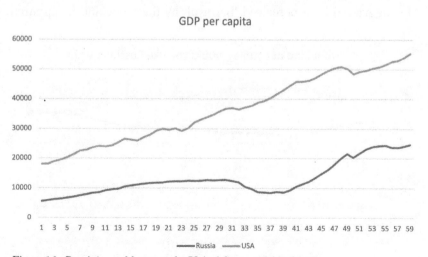

Figure 10: Russia's wealth gap to the United States, 1960–2018
Source: Our World in Data, 'GDP Per Capital, 1960 to 2018', 2023

economic policies had helped create. Now, the regime hitched its
political wagon more thoroughly to the political right.[38]

NATO Enlargement

This rightward shift happened in the context of the successful assertion
of Russia's role in the region, in particular with regards to preventing
further enlargement of NATO as well as the European Union. This
was a popular policy, although not one universally endorsed. Opinion
polls between 2003 and 2015 showed Russians split between those who
wanted a decent life rather than international status, and those who preferred to live in 'a powerful country that is respected and feared by other
countries'. Over time, the pro-great-power sentiment first declined and
then took off. By 2015 the two sides were about equally matched (see
Figure 11). Threat perceptions increased together with status anxiety.
Between 1997 and May 2022, the proportion of Russians who thought
that NATO membership for Ukraine would pose a 'big threat' to their
country rose from under half to reach 72 per cent. The proportion who
had a 'bad' attitude towards NATO went from 76 per cent in 2018 to
82 per cent in 2022.[39]

Status concerns were particularly rife within the political elite of the
country, who had long complained about NATO enlargement. They
felt aggrieved by a perceived 'betrayal' by the latter and its apparent

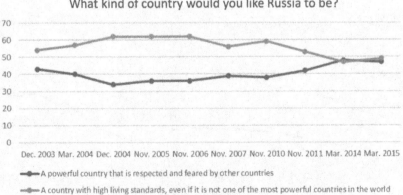

What kind of country would you like Russia to be?

Figure 11: Support for great power status in Russia, 2003–15
Source: Levada-Center, 'Russia's Role in the World', 25 March 2015

'meddling' both in Russian domestic politics and those of its closest neighbours. That 'Russia' had been given assurances that NATO would not expand into what it saw as its backyard—Eastern Europe in general and the former Soviet space in particular—became an endless refrain. How credible are such claims?

There is no doubt that, in the negotiations about German reunification in 1990, there were very explicit public and private messages that NATO would not expand eastward. To cite only one example, on 2 February 1990, German foreign minister Hans-Dietrich Genscher with US secretary of state James Baker at his side, said, on the record, during a press conference:

> Perhaps I might add, we were in full agreement that there is no intention to extend the NATO area of defense and the security toward the East. This holds true not only for GDR [communist East Germany], which we have no intention of simply incorporating, but that holds true for all the other Eastern countries.[40]

And in May, NATO secretary general Manfred Wörner noted in a speech that the alliance was 'ready not to deploy NATO troops beyond the territory of the Federal Republic [of Germany]', which would give 'the Soviet Union firm security guarantees'.[41]

Why was a moratorium on NATO expansion not inscribed in any legally binding treaty? It was not because it was unthinkable. NATO membership not only of Germany but also of the rest of Eastern Europe was on most actors' minds at the time, *pace* recent assertions to the contrary.[42] And Gorbachev, to the immense frustration of some of his more hardline advisers, gambled it away, partially in return for much-needed funds and loans from Germany, but also because he agreed with some of the principles involved. One such principle, the most important of them, was that sovereign countries could choose their alliances. As a result, the earlier willingness to concede guarantees against NATO enlargement soon dissipated, not least because the US Government was opposed to such an idea. And then, in the second half of 1991, the Soviet Union collapsed.[43]

The later complaints that assurances had been made reflected the increasing bitterness over the post-1991 status of Russia: no longer a great power, let alone a superpower, so imperial nostalgia was rife. It is important to stress that, according to the most in-depth reconstruction of these negotiations, it was the Soviets who had failed to secure the kind of guarantees which Genscher had offered earlier. It was not that assurances had been made to the Soviet great power which were then not honoured towards the Russian Federation after its demotion to regional power. It was that, during the negotiations, it became clear to the Germans and the US officials involved that such assurances were not necessary. And Gorbachev proved them right by agreeing to German unification, within NATO, and with no guarantee against further NATO expansion. Gorbachev's critics already saw this as a defeat at the time, but later they preferred to blame the West for Russia's diminished status. Talking about NATO enlargement as a betrayal of assurances given was a relatively safe way to talk about this resentment to international audiences. And as this discourse was eagerly embraced by some in the democratic world, it was useful repeating it. Eventually, this propaganda campaign yielded fruit: Russia managed to prevent both Ukraine and Georgia from entering NATO.

Who drove NATO enlargement, once it did happen? NATO had kept its options open in 1989–90, but the alliance did not press for membership of any of the former Warsaw Pact states. Again, that was not a result of such a move being unthinkable at the time. In fact, it was often seen as desirable. Even the admission of Ukraine and Russia was at times considered. But no actions followed such internal discussions. While the Bush administration had decided to open the alliance to Eastern European states, it was unable to implement this policy before the election of Bill Clinton. In the end, it was not NATO that went out to recruit new members; it was the Eastern European states themselves that worked hard 'to pry open the doors of Western institutions that were acting less than hospitably'. NATO expansion was 'demand-driven'.[44]

As other states of Eastern Europe prepared to enter the alliance, the narrative of betrayal took shape in Moscow. It was driven by the increasing realisation that NATO enlargement was unlikely to include Russia. Until that epiphany, Moscow policymakers saw it as 'perfectly acceptable': it would increase Russia's status 'as America's key partner and ally'. Once Russia's exclusion became likely, the Russian position shifted to opposition.[45] In this context, it was Yeltsin, not Putin, who first claimed there had been a commitment not to expand NATO to the east, and the new Clinton administration had 'to scramble to figure out whether his claims had any validity'.[46]

By early 1994, the residual imperial consciousness of the Russian elites had fully reasserted itself. Yeltsin was quite open about the fact that he thought Russia was still a great power, while the other successor states as well as the former satellites were not. Russia, he said to German chancellor Kohl, was different from other Eastern European countries, because it was a 'great country with a great army and nuclear weapons'. This line was also taken by Gorbachev, in the process of writing a memoir, who gave an oft-quoted 1995 interview where he asserted the country's great power status: 'Russia will not play second fiddle.' And NATO expansion without Russia, or with Russia far back in the queue, raised serious resentments. As the leading historian of this question noted: 'If Russia had been in a position to obstruct the enlargement of NATO in 1996, it would have done so.'[47]

But it wasn't, and it didn't. In 1997, Poland, the Czech Republic and Hungary were invited to join the alliance—in the case of the first two, originally with Yeltsin's explicit and public consent, later retracted.[48] They became NATO members in 1999. The price for all of this—and the United States continued to talk to Yeltsin and tried to make sure Russia would at least tolerate the enlargement—was a lot of money as well as admission of Russia to the exclusive club of the G7, now the G8 (until Russia was removed again in 2014 in response to its illegal annexation of Crimea).[49] This then set the pattern: Eastern European countries lobbied for admission and NATO increasingly accepted their approaches. Thus, Slovenia, Slovakia, Romania, Bulgaria, Estonia, Latvia and Lithuania joined in 2004.

Russia continued to oppose such moves. In an oft-cited speech at the 2007 Munich Security Conference, Putin made this opposition plain.

Avoiding 'excessive politeness and the need to speak in roundabout, pleasant but empty diplomatic terms', Putin promised 'to say what I really think about international security problems'. And he did. NATO expansion, he said, 'represents a serious provocation.' In a historically muddled sequence of sentences, he claimed that it was a violation of 'the assurances our western partners made after the dissolution of the Warsaw Pact', cited Wörner's 1990 speech as if it were an actual security guarantee rather than the expression of a potential negotiating position, and claimed that the Berlin Wall came down because of the 'historic choice ... made by our people, the people of Russia—a choice in favour of democracy, freedom, openness and a sincere partnership with all the members of the big European family'. Instead, NATO enlargement now imposed 'new dividing lines' across Europe.[50]

It was thus clear that Putin was not happy. Nevertheless, NATO remained attractive to Russia's neighbours. Ukraine and Georgia tried to join, applying for a 'Membership Action Plan' (MAP) in 2008, a first step towards accession. However, at the 2008 NATO summit, they were denied this opportunity.

This outcome was a major diplomatic victory for Russia and a 'historic US defeat'.[51] Subsequently, Russia's propaganda machine successfully presented it as a renewed affront by the West. In fact, it was the opposite: for the first time, Russia had been invited to attend a NATO summit, and NATO listened. On 2 April 2008, Putin broadcast Russia's interest in Ukraine and stated his opposition to its existence as an independent state. Ukraine, he claimed, in line with what he would assert later as well, was 'a very complicated state' which 'was created in Soviet times' and 'received huge territories' from Russia. With a nod to the imperial notion of the Russian nation, he asserted Russia's interest in the country, given that 'seventeen million Russians currently live in Ukraine'.[52] The next day, NATO decided not to offer a MAP to Ukraine and Georgia. As a consolation to both the sponsors of the MAP within NATO (the United States and Eastern European member states) and the snubbed countries, NATO asserted that, in principle, 'NATO's door will remain open to European democracies willing and able to assume the responsibilities and obligations of membership, in accordance with Article 10 of the Washington Treaty'. With regards to Ukraine and Georgia, the final Summit Declaration read:

> NATO welcomes Ukraine's and Georgia's Euro-Atlantic aspi-
> rations for membership in NATO. We agreed today that these
> countries will become members of NATO. Both nations have
> made valuable contributions to Alliance operations. We wel-
> come the democratic reforms in Ukraine and Georgia and look
> forward to free and fair parliamentary elections in Georgia in
> May. MAP is the next step for Ukraine and Georgia on their
> direct way to membership. Today we make clear that we sup-
> port these countries' applications for MAP. Therefore we will
> now begin a period of intensive engagement with both at a high
> political level to address the questions still outstanding pertain-
> ing to their MAP applications.[53]

This day never came, however. While NATO continued to enlarge, with Albania and Croatia, which had been invited to do so at the 2008 summit, joining in 2009, Montenegro in 2017 and North Macedonia in 2020, Georgia and Ukraine remained non-members. The 'in prin-ciple' recognition of their ability to join became a gesture towards an indeterminate future.

Russia, by contrast, went on the offensive. Shortly after the summit had demonstrated both the divisions within NATO and the inability of the United States to get its way within the alliance, Russia used an escalation between Georgia and South Ossetian separatists as an excuse to wage war on the country. This war was triggered by Georgian shelling of the town of Tskhinvali on the night of 7 August. This attack, even if it had been in response to South Ossetian attacks on Georgian villages, as Georgia claimed, was neither necessary nor proportionate, and hence illegal under international law, as the European Union's Independent International Fact-Finding Mission on the Conflict in Georgia found. Russia, however, exploited this violation to launch a full-scale invasion of Georgian territory. This attack, in turn, was illegal under international law: Russian peacekeepers had every right to defend themselves, but no right to violate the borders of a sovereign state. 'Russian military action went far beyond the reasonable limits of defence,' concluded the Fact-Finding Mission. 'In a matter of a very few days, the pattern of legitimate and illegitimate military action had thus turned around between the two main actors Georgia and Russia.' The latter had little trouble defeating the former in a quick five-day war. Thus, in the first half of 2008, Putin had not only verbally asserted Russia's right to its backyard, he had also shown in practice that he was willing to enforce his will militarily and in open defiance of international law.[54]

After Yanukovych won the Ukrainian presidential election in 2010, Russia's victory over Ukrainian NATO aspirations was further cemented. The new president made it clear that he had no intention whatsoever of joining NATO. Parliament agreed and passed a law which effectively 'declared Ukraine a non-aligned country'.[55]

However, Ukraine's ambitions towards the European Union (not a military alliance but an economic confederation) remained. This situation might well have been the basis for a sustainable compromise: no to NATO, yes to the EU. But Putin, emboldened by the recent successes of his hard line against the West, would have none of it. Russia opposed EU expansion with the same vigour with which it opposed the military alliance's encroachment. And again, Putin was successful, this time by convincing Ukraine's leadership to turn its back on the Association Agreement and integrate into the Russian economic sphere instead.

Encountering Euromaidan

It was in this situation that the regime encountered the 2013–14 revolution in Kyiv: economic growth had slowed from the steep increases of the first years of Putin's rule (see Figure 11), the liberal and more cosmopolitan parts of society had been alienated from the regime which had wagered more on Russian nationalism and imperialist nostalgia, and Putin's self-assertion in the international sphere had borne some fruit. The security agencies had taken a larger and larger role in monitoring and suppressing opposition, which was seen, in the typical paranoia of professional spooks, as sponsored by the West. The massive protests in 2012 showed the regime how large opposition was, despite the rosy picture the opinion polls painted. Moreover, these polls were slipping as well. And the early, somewhat half-hearted attempts at decolonisation and an embrace of democratic development internally had given way to a decisive embrace of the role of hegemon in the region.

That role was put into question by the revolution. It jeopardised Russia's ally in Kyiv, Yanukovych, and threatened to turn Ukraine back towards the West—a turn Putin had prevented with so much skill ever since 2008.

The Kremlin was unable to perceive Euromaidan as a complex event driven by a variety of domestic Ukrainian forces, which toppled an increasingly autocratic (if elected) government in an extra-constitutional but parliamentary coup followed by free and fair elections. To Moscow, it was yet another attack from the West, which needed to be fended off, like NATO expansion or the 2012 protests at home.[56]

> From the outset of Euromaidan, Russia's perspective has been that it took place as a result of direct Western involvement, and that the West manifestly failed to deal and even made a pact with extremism. Moreover, virtually all reports from media affiliated with the government maintain that Euromaidan could not have occurred without support from the EU and United States.[57]

The West seemed to be winning 'a geostrategic victory over Russia' in alliance with 'extremist neo-Nazi forces' through a coup which 'removed a democratically elected president from power'.[58]

The mediation of Poland, France and Germany, which resulted in the ill-fated compromise discussed in Chapter 3, was construed as meddling in internal Ukrainian affairs. The 'meddlers', of course, did not get what they wanted: their compromise solution was subsequently ignored by Ukrainian actors. Russia's own negotiator had refused to sign the compromise document, indicating that Moscow was not on board with this solution. But this did not stop the Kremlin later claiming that it should have been enforced after Yanukovych had fled. Foreign Minister Sergey Lavrov also maintained, without blushing because of the inconsistency of the Russian position, that the lack of implementation of the compromise solution showed that the Russian refusal to sign it had been the correct course of action.[59]

The contortions of the Russian official line were clearly improvised as the Kremlin tried to grasp the meanings of fast-moving events. But Moscow did have reasons to worry. The revolution in Kyiv questioned whether Russia really had the power to dominate what it believed was its backyard; it showed that a democratically elected strongman could be deposed by popular protests by a sizeable minority; and it seemed to yet again show the West's malicious meddling in post-Soviet affairs. The Maidan revolution could serve as an example to the opposition at home, and it seemed to have brought a bunch of fascists into power next door. And Putin was running out of options: he had tried economic coercion, economic assistance and diplomacy in order to influence the political outcome in Kyiv. None had worked. Only one option was left, if he did not want to concede defeat, and acknowledge that Russia was not, indeed, the hegemon of the post-Soviet space: use force.[60]

And he did, calculating, correctly, 'that NATO would not respond in kind to Russia's attack on Ukraine if that attack was decisive and rapidly attained its objective'. Putin thus saw an opportunity: NATO, while stronger overall, was relatively weak in the region. The Atlantic alliance 'could not fulfil its commitments to mutual defence of members in Eastern Europe for strictly logistical reasons'. Partially as a result of attempts to avoid provoking Russia, NATO 'had no forward bases there of any significance and could not establish them quickly'. There were also serious disagreements within the alliance over how to deal with Russia. Germany, France and Italy were opposed to anything looking like 'provocation', frustrating their US ally. And public opinion in the United States itself was not favourable to renewed military adventures. Putin knew all of this. This knowledge 'emboldened Russia to intervene in Ukraine at the moment of opportunity, for which it had been preparing'.[61]

The Crimean annexation of 2014, then, was 'opportunistic, unplanned and based on a snap assessment of fast-moving events'.[62] It is possible that the original intention was to put pressure on Kyiv to come back to the negotiating table to allow Moscow to shape the outcome of the revolution; or it might have been prompted by fears about the future of Russia's naval base in Sevastopol.[63] But soon, events on the ground took on their own momentum. What transpired was the interaction of a planned and well-executed special forces operation (the famous 'little green men', unmarked, polite, silent and well equipped), local militias enraged by the revolution in Kyiv (which they saw as a coup), and local politicians who hurtled towards secession. The staged referendum, where the vast majority of Crimean residents voted to join Russia, has neither validity in international law, nor can its results be trusted. But a 1996 Gallup poll had shown support for joining Russia among 59 per cent of Russians living in Crimea and among 41 per cent of Crimean Ukrainians. A 2014 poll by the Kyiv International Institute of Sociology had 41 per cent of Crimean residents supporting the integration of Ukraine into Russia. And in Russia, Putin's approval ratings soared, the media exploded into patriotic frenzy, and there was much flag waving and horn tooting on Moscow's streets. 'The Russian people were ecstatic. Putin was their leader. He had to follow them.'[64]

In 2014, the Russian Government thus partially caved in to pressures from below, albeit from a minority, breaking its pledge to respect Ukraine's borders, which it had committed itself to in both the 1994 Budapest Memorandum and the 1997 Treaty on Friendship, Cooperation and Partnership with Kyiv. It was something of a moment of no return. Russia returned to imperial expansion.

CHAPTER 5

VLADIMIR THE GREAT

War

The annexation of Crimea in 2014 was something of an improvisation. While plans had been on the shelf for such an eventuality, events on the ground developed their own momentum. But the initiative clearly originally came from Moscow: Putin sent in his 'little green men', setting off events he had not completely thought through beforehand.

Donbas, the mostly Russian-speaking industrial heartland in the east of Ukraine, was different. Here, local initiative preceded action from Moscow, although this initiative, in turn, would not have eventuated without the Crimean events. The annexation, and the language, images and symbolism used to justify it, served as signals for would-be separatists in Donbas that they might get support from Russia. This signal then triggered the self-mobilisation of these forces, which previously had been marginal.[1]

We should not be surprised that initiative was shown from below in Putin's dictatorship. Historians have long pondered the notion of 'weak dictators'—strongmen who let their underlings try to figure out what they want. Even the most iconic and 'totalitarian' dictatorships relied on such initiative from below: neither the dictator nor even his closest entourage can know, do or decide everything. Hitler was the

126

classic case of the dictator who let his entourage 'work towards' him. Stalin was more controlling (and more hard working) and kept his underlings on a shorter leash. But he, too, worked through 'signals' which officials had to decode.[2]

Putin is fairly far along the continuum towards the 'weak dictator'. The political system of Putinism is that of interrelated networks competing for influence over the leader. Putin is 'the linchpin of the system' but, after his workload had nearly crushed him early in his reign, has acted in a '"hands off" mode' since the middle of his third term. He does not pull all the strings from the top. He's often indecisive and driven by his more dynamic (and often more radical) underlings. He rules 'by signal' rather than by command, issuing 'vague directives that could, depending on the recipient, be interpreted as commands or mere opinions'. As a result, Russia's strategy towards Ukraine—as towards many other issues—remained 'confused, convoluted, unformed'. Its only constant was the attempt to strengthen the regime at home while extending Russia's power across the old imperial space. Thus, while Putin might not be the strategic genius his supporters claim, he certainly has a set of strategic goals which inform his day-to-day tactical decisions: 'It is too early to bury Russia as a great power,' he said in 1999. This statement remained his program.[3]

Putin was reluctant and at first, indeed, resistant to getting involved in Donbas. Yes, there was a gang of fifty-two veterans of other wars and World War II re-enactors, led by Igor Girkin aka Strelkov, a retired FSB agent, which trudged across the border in April 2014 and took the regional city of Slovyansk (which they would hold until the Ukrainian army pushed them out in July). But Girkin was a freelancer at this stage. Elsewhere, it was angry locals—a militant minority but still locals—who, inspired by what had happened in Crimea, took matters into their own hands, setting up would-be governments. Their grievances were local and longstanding, but they did not represent the population. Independent opinion polls showed only 30 per cent support for secession.[4]

This was a militant minority. Scared by the Revolution of Dignity, their minds saturated with Russian state television's propaganda about 'fascism' in Kyiv, and inspired by the Crimean events, they had taken power in a coup and then appealed to Moscow to bail them out once they came under pressure from Kyiv. Putin refused at first. Meanwhile, Ukraine's armed forces were on the march to reassert control of the region in an 'anti-terrorist operation', announced on 15 April.

We don't know why Putin refused to annex Donbas at this stage. But the European Union had suspended preparations for a G8 summit in Sochi on 3 March, cancelled bilateral talks with Russia on 6 March, and set about imposing sanctions against Russian officials and companies on 17 March, 20 March and 15 April. Europe also threatened 'broader economic and trade sanctions' should Russia further escalate its aggression against Ukraine. These were synchronised with a set of executive orders signed by US president Barack Obama of 6, 17 and 20 March, which imposed US sanctions on individuals in Russia's elite. The timing suggests the refusal was a retreat from exposed positions as, at that point in the process, the Kremlin found the costs of further escalation prohibitive. Putin would also have been aware that support for the insurgents was nowhere near the level of sympathy his 'little green men' had encountered in Crimea.[5]

However, the response from the United States and the European Union had a contradictory result. As a well-informed account has it, Putin was 'in a bind'. Launching a full-blown invasion would trigger 'a tougher western response and [Putin would] quite possibly find himself trying to prop up a regime with no real constituency. Yet if he backed away entirely, he would show weakness to the Americans and to his own nationalists. He could neither advance nor abandon the Donbas project.'[6]

Eventually, then, he sent in troops. Ever since the 2012 protests, he increasingly had been hitching his political wagon to the imperialist and ultranationalist right. And his right-wing constituency, both within and outside of the security agencies and the military, supported the political freelancers in Donbas. So when Kyiv's military began taking Donbas back from the putschists, his new allies managed to convince him that it was in Russia's interest to put a stop to it. Thus, he sent in troops, regular ones this time, who were fighting in Ukraine by August 2014. This 'covert Russian invasion of mainland Ukraine' stopped the Ukrainian army from re-establishing control over Ukrainian territory—it was regular Russian troops that turned the Donbas insurgency into a frozen conflict; it was regular Russian troops that won the battles of Ilovaisk in August and early September 2014 and Debaltseve in January and February 2015. Thereafter, the front lines were frozen until February 2022, when Putin escalated the crisis to all-out war.[7]

Was this escalation another case of initiative from below? The evidence strongly points towards the conclusion that this was Putin's decision, and that the dictator had undergone a process of radicalisation since the beginning of the war with Ukraine in 2014. This radicalisation was not preordained but catalysed by several outside events. One was the relatively weak response of the democratic world to the illegal annexation of Crimea, the intervention in Donbas, and the criminal war Russian forces had waged in Syria since 2015. Again and again, Putin confounded democratic countries with the radicalism and brutality of his actions. And every time he got away with it.

A second external stimulus came from the non-human environment. In December 2019, the novel coronavirus (or COVID-19) was first identified as the cause of a wave of severe respiratory syndrome in China. By the end of January 2020, the new virus was in Russia. By April, it had spread all over the country. By then, Putin, as *The Economist* reported, was already 'in hiding'. Just days after an early publicity stunt in a hazmat suit, Russia's he-man president took the advice that this illness was serious. From March, he 'holed up in his residence outside Moscow, haranguing officials by video-link as his approval ratings sank'. The years of self-isolation began.[8]

From isolation, Putin watched world events unfold. In May 2020, massive protests broke out in dictatorial Belarus, threatening another of the colour revolutions which had repeatedly rocked the post-Soviet space and which Putin and his men saw as conspiracies of the West directed against Russia. The protests showed yet again that political unrest was always just around the corner. And despite the harshness of the Belarusian dictatorship—a much more severe one than Putin's at that point—the protests continued all year.

In June 2020, Putin, from his coronavirus bunker, published a long, rambling article on the real meaning of Soviet victory in World War II. Remarkably, he empathised quite strongly with the losers of World War I: Germany. Did he have Russia after 1991 in mind when he wrote that World War II was caused by 'the decisions made after World War I'? In particular, the Treaty of Versailles was a 'symbol of grave injustice for Germany', a 'national humiliation' which 'became a fertile ground for radical sentiments of revenge' exploited by the Nazis. Next came a denunciation of British and French policy in the run-up to World War II and a vigorous defence of anything Stalin had done in the same period. The analogies with the present were obvious to any reader who knew about the way NATO enlargement and Russia's aggression of 2014 had been portrayed in Russia. The Soviet Union was pushed into invading Poland in 1939 by the actions and inactions of the western powers: 'there was no alternative'. Annexing the three Baltic republics in 1940 was similarly historically necessary, and, besides, was 'implemented on a contractual basis, with the consent of the elected authorities'.

Putin then went on the attack. Attempts by Eastern European countries to remember the problematic role the Soviet Union had played in the origin of World War II revealed 'a deliberate policy aimed at destroying the post-war world order'; these attempts were also 'mean'. Also, the Soviet occupation of Eastern Europe was not real, only 'alleged'. He threatened a 'harsh payback', before he launched into a celebration of the heroic war effort of the Soviet people.

The thrust of this argument was a defence of Russia's position in the UN Security Council—a direct outcome of World War II. It was an assertion of Russia's great power status and a defence against proposals to strip veto power from a country which no longer qualified as a great power. Putin disputed this claim with some panache: He was one of 'the leaders of the five nuclear-weapon States, permanent members of the Security Council'. And he hoped he could meet the other leaders of the world's great powers soon.[9]

Some of the revisionism in Putin's 2020 essay was breathtaking, but much of it reflected conservative historical opinion in Russia. It could be read as defending, by analogy, Russia's annexation of Crimea. But it did not imply a program of further aggression. Rather, it was a dual plea: to accept what Russia had done in the past as historically necessary and hence acceptable, and to restore its threatened standing as a great power despite the pariah status it had manoeuvred itself into with the illegal annexation of Crimea.

Ukraine as Fiction

A year later, after more time spent in isolation reading history books, Putin's stance had hardened. His next historical epistle, published in July 2021, was again in keeping with much of Russian conservative historical opinion, but its thrust was much more worrisome. It asserted that there was no Ukraine. That nation was a fiction, invented by the Bolsheviks (and other enemies of Russia). The essay was 'a manifesto for upheaval and revisionism'.[10]

Putin imagined a Russian people going back to medieval Rus, which had been united by the political rule of the princes of Kyiv (or, rather, 'Kiev'), the Orthodox faith and a common language, 'Old Russian'. He acknowledged that, after the decline of the Kievan state and the Mongol invasion, the historical development of north-eastern and south-western Rus was strikingly different, with the former being 'gathered' by the principality of Moscow, while the latter came under the rule of the Polish-Lithuanian Commonwealth. However, this bifurcation had no cultural or political impact on the 'Russian' population, who remained Orthodox and did not speak Polish. Khmelnytsky's uprising he rendered not as a Cossack rebellion but as a liberation movement of essentially Russian people, which led to the reunification of Russia in 1654. Thereafter, the great Russian nation flourished. Ukrainians were not repressed or Russified but integrated into the great imperial project, which indeed linked the tsarist empire with the Soviet Union.[11]

So far, so wonderful. But why did a Ukrainian state then break away from this heartfelt union? Why did it form a new state in 1991, a state which now refused to subject itself to Russian rule, seeking affiliation with the European Union and, most horrible of all thoughts, NATO protection from its brother to the east? What had happened? The great Russian people were divided by spoilers: Austrians, Germans, Bolsheviks. Correctly noting the role of Galicia in the national awakening of the nineteenth century, Putin blamed the Austro-Hungarian government for the rise of the national movement.

He ran quickly over the most important event of modern Ukrainian history: the independent state of 1918–20. His account left out any mention of Bolshevik aggression against the new Ukrainian state and the role this aggression played in the declaration of independence and the peace treaty with Germany in 1918. He obscured all continuities between the various Ukrainian regimes of 1917–20, instead telling a story of ceaseless ruptures. Ukrainian regimes and national consciousness were unreal forces in his telling, motivated only by foreign powers intent on dominating Russia—first Austria and Germany, then Poland. Ukrainians had no agency in his narrative. They were but puppets manipulated by nefarious outside forces. Ukraine as a state and as a nation was the artificial creation of Bolshevism—a somewhat mysterious event in Putin's rendering, given that the Bolsheviks were Marxists and, as such, enemies of nationalism and the nation-state. This was the original sin, Lenin's original sin, which led to the current lamentable state of affairs.

The Decision

With this essay, Putin moved beyond claiming Russia's great power status in the borders it had inherited after 1991 (together with the Soviet Union's seat on the security council and the old empire's nuclear arsenal). He instead denied a neighbouring state its right to exist. It was the intellectual program for the war of aggression which Putin would unleash a bit over half a year later. It signalled 'a change in Putin's thinking'. Ukraine was 'becoming an obsession'.[12] And on 7 October 2021, still in his corona-bunker, he turned sixty-nine.

By now, world events had improved from Putin's perspective. The threat of a democratic revolution in Belarus had been clubbed out of existence. Putin had checked the resolve of the outside world by amassing troops at Ukraine's border in March and April. This deployment preceded, but was then enhanced in reaction to, a large-scale

NATO exercise in Europe. Results were encouraging: US President Joe Biden, who just weeks earlier had labelled his Russian counterpart 'a killer', now called the Kremlin and suggested a meeting. Russian state television hosts were gloating: Biden's 'nerves had failed him'.[13] The build-up, however, was more than just 'heavy-metal diplomacy'. It also put military equipment in place close to the border, which was not removed with the troops but made a renewed mobilisation easier once the time was ripe.[14]

Ukraine reacted to Russia's military grandstanding with a renewed call for NATO membership, now made more urgent by the suggestion that the alternative was the acquisition of nuclear weapons. Like all earlier such pleas, it fell on deaf ears, but Putin would later use the 'nuclear threat' when legitimising his aggression. Meanwhile, his own, much more material threats bore fruit. In the run-up to the Biden–Putin summit in Geneva on 16 June, the White House halted the delivery of a military aid package to Ukraine.[15] And at the summit itself, Biden started proceedings by saying what Putin wanted to hear: that Russia was not a 'regional power', as Obama had (correctly) noted, but one of the 'great powers'.[16]

So far, so good. Then things got better. In August, Putin watched the chaotic retreat of the United States from Afghanistan—'a gift from the heavens, a thunderbolt'.[17] The ongoing political chaos in Britain and the increasingly disunited European Union seemed to point in the same direction: Russia's enemies, long on the march with NATO expansion, colour revolutions and unfair sanctions, were at their weakest in decades. 'A narrative of Western ineptitude and division, stretching from the EU to NATO, seemed to have gained currency in the Kremlin during 2021, emboldening Putin,' one observer later wrote.[18] In Ukraine, Volodymyr Zelensky seemed a joke as a president. By the middle of the year, support among likely voters stood at 30 per cent, way below the 73 per cent who had voted him into office. By November, an analyst writing on the blog of the Wilson Center asked if this was 'the end of the Zelensky alternative'.[19]

Meanwhile, Putin's approval ratings in early 2022, before the invasion, stood at 69 per cent.[20] For Putin, of course, around 70 per cent approval was low. And the last foreign adventures in 2014 had significantly boosted the number. Surely, now was the time to strike?

In preparation, Putin's regime had become more menacing internally. In January 2021, opposition figure Alexey Navalny, whose assassination Putin's minions had botched in 2020, returned to Russia. He also released a video about one of Putin's more outrageous residences, a veritable palace in the Krasnodar region. The video went viral nearly instantly. Navalny was arrested at the border, with protesters subjected to the already well-known police brutality. Navalny disappeared into prison, the protests ended in late April, and in early June, organisations linked to Navalny were declared 'extremist' and liquidated. Two of the last independent media outlets, TV Rain and Meduza, were declared 'foreign agents' shortly thereafter. And at the end of December, the human rights organisation Memorial, a long-term critic of both the Stalinist past and Russia's dictatorial present, was finally shut down.

This rapid-fire assault on what remained of civil society and an independent public sphere should have served as a warning, as in Putin's mind, internal repression and external war were linked. As he implied in another of his many excursions into history, World War II, the war he thought about most, was unlikely to have been won had the Stalinist state 'been less brutal'.[21]

By the summer of 2021, the decision, in principle, to go to war had been taken. The July 2021 essay on 'the unity of Russians and Ukrainians' was a general ideological statement of intent. One could argue that the goal—a return of Ukraine into Russia's orbit—could have been achieved in a variety of ways, and hence diplomacy still had a chance. Given that the essay was not an internal document but widely publicised, it was clearly also intended to send a message to the world, maybe even convince the outside world of its interpretation's merits. And the precedent established in 2020–21 suggested that a historical essay asking for a summit would get more traction if enhanced by a military threat. Hence, at the start of November a new military build-up at Ukraine's border took place, amid the already well-known claims that reports of an impending invasion were Russophobic hysteria.

However, Putin's essay was not the only preparation put in place in July 2021. In the same month, Russia's FSB began planning the occupation of Ukraine. Putin's spooks conduced survey work to gauge the popular mood in the neighbouring country. They found an apathetic population which distrusted the political leadership, did not expect war with Russia, and was preoccupied by economic concerns—encouraging data for any invader.[22] Hence, by the middle of 2021, Putin had set the general policy direction towards further confrontation. But he was as indecisive as ever. He made the final decision at the last minute. Military commanders only learned of it—'with bulging eyes'—the week before they led their men into action.[23] According to Ukrainian intelligence, Putin postponed the start of the war at least three times, the last in mid-February.[24]

At the end of 2021, Putin opened another window for negotiations, however insincere. Typically, it revolved around Ukraine's potential membership of NATO. Russia's demands were presented in the form of a draft treaty which, for example, would have obliged the United States to 'rule out further expansion of the North Atlantic Treaty Organization in an easterly direction' and to 'refuse admission' to NATO to successor states of the Soviet Union. Moreover, no troops or weapons could be deployed anywhere Russia 'perceived' them as a 'threat to its national security' (essentially a veto over any deployment outside the United States).[25] These proposals were a 'major overshot'. They were so maximalist that they were nearly meaningless—'demands so imperious and swaggering you could only marvel at their audacity'.[26] But it is not clear that this was clear to Putin.

Why issue such demands unless you are so enmeshed in your own interpretation of the situation that you no longer perceive the limits of the possible? When journalists asked Deputy Foreign Minister Sergei Ryabkov if the proposals were unreasonable, he emphatically denied this. He sounded desperate: 'This is not about us giving some kind of ultimatum, there is none. The thing is that the seriousness of our warning should not be underestimated.' Russia, he said, wanted to begin negotiations as soon as possible. 'We can go any place and any time, even tomorrow,' he proclaimed in 'animated remarks'.[27]

In fact, the last-minute, drop-of-a-hat request to reverse decades of diplomacy were in line with the utopian hope expressed in the 2020 World War II essay: that the great powers of the world, Russia among them, would sit down and divide up the globe as they had done in the good old days at the end of World War II. And why not? The build-up in early 2021 had gotten Putin a 'historic summit' with Biden. Maybe this even more menacing military posturing would finally push NATO to accept that Russia was still the great power Putin so desperately wanted it to be. Putin's experience with the West suggested that the 'so-called democrats' would buckle if you pushed them. They were weak, while Russia was strong. But he had overplayed his hand this time. No new invitation was forthcoming. Instead, US intelligence warned an incredulous world that a full-scale land war was in the offing.

We can be certain that, when war came, it was Putin's snap decision. Journalists in the state media had not been prepared— either by instructions or by rumour—that war was coming. Instead, they were presented with an abrupt change of the official line on 21 February 2022.[28] On the same day, even some of Putin's closest associates acted stunned and confused when they were called to a televised meeting of the Security Council, one of the most powerful bodies in the land.[29] According to a well-informed journalist, 'only three people in the room apart from Putin himself knew the full extent' of the plan: Defence Minister Sergei Shoigu, Chairman of the Security Council Nikolai Patrushev and FSB chief Aleksander Bortnikov.[30] Towards the rest, Putin behaved like a mixture of King Lear and James Bond villain Ernst Stavro Blofeld.[31] It was a spectacle designed to ensure everybody knew who was boss. One by one, some of the most powerful men in Russia had to declare their support, 'like frightened boyars pledging allegiance'. The entire episode had 'over-tones of megalomania'.[32] As a veteran observer of Russian politics put it, this 'was not a politician convening his team for discussions, this was a supreme leader marshalling his minions and ensuring collective responsibility for a decision that, at minimum, will change the security architecture in Europe, and may well lead to a horrific war that consumes Ukraine.'[33]

On a Mission

Putin's speech, given at 10 p.m. on 21 February, implied that he had finally made up his mind. He repeated his history lesson on the unity of the Russian and Ukrainian peoples: Ukraine was historically Russian land; the Ukrainian state had been created 'entirely' by Bolshevik Russia; later, Ukraine got other lands gifted by Stalin and Khrushchev etc. etc. Rehashing this history was important in order 'to explain the motives behind Russia's actions and what we aim to achieve'. The problem was, as many observers noted, that his speech was so angry and so rambling, it was difficult to figure out what the conclusions were that he wanted to draw.

What followed were views Putin had expressed ever since the 1990s. Almost nothing was new. It was an angry summary of a Russian imperialist's long-held resentments. Ukraine was an artificial creation and a historical mistake. The Soviet Union was the successor state of the Russian Empire and de facto a centralised state. The problem was that Stalin had failed to 'cleanse' the Soviet constitution of 'the odious and utopian fantasies inspired by the revolution' and hence left formal Ukrainian statehood intact. In a heroic effort at mixing his metaphors, Putin then declared that the result of all this was that the 'virus of nationalist ambitions is still with us, and the mine laid at the initial stage to destroy state immunity to the disease of nationalism was ticking'. He then rambled on about the prehistory of the implosion of the Soviet Union. Significantly, he described it as the 'collapse of the historical Russia known as the USSR'. [34]

Russia, thus, had been wronged. But despite 'all the injustices, lies and outright pillage of Russia', the Russian people had magnanimously 'accepted the new geopolitical reality that took shape after the dissolution of the USSR'. Selflessly, Russia had helped the other successor states, including Ukraine. But the Ukrainians had been treacherous, exploiting Russia's help and reneging on their obligations. Ukraine's decolonising choices, a history outlined in Chapter 3 of this book, he rendered as an attempt by the Ukrainian authorities, assisted by 'external forces', to build 'their statehood on the negation of everything that united us, trying to distort the mentality and historical memory of millions of people, of entire generations living in Ukraine'. The rise of Neo-Nazism was the result.

Ukraine's drift towards European constitutional models, closely related to its attempts at post-imperial reconstruction, Putin described as 'mindlessly emulating foreign models, which have no relation to history or Ukrainian realities'. This 'so-called pro-Western civilisational choice' had nothing to do with pressures from below (never mind the Orange Revolution, which went unmentioned) but rather was an attempt by 'the oligarchic Ukrainian authorities' to keep the 'billions of dollars' they had stolen from the people. A stable statehood thus never developed; corruption was rife; democracy was just a 'screen for the redistribution of power and property between various oligarchic clans'. This led to 'justified public discontent', exploited by 'radical nationalists' (in the pay of foreign governments) in the Maidan protests, which became a 'coup d'état', followed by terror and civil war. The result was 'an acute socioeconomic crisis'. It had been caused by the Ukrainian elites not respecting the legacies left to them by the great Russian Empire: 'They spent and embezzled the legacy inherited not only from the Soviet era, but also from the Russian Empire.'

What's more, they also put foreigners in charge: 'Ukraine itself was placed under external control, directed not only from the Western capitals, but also on the ground, as the saying goes, through an entire network of foreign advisors, NGOs and other institutions present in Ukraine.' Ukraine had 'been reduced to a colony with a puppet regime'. Russian language and culture were suppressed, Russians were sent the signal 'that they are not wanted in Ukraine', and the Moscow-controlled Orthodox Church was destroyed.

What Putin outlined was a program to rebuild the Russian Empire: Ukraine was Russian land, the Soviet Union just one instantiation of the Russian Empire, Ukraine a fiction. The Ukrainian authorities had gotten their chance to do something with this inheritance and they had embezzled it all. Thus, they had lost all legitimacy. Russia had selflessly supported Ukraine, the brother country, after 1991, but seeing that the little brother could not govern himself, the bigger brother needed to intervene.

The invasion of Ukraine was both revenge for the humiliations Russia had suffered at the hands of Ukraine and the West after 1991 *and* a rescue mission: the Ukrainians, who were really just Russians with an accent, needed to be saved from their own government and from foreign domination, the people of Donbas from 'genocide'. Putin, who had re-established the power of the Russian state since he had become president in 2000, and who had broken the power of the oligarchs in Russia, now proposed to do the same in Ukraine. He was an angry, resentful man on a historical mission.

Moreover, this was also a pre-emptive strike, Putin claimed. Ukraine's military strategy of March 2021 was an aggressive preparation for war against Russia and Kyiv was in the process of creating its own nuclear forces, quite possibly with western aid. This was a typical case of Putin's gaslighting. Ukraine's strategy document instead was focused on the 'repulsion and deterrence of armed aggression'. It reaffirmed Ukraine's non-nuclear status and explicitly did not call for military parity with Russia, to avoid the horrendous costs and militarisation of the state this would involve.[35] Similarly, Putin turned US military support for Ukraine since 2014 from an attempt to increase its defence capability in the context of Russia's illegal annexation of Crimea and the support for the insurgency in Donbas, into preparation for offensive war.

The conclusion of the speech was something of an anticlimax. Everything Putin had said in the preceding fifty-four minutes should have prepared his audience for a declaration of war. Instead, he said, 'I consider it necessary to take a long overdue decision and to immediately recognise the independence and sovereignty of the Donetsk People's Republic and the Luhansk People's Republic.'[36] But on the same night, Russian troops entered Donbas. Three days later, Russia's all-out assault on Ukraine was underway.

Reasons for Going to War

Putin's aggression had several longer-term motives. Most important were geopolitical aspirations. Putin understood the Ukrainian revolutions of 2004 and 2014 not as domestically generated upheavals but as

plots by the United States and the European Union to pull Ukraine out
of Russia's orbit. He read NATO enlargement, against which he had
'railed' ever since the mid-1990s,[37] in the same way: as an aggressive
move of a geopolitical foe—'the West' (by which he meant the United
States, the old adversary of the Cold War days of his youth and early
adulthood). While there had been some successes along the way—the
2008 derailing of the MAP for Ukraine among them—overall, the
Russian President had failed in his bid to bind Ukraine more strongly
to Russia and pull it out of the European and transatlantic orbits. His
attempts to keep Ukraine from signing the Association Agreement with
the European Union had led to the Revolution of Dignity of 2014, a
decisive shift away from Russia. Russia's aggression in 2014—Crimea
and Donbas—had furthered this drift: the 2010 neutrality law was
repealed at the end of 2014.

True, more than a decade after the 2008 refusal of a MAP to
Ukraine, NATO had still not issued one, let alone admitted the country.
Nevertheless, relations between Ukraine and NATO were prosper-
ing. Since 2016, a Comprehensive Assistance Package for Ukraine
had helped build up its military; in 2017, legislation made NATO
membership 'a strategic foreign and security policy objective'; and in
2019 this goal was enshrined in Ukraine's constitution. In September
2020, Ukraine issued a new National Security Strategy, centred,
again, on gaining membership.[38] NATO, of course, did not respond
to these clearly articulated wishes, but cooperation between NATO
and Ukraine had increased since 2014, in particular with regards to
training and participation in NATO exercises. In June 2020, Ukraine
joined a NATO program to update its weaponry and communications,
as well as its command and control systems, to ensure they would work
with those used by the alliance.[39]

There was also the bad example Ukraine was setting, which might
well play into the hands of Russia's enemies by weakening the Russian
state Putin himself embodied. His increasingly authoritarian regime
was threatened by the troubled but nevertheless vibrant democracy
at its doorstep, which could serve as encouragement to the opposition
in Russia. This was, of course, part of the reason why 'Western elites'

had 'installed' the 'Kiev regime' as an 'anti-Russian bridgehead' in the first place. This plan needed to be pre-empted, lest Russia broke apart into squabbling regions. The invasion was the foreign-policy equivalent of the strategy of 'preventive counter-revolution' Putin had long pursued at home.[40]

And then there was ideology. The notion that Ukraine was not a separate country or nation needs to be taken seriously. Putin is a Russian imperialist. Like many Russians of his generation, he grew up thinking of the Soviet Union as Russia's state, and he experienced Russians and Ukrainians interacting as one. Given the effort he put into the historical research for his 'Ukraine does not exist' essay, and given its consistency with earlier pronouncements he made on the same topic, we can assume that he means what he writes.

Finally, there was the influence of Putin's immediate entourage, dominated by former KGB men like himself. They had been trained to perceive the world as an anti-Russian conspiracy and acted accordingly.

But none of these larger structural forces explains the timing: in 2021–22, there was no new democratic revolution in Kyiv, nor was there an attempt to expand NATO. The claim that Ukraine, by 2021, 'was becoming a de facto member of NATO' is good polemics, but even if it were true, it would denote an ongoing process and hence cannot explain why Russia reached the tipping point into all-out aggression.[41] Despite support from the United Kingdom, Ukraine had again failed to receive a MAP at the NATO summit in Brussels in June 2021.[42] The US–Ukraine charter on Strategic Partnership, signed on 10 November 2021, hardly qualified as upping the ante. Far from 'accepting Ukraine's application for NATO membership',[43] it instead confirmed the status quo. In principle, the United States supported 'Ukraine's right to decide its own future foreign policy course free from outside interference, including with respect to Ukraine's aspirations to join NATO'. But both sides stressed the need 'to further pursue a comprehensive reform agenda to keep transforming the country'.[44]

This was the old line, in place since 2008: in principle, Ukraine might join someday, but that day was not here. Like the horizon, it kept receding as you marched towards it. When Russia demanded in

December that NATO no longer expand into the post-Soviet space and issue security guarantees, the charter was not even mentioned.[45] Nor did Putin mention this document in his angry speech of 21 February 2022 (where he did drag out the well-rehearsed history of NATO enlargement as a betrayal of Russia by Russophobes).

The whole issue of NATO expansion was a red herring to justify Russia's aggression. It was part of the background irritation Russian elites had long felt about their decreased status in the world, but not a proximate cause of the war. The escalation came from Russia, not Ukraine or NATO.

The Personal Is Historical

But what *was* about to happen in 2022 was something more personal: Putin would turn seventy. This circumstance, more than any other, explains the timing of the invasion.[46] Time seemed to be running out for the president to leave a lasting legacy. Domestically, he was a failure: by 2022, his earlier attempt to be remembered as the president who brought prosperity and the good life to his people had disappeared among corruption, the personal enrichment of the few, and the immiseration of the many. Putin is an ageing macho with a history obsession. In 2008, he asked Alexei Venediktov, then editor-in-chief of the independent radio station Ekho Moskvy (now shut down): 'You're a historian. What are the history books going to say about me?' Venediktov's evasive response did not satisfy the great man, so after the annexation of Crimea in 2014, he asked him again: 'Now what are they going to write about me?'[47]

On a fundamental level, then, Putin's aggression was the result of an unhealthy obsession with history and with his own role in it. In particular, he had long pondered the history of the Soviet Union's World War II, an obsession he shared with many of his compatriots. As he wrote in 2020, his family had suffered, like the majority of families in the Soviet Union, immensely:

> For my parents, the war meant the terrible ordeals of the Siege of Leningrad where my two-year-old brother Vitya died. It was

the place where my mother miraculously managed to survive. My father, despite being exempt from active duty, volunteered to defend his hometown. He made the same decision as millions of Soviet citizens. He fought at the Nevsky Pyatachok bridgehead and was severely wounded. And the more years pass, the more I feel the need to talk to my parents and learn more about the war period of their lives.[48]

This personal investment in the Soviet Union's World War II led to a series of interventions into the debate on how to remember this war. Putin's government sponsored Victory Day (9 May), long the most popular of holidays, as an increasingly bombastic celebration of Russian military prowess, complete with children in uniform and other cringe-worthy elements. This cult of the 'Great Patriotic War', as the German–Soviet war of 1941–45 is still called in Russia, was clearly used for political purposes: pride in Soviet victory was maybe the only thing everybody could agree on in an otherwise disunited society. But this war is also a truly personal obsession of the president.[49] 'According to people with knowledge of Mr Putin's conversations with his aides over the past two years,' wrote a well-connected Russian journalist less than a month after Putin's tanks had rumbled into Ukraine, 'the president has completely lost interest in the present: The economy, social issues, the coronavirus pandemic, these all annoy him. Instead, he … obsess[es] over the past.'[50] Putin's biographer concurred: 'Instead of focusing on Russia's future', Putin 'spends more and more time thinking about the past'.[51]

This past began to expand. His 2020 essay still covered familiar ground: it was a defence of Soviet imperialism during World War II. The 2021 essay on Ukrainian history, by contrast, was an unapologetically imperialist history of Russia since medieval times. They both fit into a wider pattern. In 2016, Putin unveiled a memorial to Volodimer ('Vladimir') the Great, ruler of Kyiv from 980 to 1015, a 'Russian' ruler, according to Putin (and most historically conscious Russians).[52] In June 2022, the more modern Vladimir compared himself, without too much false modesty, to Peter the Great.[53]

This was the culmination of a long obsession with history and his own role within it. Putin was the heir of a long line of glorious rulers of Russia. He had started his rule with a successful campaign in Chechnya, which had taught him, according to an official who knew him well, that 'Russia's might and empire could indeed be restored through military aggression'. [54] Now, he applied this lesson from history to Ukraine. Thereby, he would cement his place in the Russian history books.

Analogies at War

The event which loomed largest in Putin's historical imagination continued to be World War II. Analogies with the war that had traumatised his parents helped the decision to go to war. These parallels were alarming. While the aspirations of Ukraine to join NATO had gone nowhere since 2008, its army had clearly gotten better trained, better equipped and better led since 2014, when Russia had been able to take over Crimea without so much as a single shot fired. It had also acquired significant combat experience in the ongoing war over Donbas with Russian-sponsored proxy forces and, at times, regular Russian forces. If Ukraine's military potential continued on this upward trajectory, would it not possibly threaten Russia in the foreseeable future? Was Russia facing a situation similar to the Soviet Union in 1940 and early 1941, when Germany prepared for its attack? Maybe now was the time to strike, just as Stalin should have done then in order to pre-empt German aggression.

Putin explicitly made these analogies when he announced his 'special military operation' on 24 February 2022, showing that his perception of reality was fundamentally warped by the 'lessons of the Second World War':

> We know that in 1940 and early 1941 the Soviet Union went to great lengths to prevent war or at least delay its outbreak. To this end, the USSR sought not to provoke the potential aggressor until the very end by refraining or postponing the most urgent and obvious preparations it had to make to defend itself from an imminent attack. When it finally acted, it was too late.

As a result, the country was not prepared to counter the invasion by Nazi Germany, which attacked our Motherland on June 22, 1941, without declaring war. The country stopped the enemy and went on to defeat it, but this came at a tremendous cost. The attempt to appease the aggressor ahead of the Great Patriotic War proved to be a mistake which came at a high cost for our people. In the first months after the hostilities broke out, we lost vast territories of strategic importance, as well as millions of lives. We will not make this mistake the second time. We have no right to do so.[55]

All of what he said was true, of course, except the analogy.[56] Ukraine was not preparing to invade Russia. That this was a fantasy did not mean that it was not real enough for a leader who lived increasingly isolated from even his closest advisers while reading history books. His obsession with the war was tinged with resentment about the outside world allegedly not recognising the centrality of the Soviet effort in the outcome of World War II. As he wrote in 2020: 'The Soviet Union and the Red Army, no matter what anyone is trying to prove today, made the main and crucial contribution to the defeat of Nazism.'[57] Again, he was right about history and wrong about the present. The Red Army did indeed play the decisive role in the war in Europe, but historians in the democratic world have long recognised this fact. Only historiographical outliers claim the opposite, and they have to contend with serious scholarly critiques when doing so.[58]

Where Putin is also wrong is in construing victory as the essence of this war, which had numerous other facets, many of them dark and unedifying. The Soviet Union was not always the victim of outside aggression; at other times, it was a perpetrator of violence against its own soldiers and civilians, and of aggression against some of its neighbours—Poland and Finland come to mind, as well as Estonia, Latvia and Lithuania. Collaboration with the enemy was not a Ukrainian specialty: the largest number of collaborators were, in fact, Russians. Many more Ukrainians fought with the Red Army than joined the nationalist underground or the various German armed formations.

The notion that this was 'Russia's war' fundamentally misrepresents the multinational character of this struggle. The Soviet Union was a multinational empire and the Red Army a multinational fighting force.[59]

Putin, then, is both an avid reader and the occasional author of history. The point here is not so much that he is a good or a bad historian, but that his sense of history is deeply entangled with his sense of self. And given both the irrationality of the attack on Ukraine and the centrality of Putin as the decision-maker, we do need to come to terms with Putin the man.

Toxic Masculinity

Putin's actions have been analysed as the result of his socialisation in the KGB. Likewise, his propensity for risk-taking, his tendency to prioritise tactics over strategy, and the fact that he simply got away with breaking the rules of polite international discourse between nations, all go some way to explaining how we got to 24 February 2022. But there is another aspect which cannot be overlooked. Putin has carefully crafted the personality of the macho. Before his current physical decline began, he regularly arranged for photo-ops while fishing, hunting and horse-riding, ideally with no shirt on. There was no hint of homosexuality in this 'Marlboro manhood', which was flanked by a nasty state campaign against LGBTQIA+ people. This was in line with a performance of 'street masculinity' that Putin also embraced: he regularly used the crude language of the Russian criminal subculture, laced with references to bodily fluids of all kinds, as well as sexuality and physical brutality. This persona was, of course, carefully crafted to create 'charisma where there was none' and thus shore up his regime: Putin's masculine image rhymes with mainstream Russian male fantasies. But nobody can engage in this kind of cosplay for very long if he sees it as a ridiculous display of an outdated version of manhood. Putin clearly relishes this image; he projects to his followers what he himself hopes to represent.[60]

In international politics and in history-writing, a macho is politely called a 'great man'. Putin clearly aspires to become one. But this historically conscious he-man is ageing. He no longer poses half-naked, he no longer plays ice hockey with fellow dictator Alexander

Lukashenko, and he no longer invites cameras to judo matches he competes in (and, of course, usually wins). His oft-cited use of Botox, his much younger lover, his attempts at flirting with female journalists at press conferences—they all indicate a man unwilling to age gracefully.[61] Prior to the war, he knew he was running out of time and he knew he had not accomplished much worth writing about in the history books. The narrative the opposition developed about him was of a corrupt thief of the nation's riches, while the hard right saw him as flaccid and lacking toughness. He had evidently failed to make Russia into the kind of 'normal country' many hoped it would become from 1991: democratic, prosperous and thriving. He failed in what he originally set out to do: to make the lives of ordinary Russians better. He also failed to make Russia great again. So would he enter the history books as a failure?

The Russian Everyman

Clearly, imperial glory was the best option to ensure immortality. And Putin had reason to believe that the West was weak and he had the whip hand. A successful little war against Ukraine would also finally wash away the long years of humiliation many in the Russian elite felt vis-a-vis their old Cold War opponent the United States and, as they saw it, its imperial arm—NATO.

The timing of the war with Ukraine, then, was 'about one man and his vendetta'.[62] Putin's resentments, his disappointments, his obsession with history and his own role in it, all came together in his seventieth year to move him to war. This was the decision of an ageing, increasingly isolated and obsessed man, who had been steaming in his own resentments for two long years of COVID isolation. With his seventieth birthday just around the corner, with the countries he saw as Russia's geopolitical rivals weak, and with not much to show for nearly a quarter of a century in power other than obscene wealth and tasteless mansions, now was the time to strike.

But the obsessions themselves, the underlying resentments, geopolitical dreams and hopes for imperial greatness were far from Putin's alone. 'His grievance at Russia's loss of empire and international standing,' writes the leading historian of NATO expansion, 'is widely shared among other displaced servants of the Soviet state.'[63] Putin 'represents the hopes and fears, the aspirations and resentments of a substantial part of the Russian population,' concludes his biographer.[64] In this, as in much else, he is a Russian everyman. In this sense, Putin's war is also Russia's war.[65]

CHAPTER 6

THE FUTURE

Consequences

What will the consequences of Russia's aggression be? The physical, economic and human toll of this war on Ukraine has already been mentioned in the introduction to this book. Ukraine will need long-term support from the outside world not only to survive this war but also to rebuild once the war is over. For Russia, the physical toll has been much less, as Ukraine has, thus far at least, not retaliated for Russia's systematic campaign of destruction of civilian infrastructure and bombing of cities. Assaults on Russian soil have been restricted to military targets. But battlefield losses are enormous, both in matériel and, crucially, in human beings.

Economically, Russia has suffered from sanctions. While a collapse of its economy has been avoided, the impact has nonetheless been severe. The country faces 'a prolonged, painful recession'. This crisis is survivable: with a forecast of a 7–8 per cent decline in GDP in 2022–23, it is similar to what the country suffered in 1998 and 2008, and nowhere near the catastrophe of the early 1990s. But it will come on top of already stunted growth, 'unfavourable demographic trends, low investment rates, and low levels of productivity'. If Putin went to war in a bid to make Russia into a great power again, the conflict he unleashed has only further undermined the economic basis for such a claim.[1] Whether or not military production can be maintained in the medium to long term under the sanctions regime remains to be seen. The evidence thus far is mixed. There clearly was no complete breakdown, and sanctions can be circumvented in a variety of ways. But there are also reports on limits, in particular on precision weapons and more modern supplies.[2]

Politically, the war has led to a temporary truce in Ukraine. The various fault lines—political, economic, generational, regional—have lost their power as society faces outside aggression. The trajectory towards a civic form of nationalism, which allows for the inclusion of a variety of ethnic groups into the polity, has been accelerated, as it proves its power to mobilise the citizenry in defence of their country. As we also saw in Chapter 3, however, there are some early indicators that the inevitable siege mentality of wartime has increased support for at least the temporary suspension of democratic processes and a 'strong hand'. Ukraine's overall trajectory since 1991, however, where autocratic tendencies have been stopped in their tracks again and again, is cause for cautious optimism. If anything, civic mobilisation has increased in wartime.

Ukraine's drift away from Moscow has sped up since the 2022 invasion. By July, 81 per cent of respondents would participate in a referendum to join the European Union and vote in favour, up from only 47 per cent in 2013; and if NATO membership were to be put in front of Ukraine's citizens, 71 per cent would cast their ballot in favour, as opposed to 20 per cent in 2009. Moreover, regional divisions have lessened dramatically. In 2009, the west of the country supported NATO membership with 40 per cent, while in the centre, south and east, the corresponding shares were only 17 per cent, 11 per cent and 1 per cent, respectively. In 2022, by contrast, the majority in each region were ready for membership: 81 per cent in the west, 73 per cent in the centre, 65 per cent in the south and 56 per cent in the east. Support for EU membership has always been stronger than for the defence alliance, but the trend is the same. If in 2013 a majority in the east and a plurality in the centre were in favour of the European

Union, pluralities in the south and east were opposed to such a west-ward integration of their country. In 2022, by sharp contrast, 88 per cent in the west, 81 per cent in the centre, 77 per cent in the south and 71 per cent in the east were prepared to vote for membership.[3] The European Union reciprocated by granting candidate status on 23 June 2022. At the end of September, Ukraine also applied to join NATO. If one reason for Putin's war was stopping the drift of Ukraine towards Europe and the North Atlantic, he achieved the exact opposite.

Meanwhile, Russia's trajectory towards dictatorship has accelerated. The scholarly discussion about whether Russia is now 'fascist' is largely terminological. Most analysts agree that Russia has shifted towards 'a chillingly more repressive imperialist order', complete with calls for 'self-purification' of society from 'scums and traitors'; militarism and militarisation; a cult of masculinity encircling the leader, Putin, as 'the man-soldier, the man-defender of the nation, but also potentially the man-aggressor'; and calls for the 'eradication' of Ukraine in a war that is construed as a civilisational and spiritual contest with a decadent 'West'. There is no doubt that Russia's political system is now 'a closed, personalist authoritarian regime, potentially en route to becoming a more totalitarian model'. The disagreement is largely over whether the label 'fascism' should be attached to this system, with critics wor-rying mostly about the policy implications: given that in non-scholarly discussions 'fascism' quickly gets equated with 'Nazism' or 'Hitlerism', embracing the label might encourage the disastrous idea that the only way to deal with Russia under Putin is to march on Moscow.[4]

In such a system, revolution is unlikely. And thus far there has been no massive groundswell in Russia against the war. It is remarkable, given the repression and propaganda campaigns, that while 21 per cent of respondents to a late September 2022 poll did not support the 'actions of Russian military forces in Ukraine', and another 8 per cent 'can't say' (with larger shares among the young and smaller shares among older people), and while the share of those who backed the war decreased from 80 per cent in March to 72 per cent in September, there was still overwhelming support for the conflict, even among the most anti-war cohort—those aged eighteen to twenty-four (55 per cent).[5] Opinion polls are not good predictors of revolutions, not least in a country where speaking out against the war or the government can land you in prison. But both the level of repression and Russia's overall record of civil unrest since 1991 do not indicate the likelihood of a major eruption from below, or, should it eventuate, its success.

A palace coup, by contrast, might happen, or Putin might resign or die, but it is unwise to bank on any such eventuality. Making regime change in Russia a strategic goal of support for Ukraine, moreover, only limits Russia's options to find a way out of the war it is bogged down in. And if regime change were to happen, it is unlikely that the resulting government would suddenly drop Russia's imperial pretensions or shift to democratic nation-building. As Philip Short has suggested in his well-researched biography of Putin, whoever succeeds the current dictator 'is unlikely to put Russia on a fundamentally different course'.[6] For the democratic world, that implies the unpleasant choice between giving in to Russia's imperialist demands of hegemony over the post-Soviet space and at least a medium-term containment of Russia.

This choice might well also depend on the extent to which the rifts within both NATO and the European Union can be managed in the months, years and quite possibly decades ahead. Initially, both the European Union and NATO, as organisations, were united by the shock of the full-scale Russian invasion of Ukraine in 2022. Citizens, too, have rallied behind the organisations. Seventy-two per cent of European citizens now have favourable views of the European Union, with Greeks being least fervent (50 per cent) and Poles the most enthusiastic (89 per cent).[7] NATO is only slightly less popular, with 65 per cent of those surveyed in member states viewing it positively. Again, Greece brings up the rear with 33 per cent and Poland leads the pack with 89 per cent. Approval for the alliance has grown in Germany, the United Kingdom, Poland, the United States and the Netherlands.[8] Sweden and Finland have decided to join in light of Russia's aggression. Whether or not this new popularity of the transnational organisation will outlast a longer war and its economic consequences remains to be seen. Moreover, the old divisions in both NATO and the European Union have not suddenly disappeared, as Turkey's obstructionism over the admission of Sweden and Finland, and the rift between Germany and Poland over the question of delivery of tanks to Ukraine, demonstrated throughout 2022 and early 2023.

What the long-term consequences of this war might be depends to a significant degree on how and when it ends. At the beginning of 2023, when the manuscript of this book was finished, most serious analysts saw the war continuing throughout the year and possibly into 2024. Such a long-term conflict would deepen the economic fallout in Russia, in Ukraine and in the world at large. It would also see deepened destruction and misery. The longer this conflict lasts, the more it will force both Russia and Ukraine, but also the outside world, to further militarise their societies and economies. Even if a way out of the war is found in 2023, it is likely that the post-1985 decrease of military expenditure from 4.2 per cent of global GDP to 2.2 per cent in 2021 will see a reversal. As stockpiles are running low, production will need to be increased in countries which want to continue to support Ukraine. And the war has shown that the illusions after 1991 that soft power would replace military might in a new world order of rules and polite conduct were just that: utopian pipedreams.[9]

How This War Will End

There is no lack of speculation on how this war will end, often presented with the strength of historical laws ('Wars always end in x'). None of these alleged certainties hold up to actual historical comparison: wars end, or do not end, in all sorts of ways, and acquaintance with what happened in the past does not help predict the future. The truth of the matter is that we do not know how this war will end. But we can speculate about possible paths, their likelihood and likely consequences.

The war could end in a Russian victory. This seems unlikely but not inconceivable. As the most in-depth military analysis of the first phase of the war warned, Russia's armed forces 'have considerable military potential, even if deficiencies in training and the context of how they were employed meant that the Russian military failed to meet that potential'.[10] Winning the war would require Russia to ramp up its military production and mobilisation of manpower, and increase the quality of its training and leadership. It could do that over the long run, just as the Soviet Union did during World War II, where it came back from stunning defeats to win the campaign. It could do so particularly if some of the countries which today are sitting on the fence decide to defy the United States, NATO and the European Union and circumvent or ignore sanctions; the United States reverts to isolationism; NATO disintegrates into squabbles between its members; and the European Union implodes among disagreements between old and new, and rich and less prosperous nations. All of this seems unlikely from the vantage point of early 2023, but not impossible. Indeed, as far as one can tell, this is the long-term strategy of the Kremlin: to outlast the West and Ukraine itself, to mobilise the Russian population's allegedly superior ability to suffer, and to wait until its adversaries run out of steam and patience, and then strike.

The results of such a victory would be devastating for the future of both democracy and peace in the east of Europe. Ukraine would cease to exist, either entirely or as an independent country. Given the strength of civic patriotism and anti-Russian sentiment in the country, this would require severe repression by the occupier or a puppet regime. It would strengthen the war party in Moscow and further fuel imperialist fantasies. Ukraine is certainly central to Putin's project of resurrecting Russia's great power status, but it is not the only territory he thinks belongs to Russia's sphere of influence. He has long sought to re-establish 'links' to all successors of the Soviet Union, uniting them around Russia as the imperial core. His anger at Baltic independence in the early 1990s was only rivalled by his disgust over Ukraine's treachery. Many in his native Petersburg saw Estonia as their backyard (quite literally so, as they owned weekend homes, or dachas, across the border), and militarily, the small nations of the Baltics would be much easier to defeat than Ukraine. NATO membership will be a deterrent only as long as the alliance can convince Russia that it will truly fight for them, which under the scenario of NATO disintegration assumed here would not be the case.[11]

Another nightmare scenario is nuclear war. There are two variants of this prospect: an escalation of the war into a Russia–NATO confrontation which spirals into a nuclear holocaust, or the use of tactical nuclear weapons by Russia on the battlefield. The latter is more likely than the former, given the extreme care with which NATO is keeping itself away from the front lines. Putin also does not have a death wish, as critical Russian journalist Yevgenia Albats has pointed out: 'Look at the size of the table he got out for Macron—does it look like someone who is willing to die in a nuclear war?'[12] If the analysis provided in this book is correct, his chief motivation is the re-establishment of Russia as a great power and the securing of his own position in the history books. Bringing the world to an end would help advance neither goal. Nevertheless, the mere possibility of such a future should keep everybody in a decision-making position alert. And it might be a second reason not to tie an end to the war to a demand for regime change in Russia.

Tactical nuclear weapons are a different matter. If Putin perceives an advantage in their use—such as breaking Ukraine's will to fight or its allies' will to support Ukraine—he might consider using them. Much depends here on the signals he receives about the likely consequences, not only from his adversaries but also from putative friends like China. This is a central task for ongoing diplomacy.

If an outright Russian victory requires a coincidence of many factors in Russia's favour, outright victory for Ukraine seems somewhat more likely. Ukraine's armed forces have performed better than anybody expected. They have proven able to quickly integrate new weapons, shown an aptitude for tactical innovation, and have been led by strategically well-versed leaders. With the right equipment—main battle tanks, combat aircraft—they might achieve victory on the battlefield. 'Ukraine's victory is possible,' write the authors of a major study of the first phase of the war, 'but it requires significant heavy fighting. With appropriate support, Ukraine can prevail.'[13]

But in war there are no guarantees. And the overall constellation of forces is not in Ukraine's favour: Russia has an advantage of 3:1 in population size and available manpower, nearly as large a gap in the defence budget, and nearly eight times Ukraine's purchasing power. It counts more than six times the number of tanks and thirteen times more aircraft. And on the list goes: for any material indicator, Russia has superiority.[14] Taking Donbas back might be one thing, moreover, but Crimea would be a hard nut to crack tactically and operationally. Much will depend on what weapons Ukraine receives and in what numbers. Much will also depend on the ability, or lack thereof, of the Russian side to regroup, retrain and re-equip their troops, and to reimagine their war.

A more likely scenario, therefore, would be a stalemate on the battlefield—a frozen conflict interrupted by intermittent fighting, maybe with some gains for one side or the other. This would be, in a way, a return, though on a larger scale, of the situation in early 2015, when the Donbas war froze. But now, it might well be accompanied by continued missile strikes on cities and civilian infrastructure, which would make the normalisation of life away from the front line impossible. Even with further improved air defences, this amounts to another horror scenario for Ukraine, even if better than outright defeat. It would lock Ukraine into poverty for the foreseeable future, as too many resources would have to go to the war, destruction would continue, and postwar reconstruction would be hampered.

There could be a negotiated peace. At the moment, it is unlikely that one would succeed—the two sides are too far apart, with Russia demanding appeasement for its land grab in Donbas and Crimea, and Ukraine requesting full retreat from all territories captured since 2014. The realities on the battlefield might eventually change the calculus, but that seems, at best, a medium-term prospect. It is likely that peace will be quite some time off.

One particularly nasty scenario remains. Realising that he is unlikely to win, Putin could decide he needs to pull back his troops. But how to do that without losing face? The answer could be, again, taken from the German playbook of World War II: *Verwüstung*—'desertification'. After employing decisive strikes on infrastructure and housing, possibly including nuclear weapons, Putin could make a convincing case at home that he has neutralised the alleged military threat posed by Ukraine. Then he could retreat, using the 'off ramp' some in Europe insist he needs. Avoiding this not unrealistic scenario will require some fairly tough diplomacy, backed up by credible threats of retaliation.

Involving China in this quest will be vital—it is the most influential temporary friend of Russia.

A Decisive Rift

As long as the war continues, the rift between Russia and Ukraine will deepen. This might well be the most long-term, and in many ways the most tragic, consequence of this war. The growing gulf is not just between states or governments but also between societies. This major discontinuity could potentially disentangle centuries of entangled histories. The two were not always violent and adversarial, as chapters 1 and 2 tried to drive home. Ukrainians and Russians speak related languages, which are mutually intelligible, with relatively little training. Most Ukrainians are bilingual in the first place, many having grown up speaking Russian at home and in public. There is plenty of intermarriage and a plethora of family ties between both nations. Russians work in Ukraine and Ukrainians in Russia, or at least they used to. Little wonder, then, that significant numbers of both Russians and Ukrainians until recently expressed their goodwill and positive perceptions of each other. In August 2020, for example, 48 per cent of Russian respondents to a survey reported a positive attitude towards Ukraine, while 43 per cent held negative sentiments. In Ukraine a month later, the corresponding numbers were 42 per cent for both positive and negative attitudes. Only minorities (16 per cent of Russians and 5 per cent of Ukrainians) supported a unification of the Russian and Ukrainian states. Majorities supported the notion that their states should be 'independent yet friendly nations' with open borders and no visa and customs barriers (51 per cent in both Russia and Ukraine).[15]

The war has led to shifts on all levels. As a polling agency discovered, between April and August 2022, the share of Ukrainians who reported speaking Ukrainian at home grew from 48 per cent to 51 per cent, and 'the use of Russian in everyday life has decreased by about half'. Meanwhile, 86 per cent supported Ukrainian as the sole state language, close to 70 per cent were not watching Russian television, and 81 per cent reported negative attitudes towards residents of Russia (up from 69 per cent in April, and from only 41 per cent in 2021).

Most (64 per cent) had either neutral or positive relationships with Russians living in Ukraine. About half of the respondents thought that reconciliation was impossible between Russia and Ukraine. Of those who thought it was a prospect in principle, a third thought it would take two to three decades to achieve.[16]

That might well be optimistic. If Putin unleashed this war on the basis of an ideological and historical program which denies that Ukrainians and Russians are different peoples with different histories, different languages and different cultures, then his war, and his army's behaviour, have instead cemented this very bifurcation. Ukraine and Russia had developed both together and apart since the Middle Ages; their difference was recognised and celebrated by intellectuals in the nineteenth century; it was tried out during the Ukrainian and Russian revolutions of 1917–21 and in the subsequent Ukrainian and Russian republics within the USSR; and it became institutionalised in two states in 1991. Now, the rift is wider than ever. Ukraine is unlikely ever to return to the Russian Empire. The empire itself is a thing of the past. It remains to be seen how much blood will need to flow until this reality is accepted in Moscow.

NOTES

1 Martin Kimani, 'Statement of Emergency Session of the UN Security Council on the Situation in Ukraine', delivered 22 February 2022, *American Rhetoric*, https://www.americanrhetoric.com/speeches/martinkimaniunitednationsrussiaukraine.htm (accessed April 2023).

Putin's War? An Introduction

1 Mykhaylo Zabrodskyi, Jack Watling, Oleksandr V Danylyk and Nick Reynolds, *Preliminary Lessons in Conventional Warfighting from Russia's Invasion of Ukraine: February–July 2022*, Royal United Services Institute for Defence and Security Studies, London, 2022, pp. 1, 8, https://static.rusi.org/359-SR-Ukraine-Preliminary-Lessons-Feb-July-2022-web-final.pdf (accessed April 2023). If not otherwise indicated, the account of the fighting until July 2022 comes from this source.

2 Ibid., pp. 10–11.

3 Number of bomb shelters and guns: Owen Matthews, *Overreach: The Inside Story of Putin's War against Ukraine*, Mudlark, London, 2022, pp. 216, 217.

4 Ibid., pp. 220–25; and Zabrodskyi et al., *Preliminary Lessons in Conventional Warfighting*, p. 26.

5 Matthews, *Overreach*, pp. 219–22.

6 Zabrodskyi et al., *Preliminary Lessons in Conventional Warfighting*, pp. 2, 17.

7 Ibid., p. 9.

8 *Reuters*, 'Ukraine Has Lost between 10 000 and 13 000 Soldiers in War: Official', 2 December 2022.

9 *VOA*, 'At 100 Days, Russia–Ukraine War By the Numbers', 3 June 2022,
   https://www.voanews.com/a/at-100-days-russia-ukraine-war-by-
   the-numbers/6601899.html (accessed April 2023). The 74 000-
   square-kilometres of liberated territory are as of 14 November 2022.
   @TheStudyofWar&@criticalthreats, '#Ukraine Has Liberated
   Approximately 74 443 Square Kilometers of Ukrainian Territory
   since Russia's Full-Scale Invasion Began on February 24, 2022',
   Twitter, 13 November 2022, https://twitter.com/TheStudyofWar/st
   atus/1591628604525645824?s=20&t=dfh6qj7zT7g8-6MdT4vJSQ
   (accessed April 2023).

10 Australian Department of Foreign Affairs and Trade, 'Invasion of
   Ukraine By Russia', media release, https://www.dfat.gov.au/crisis-
   hub/invasion-ukraine-russia (accessed November 2022); Australian
   Department of Foreign Affairs and Trade, 'Ukraine Visa Support',
   2023; Australian Department of Defence, 'Additional Support for
   Ukraine', 27 October 2022, https://www.minister.defence.gov.au/
   media-releases/2022-10-27/additional-support-ukraine   (accessed
   April 2023); Australian Bureau of Statistics, 'Population Clock',
   14 November 2022, https://www.abs.gov.au/ausstats/abs%40.ns
   f/94713ad445ff1425ca25682000192af2/1647509ef7e25faaca256
   8a900154b63?OpenDocument (accessed April 2023); Australian
   Bureau of Statistics, 'Cultural Diversity Data Summary, 2021',
   28 June 2022, https://www.abs.gov.au/statistics/people/people-
   and-communities/cultural-diversity-census/latest-release   (accessed
   March 2023); Embassy of Ukraine in Australia, 'Ukrainians in
   Australia',   23   August   2012,   https://australia.mfa.gov.ua/en/
   partnership/320-ukrajinci-v-avstraliji (accessed November 2022);
   and Daniel Hurst, 'Australian Troops Fly to UK to Teach Ukrainian
   Recruits "Infantry Tactics for Urban and Wooded Environments"',
   The Guardian, 17 January 2023, https://www.theguardian.com/
   world/2023/jan/17/australian-troops-fly-to-uk-to-teach-ukrainian-
   recruits-infantry-tactics-for-urban-and-wooded-environments
   (accessed January 2023).

11 Aston Brown, '"Not a F—ing Game": Australians Who Went to
   Ukraine Have Stark Warning for Others', *Central News*, 28 June

2022, https://centralnews.com.au/2022/06/28/not-a-f-ing-game-australians-who-went-to-ukraine-have-stark-warning-for-others/ (accessed April 2023).

12 Statista Research Department, 'Total Bilateral Aid Commitments to Ukraine 2022, By Country and Type', 7 December 2022, https://www.statista.com/statistics/1303432/total-bilateral-aid-to-ukraine/ (accessed April 2023).

13 Russian Federation Constitution, edn 2020, § 67.1.2.; available in Russian: http://duma.gov.ru/news/48953/ (accessed April 2023).

14 Richard Pipes, *The Formation of the Soviet Union, Communism and Nationalism, 1917–1923*, 3rd edn, Harvard University Press, Cambridge, MA, 1997, p. x.

15 Serhii Plokhy, *The Last Empire: The Final Days of the Soviet Union*, Basic Books, New York, 2014, p. 393.

16 This point has been made eloquently by Jeffrey Mankoff, *Empires of Eurasia: How Imperial Legacies Shape International Security*, Yale University Press, New Haven, 2022, pp. 16–79; see also Marcel H Van Herpen, *Putin's Wars: The Rise of Russia's New Imperialism*, 2nd edn, Rowman & Littlefield, Lanham, 2015.

17 'Empire of nations' is Francine Hirsch's term: see Francine Hirsch, *Empire of Nations: Ethnographic Knowledge and the Making of the Soviet Union*, Cornell University Press, Ithaca, NY, 2005.

18 Jeffrey Mankoff, 'The War in Ukraine and Eurasia's New Imperial Moment', *The Washington Quarterly*, vol. 45, no. 2, 2022, pp. 127–47.

19 F Hill and CG Gaddy, 'The History Man', in Fiona Hill and Clifford G Gaddy, *Mr Putin: Operative in the Kremlin*, Brookings Institution, Washington, DC, 2013, ch. 4.

20 I first grappled with Putin and his views on history in Mark Edele, 'Fighting Russia's History Wars: Vladimir Putin and the Codification of World War II in Russia', *History and Memory*, vol. 29, no. 2, 2017, pp. 90–124; an updated version of this essay became Chapter 8 of Mark Edele, *Debates on Stalinism*, Manchester University Press, Manchester, 2020.

21 The role of the individual agency in history has long animated historians and philosophers of history. For a clear-sighted guide

to this discussion, with a wealth of case studies, see Ian Kershaw, *Personality and Power: Builders and Destroyers of Modern Europe*, Allen Lane, London, 2022.

22 Sara Meger, 'Why Russia Isn't about to Invade Ukraine Soon', *Pursuit*, 15 February 2022, https://pursuit.unimelb.edu.au/articles/why-russia-isn-t-about-to-invade-ukraine-soon (accessed January 2022).

23 Caroline de Gruyter, 'Putin's War Is Europe's 9/11', *Foreign Policy*, 28 February 2022, https://foreignpolicy.com/2022/02/28/putins-war-ukraine-europe-hard-power/ (accessed April 2023).

24 Karl Schlögel, *Ukraine: A Nation on the Borderland*, Reaction Books, London, 2015, p. 38.

25 World Population Review, 'Largest Countries in the World', https://worldpopulationreview.com/country-rankings/largest-countries-in-the-world (accessed November 2022).

26 World Population Review, 'Total Population By Country', https://worldpopulationreview.com/countries (accessed November 2022).

27 The World Bank, 'GDP Current (US)', https://data.worldbank.org/indicator/NY.GDP.MKTP.CD?most_recent_value_desc=true (accessed November 2022).

28 Esteban Ortiz-Ospina, 'Long-Run Trends in Military Spending and Personnel: Four Key Facts from New Data', Our World in Data, 22 April 2018, https://ourworldindata.org/military-long-run-spending-perspective (accessed November 2022).

29 World Population Review, 'Military Size By Country, 2022', https://worldpopulationreview.com/country-rankings/military-size-by-country (accessed November 2022).

30 The overwhelming superiority of Russia over Ukraine in every single quantitative measure is indeed striking: see *Global Firepower*, 'Comparison of Ukraine and Russia Military Strengths (2022)', https://www.globalfirepower.com/countries-comparison-detail.php?country1=ukraine&country2=russia (accessed April 2023).

31 Union of Concerned Scientists, https://www.ucsusa.org/nuclear-weapons/worldwide (accessed November 2022).

32 These efforts are chronicled in detail in Mary E Sarotte, *Not One Inch: America, Russia, and the Making of Post-Cold War Stalemate*, Yale

University Press, New Haven, 2021, pp. 149, 158–60, 182–3, 188, 203–5.

33 Samuel Charap and Timothy Colton, *Everyone Loses: The Ukraine Crisis and the Ruinous Contest for Post-Soviet Eurasia*, Routledge, Abingdon, 2017, p. 39.

34 Mark Edele, *The Soviet Union: A Short History*, Wiley Blackwell, Hoboken, NJ, 2019, p. 77.

35 John Mearsheimer, 'Why the Ukraine Crisis Is the West's Fault', *Foreign Affairs*, September/October 2014. While he has held his ground after Russia's all-out invasion in 2022, Mearsheimer moved from 'the West's fault' to 'the West is principally responsible', a small but significant shift: John Mearsheimer, 'Why the West Is Principally Responsible for the Ukrainian Crisis', *The Economist*, 11 March 2022.

36 Rodric Braithwaite, 'Hope Deferred: Russia from 1991 to 2021', *Survival: Global Politics and Strategy*, vol. 64, no. 1, 2022, pp. 29–44, quotations pp. 30, 41, 31. On Kosovo, see Regina Heller, 'Russia's Quest for Respect in the International Conflict Management in Kosovo', *Communist and Post-Communist Studies*, vol. 47, 2014, pp. 333–43.

37 *Time*, 'Putin Q&A: Full Transcript', 19 December 2007, p. 7, https://content.time.com/time/specials/2007/personoftheyear/article/0,28804,1690753_1690757_1695787-6,00.html (accessed April 2023).

38 Philip Short, *Putin*, Henry Holt, New York, 2022, pp. 223, 224.

39 'Post-imperial phantom pains' is Karl Schlögel's metaphor: Karl Schlögel, *Ukraine: A Nation on the Borderland*, Reaction Books, London, 2015, p. 7.

40 Odd Arne Westad, *The Cold War: A World History*, Basic Books, New York, 2017, p. 623.

41 Sergey Radchenko, '"Nothing but Humiliation for Russia": Moscow and NATO's Eastern enlargement, 1993–1995', *Journal of Strategic Studies*, vol. 43, nos 6–7, 2020, pp. 769–815, quotations pp. 812, 809, 782. See also the sober assessment by Sarotte, *Not One Inch*, pp. 344–50.

42 Kimberly Marten, 'Reconsidering NATO Expansion: A Counterfactual Analysis of Russia and the West in the 1990s', *European Journal of International Security*, vol. 3, no. 2, 2017, pp. 135–61, quotation p. 138.

43 Şafak Oğuz, 'NATO's Mistakes that Paved the Way for Russia-Ukraine Crisis', *Journal of Black Sea Studies*, vol. 12, no. 45, 2015, pp. 1–12.

44 For the multiple imperial breakdowns of World War I and their aftermaths, see Robert Gerwarth, *The Vanquished: Why the First World War Failed to End, 1917–1923*, London, Allan Lane, 2016.

45 For a systematic comparison of the two cases: Gorana Grgić, *Ethnic Conflict in Asymmetric Federations: Comparative Experience of the Former and Yugoslav Regions*, Routledge, London, 2017.

1 Ukraine: A Short History to 1991

1 The text of the Fourth Universal can be found here: 'Chetvertyi Universal Ukrains'koi Tsentral'noi Rady', *Vikidzherela*, vidredahovano Serpnia 14, 2021, https://uk.wikisource.org/wiki/Четвертий_Унів ерсал_Української_Центральної_Ради (accessed April 2023).

2 In addition to the excellent overviews of Ukraine's history listed in the 'Guide to Further Reading' in this book, I have also benefited greatly from Andreas Kappeler's *Kleine Geschichte der Ukraine*, 4th edn, C. H. Beck, Munich, 2014; and from the weighty and authoritative *Ukraina: politychna istoria. XX- pochatok XXI stolittia*, Parlaments'ke vydavnytstvo, Kyiv, 2007.

3 Bernhard Schalhorn, 'Moskau', in *Lexikon der Geschichte Rußlands: Von den Anfängen bis zur Oktober-Revolution*, C. H. Beck, Munich, 1985, pp. 240–1.

4 Valerie A Kivelson and Ronald Grigor Suny, *Russia's Empires*, Oxford University Press, Oxford, 2017, p. 20.

5 Christian Raffensperger, *Reimagining Europe: Kievan Rus' in the Medieval World*, Harvard University Press, Cambridge, MA and London, 2012, pp. 134, 117, and ch. 4 more generally.

6 VP Adrionova-Perets (ed.), *Povest' vremennykh let. Chast' pervaia. Tekst i perevod*, Iz–vo Akademii Nauk SSSR, Moscow and Leningrad, 1950, p. 60. The phrase is recorded under the year 986: '*Rusi est' vesel'e pit'e, ne mozhem' bes togo byti.*'

7 Simon Franklin and Jonathan Shepard, *The Emergence of Rus 750–1200*, Longman, London and New York, 1996, pp. 158–64. Marriage

to Anna of the 'barbarian chieftain': Serhii Plokhy, *The Gates of Europe: A History of Ukraine*, Basic Books, New York, 2015, p. 33.

8   Franklin and Shepard, *The Emergence of Rus 750–1200*, pp. 218, 220. On the language issue: Michael Moser, *New Contributions to the History of the Ukrainian Language*, Canadian Institute of Ukrainian Studies Press, Edmonton and Toronto, 2016, pp. 5–17.

9   Quotations: Martin Dimnik, 'The Rus' Principalities (1125–1246)', in Maureen Perrie (ed.), *The Cambridge History of Russia*, vol. 1: *From Early Rus' to 1689*, Cambridge University Press, Cambridge, 2008, p. 125.

10 Plokhy, *The Gates of Europe*, p. 50.

11 Ibid., pp. 57–8; and Janet Martin, 'North-Eastern Russia and the Golden Horde (1246–1359)', in: *The Cambridge History of Russia*, vol. 1, pp. 127–57, quotation p. 128.

12 Plokhy, *The Gates of Europe*, pp. 59–60, quotation p. 60.

13 Ibid., ch. 7, quotation p. 72.

14 Ibid., ch. 9, quotations pp. 85, 120.

15 G Stefan, M Pugh and Ian Press, *Ukrainian: A Comprehensive Grammar*, Routledge, London, 1999, p. 1.

16 Ihor Ševčenko, *Ukraine between East and West: Essays on Cultural History to the Early Eighteenth Century*, 2nd rev. edn, Canadian Institute of Ukrainian Studies Press, Edmonton, 2009, p. 187.

17 Plokhy, *The Gates of Europe*, p. 105.

18 Kappeler, *Kleine Geschichte der Ukraine*, p. 66.

19 Mykhailo Hrushevsky, *A Short History of Ukraine*, International Books, 2022, p. 28.

20 Ibid., p. 66.

21 Ibid.

22 Natalia Yakovneko, 'Choice of Name Versus Choice of Path: The Names of Ukrainian Territories from the Late Sixteenth to the Late Seventeenth Century', in Georgiy Kasianov and Philipp Ther (eds), *Laboratory of Transnational History: Ukraine and Recent Ukrainian Historiography*, Central European University Press, Budapest, 2009, pp. 117–48, esp. 133–40; Kappeler, *Kleine Geschichte der Ukraine*, p. 21; Plokhy, *The Gates of Europe*, pp. 32, 127; Iaroslav Gritsak [Hrytsak], 'Kogda poiavilsia ukrainskii narod?', *Meduza*, 28 November 2022,

https://meduza.io/feature/2022/11/28/kogda-poyavilsya-ukrainskiy-narod-byla-li-ukraina-rossiyskoy-koloniey-chto-ukraintsy-dumayut-o-bandere (accessed April 2023); and OB Vovk, 'Konstytutsiia Pylypa Orlyka: oryhinal ta ioho istoriia', *Arhivy Ukrainy*, nos 3–4, 2010, pp. 146–66.

23 Gritsak, 'Kogda poiavilsia ukrainskii narod?' On the elections: Kappeler, *Kleine Geschichte der Ukraine*, p. 171.

24 Ševčenko, *Ukraine between East and West*, p. 187.

25 Plokhy, *The Gates of Europe*, pp. 150–1.

26 Andreas Kappeler, *The Russian Empire: A Multi-Ethnic History*, Traylor and Francis, Hoboken, NJ, 2014, ch. 9. The classic English-language study, still worth reading, is John Reshetar, *The Ukrainian Revolution, 1917–20: A Study in Nationalism*, Princeton University Press, Princeton, 1952. A short but effective review of what is at stake for historians embracing this term is Serhy Yekelchyk, 'Searching for the Ukrainian Revolution', *Slavic Review*, vol. 78, no. 4, 2019, pp. 942–8.

27 Plokhy, *The Gates of Europe*, p. 205.

28 'Tretii Universal Ukrains'koi Tsentral'noi Rady', *Vikidzherela*, vidredahovano Serpnia 14, 2021, https://uk.wikisource.org/wiki/Третій_Універсал_Української_Центральної_Ради/ (accessed April 2023).

29 Mark von Hagen, *War in a European Borderland: Occupations and Occupation Plans in Galicia and Ukraine, 1914–1918*, University of Washington Press, Seattle, 2007, ch. 5.

30 For a short summary of this recent re-evaluation of Skoropadsky, see Mark Edele, *The Soviet Union: A Short History*, Wiley Blackwell, Hoboken, 2019, pp. 39–40. For more details, see Paul du Quenoy, 'The Skoropads'ky Hetmanate and the Ukrainian National Idea', *The Ukrainian Quarterly*, vol. 56, no. 3, 2000, pp. 245–71.

31 Edele, *The Soviet Union*, p. 23.

32 Yekelchyk, 'Searching for the Ukrainian Revolution', p. 943.

33 Georgiy Kasianov, 'Die Ukraine zwischen Revolution, Selbständigkeit und Fremdherrschaft', in Wolfram Dornik et al. (eds), *Die Ukraine zwischen Selbstbestimmung und Fremdherrschaft 1917–1922*, Leykam, Graz, 2011, pp. 1331–79. On the army: pp. 161–3.

34 Mark von Hagen, 'The Ukrainian Revolution of 1917 and Why It Matters for Historians of the Russian Revolution(s)', *Euromaidan Press*, 15 September 2017, http://euromaidanpress.com/2017/09/15/ukraines-1917-1921-statehood-and-why-it-matters-for-historians-of-the-russian-revolution (accessed April 2023).

35 Peter D Stachura, *Poland, 1918–1945: An Interpretive and Documentary History of the Second Republic*, Routledge, London and New York, 2004; and Jerzy Lukowski and Hubert Zawadzki, *A Concise History of Poland*, 2nd edn, Cambridge University Press, Cambridge, 2006, p. 245.

36 The classic study of the making of this empire is Richard Pipes, *The Formation of the Soviet Union*.

37 Terry Martin, *The Affirmative Action Empire: Nations and Nationalism in the Soviet Union, 1923–1939*, Cornell University Press, Ithaca and London, 2001; 'Discursive cloak' and 'self-denying empire': Kivelson and Suny, *Russia's Empires*, pp. 288, 299.

38 Vladimir Putin, 'On the Historical Unity of Russians and Ukrainians', President of Russia, 12 July 2021, http://en.kremlin.ru/events/president/news/66181 (accessed March 2022). For more on Putin and history, see Chapter 6 of this book.

39 Terry Martin, 'The Origins of Soviet Ethnic Cleansing', *The Journal of Modern History*, vol. 70, no. 4, 1998, pp. 813–61.

40 Kappeler, *Kleine Geschichte der Ukraine*, pp. 194, 196. 'Shumskysm': *Ukraina: politychna istoriia*, p. 506. On Shumsky, see also Filip Slaveski and Yuri Shapoval, *Stalin's Liquidation Game: The Unlikely Case of Oleksandr Shumskyi, His Survival in Soviet Jail, and Subsequent Arcane Assassination*, Harvard University Press, Cambridge, MA, forthcoming.

41 George Liber, *Total Wars and the Making of Modern Ukraine, 1914–1954*, University of Toronto Press, Toronto, 2016, p. 193.

42 John Vsetecka, 'In the Aftermath of Hunger: Rupture, Response, and Retribution in Soviet Ukraine', 1933–1947, PhD dissertation in progress, Michigan State University; Yuri Shapoval, 'The Holodomor: A Prologue to Repressions and Terror in Soviet Ukraine', in Andrea Graziosi, Lubomyr Hajda and Halyna Hryn (eds), *After the Holodomor: The Enduring Impact of the Great Famine on Ukraine*, Harvard University Press, Cambridge, MA, 2013, pp. 99–121, here: p. 118; Hennadii

Yefimenko, 'The Kremlin's Nationality Policy in Ukraine after the Holodomor of 1932–33', in Graziosi, Hajda and Hryn, *After the Holodomor*, pp. 69–98, here: p. 83; and Liber, *Total Wars*, pp. 183, 186.

43 Plokhy, *The Gates of Europe*, p. 255; Serhy Yekelchyk, *Ukraine: Birth of a Modern Nation*, Oxford University Press, Oxford, 2007, p. 115; and Liber, *Total Wars*, pp. 187–8.

44 Jan T Gross, *Revolution from Abroad: The Soviet Conquest of Poland's Western Ukraine and Western Belorussia*, expanded edn, Princeton University Press, Princeton and Oxford, 2002.

45 Mark Edele, *Stalinism at War: The Soviet Union in World War II*, Bloomsbury, London, 2021, pp. 62–3.

46 Anna Wylegała, 'Entangled Bystanders: Multidimensional Trauma of Ethnic Cleansing and Mass Violence in Eastern Galicia', in Ville Kivimäki and Peter Leese (eds), *Trauma, Experience and Narrative in Europe during and after World War II*, Palgrave Macmillan, Cham, 2021, pp. 119–48.

47 Edele, *Stalinism at War*, ch. 8; and Alexander Statiev, *The Soviet Counterinsurgency in the Western Borderlands*, Cambridge University Press, Cambridge, 2010.

48 This is, of course, part of the argument of Timothy Snyder in *Bloodlands: Europe between Hitler and Stalin*, Bodley Head, London, 2010.

49 Plokhy, *The Gates of Europe*, p. 298; Serhii Plokhy, *Lost Kingdom: The Quest for Empire and the Making of the Russian Nation, from 1470 to the Present*, Basic Books, New York, 2017, p. 283.

50 Plokhy, *Lost Kingdom*, p. 288; on the falling number of students choosing Ukrainian before 1957, see ibid., p. 289.

51 Ibid., p. 290.

52 Ibid., p. 296.

53 Yekelchyk, *Ukraine*, pp. 188–92.

2 Russia: A Short History to 1991

1 Serhii Plokhy, *Lost Kingdom: The Quest for Empire and the Making of the Russian Nation, from 1470 to the Present*, Basic Books, New York, 2017, ch. 1.

2 Valerie A Kivelson and Ronald Grigor Suny, *Russia's Empires*, Oxford University Press, Oxford, 2017, pp. 36–37.

3 Richard Hellie, 'The Structure of Russian Imperial History', *History and Theory*, vol. 44, 2005, pp. 88–112.

4 Kivelson and Suny, *Russia's Empires*, p. 44.

5 VL Ianin, 'Medieval Novgorod', in Maureen Perrie (ed.), *The Cambridge History of Russia*, vol. 1: *From Early Rus' to 1689*, Cambridge University Press, Cambridge, 2008, pp. 188–210: see 'Boyar republic', p. 195. 'Significant alternative': Hans-Joachim Torke, 'Novgorod', in *Lexikon der Geschichte Rußlands: Von den Anfängen bis zur Oktober-Revolution*, C. H. Beck, Munich, 1985, p. 265.

6 Lindsey Hughes, *Russia in the Age of Peter the Great*, Yale University Press, New Haven and London, 1998.

7 Andreas Kappeler, *The Russian Empire: A Multi-Ethnic History*, Traylor and Francis, Hoboken, 2014, pp. 115–17; and census of 1897, *Demoscope*, 3 March 2013, http://www.demoscope.ru/weekly/ssp/rus_lan_97.php (accessed April 2023).

8 Alexander Etkind, *Internal Colonization: Russia's Imperial Experience*, Polity, Cambridge, 2011, ch. 5.

9 Richard Hellie, *Enserfment and Military Change in Muscovy*, University of Chicago Press, Chicago, 1971; and Marshall Poe, 'The Consequences of the Military Revolution in Muscovy: A Comparative Perspective', *Comparative Studies in Society and History*, vol. 38, no. 4, 1996, pp. 603–18.

10 The original formulation is from Geoffrey Hosking, 'The Freudian Frontier', *The Times Literary Supplement*, 10 March 1995, p. 27. The implications of this statement are explored in Chapter 4.

11 Paul Bushkovitch, 'Princess Cherkasskii or Circassian Murzas: The Kabardinians in the Russian Boyar Elite 1560–1700', *Cahiers du Monde russe*, vol. 45, nos 1–2, 2004, pp. 13–18, quotation p. 18.

12 Sidney Harcave, *Count Sergei Witte and the Twilight of Imperial Russia: A Biography*, Routledge, London, 2015; and Jonathan Clements, *Mannerheim. President, Soldier, Spy*, Haus Publishing, London, 2014; quotation: Bushkevitch, 'Princes Cherkasskii', p. 10. State council: Dominic Lieven, *Russia's Rulers under the Old Regime*, Yale University Press, New Haven, 1989, pp. 31, 34.

13 Plokhy, *Lost Kingdom*, ch. 8.

14 Philip Dwyer, *Citizen Emperor: Napoleon in Power*, Yale University Press, New Haven, 2013, pp. 369–428; numbers: pp. 370, 425; quotation p. 392.

15 W Bruce Lincoln, *In the Vanguard of Reform: Russia's Enlightened Bureaucrats, 1825–1861*, Northern Illinois University Press, DeKalb, IL, 1982.

16 W Bruce Lincoln, *The Great Reforms: Autocracy, Bureaucracy, and the Politics of Change in Imperial Russia*, Northern Illinois University Press, DeKalb, IL, 1990; quotation: Mark B Smith, *The Russia Anxiety and How History Can Resolve It*, Allan Lane, London, 2019, p. 113.

17 Quotation: Smith, *The Russia Anxiety*, p. 117.

18 Jeffrey Brooks, *When Russia Learned to Read: Literacy and Popular Culture, 1861–1917*, Princeton University Press, Princeton, 1985; and Susan K Morrissey, *Heralds of Revolution: Russian Students and the Mythologies of Radicalism*, Oxford University Press, New York, 1998.

19 Joshua A Sanborn, *Imperial Apocalypse: The Great War and the Destruction of the Russian Empire*, Oxford University Press, Oxford, 2014.

20 A landmark study is Aminat Chokobaeva, Cloé Drieu and Alexander Morrison (eds), *The Central Asian Revolt of 1916: A Collapsing Empire in the Age of War and Revolution*, Manchester University Press, Manchester, 2020.

21 The classic study of the problem is Evan Mawdsley, *The Russian Civil War*, Allen & Unwin, Boston, 1987.

22 Joshua Sanborn, 'The Genesis of Russian Warlordism: Violence and Governance during the First World War and the Civil War', *Contemporary European History*, vol. 19, no. 3, 2010, pp. 195–213.

23 I first attempted to answer it in Mark Edele, *The Soviet Union: A Short History*, Wiley Blackwell, Hoboken, 2019, pp. 62–3.

24 Quotation: Shoshana Keller, *Russia and Central Asia: Coexistence, Conquest, Convergence*, University of Toronto Press, Toronto, 2020, p. 152.

25 Lenin quotation: telegram from Lenin to IT Smigla and GK Ordzhonikidze, 28 February 1920, https://leninism.su/works/99-v-i-lenin-neizvestnye-dokumenty-1891-1922/3652-dokumenty-1920-g-fevral.html (accessed November 2022). Other quotations

and statistics on Ukraine: Andrea Graziosi, 'At the Roots of Soviet Industrial Relations and Practices: Piatakov's Donbass in 1921', *Cahiers du Monde russe*, vol. 96, nos 1–2, 1995, pp. 95, 101. On cotton: Jeff Sahadeo, *Russian Colonial Society in Tashkent, 1865–1923*, Indiana University Press, Bloomington and Indianapolis, 2007, pp. 226–8.

26 Keller, *Russia and Central Asia*, pp. 149–50, 153–4; Sahadeo, *Russian Colonial Society*, chs 7–8 give a good overview of the confusing, and confused, lines of division.

27 Mark Edele, *Stalinism at War: The Soviet Union in World War II*, Bloomsbury, London, 2021.

28 Adeeb Khalid, *Central Asia: A New History from the Imperial Conquests to the Present*, Princeton University Press, Princeton, 2021, ch. 17; David Marples, *Ukraine under Perestroika: Ecology, Economics and the Workers' Revolt*, Macmillan, London, 1991, ch. 1, quotation p. 1; and Marko Bojcun, *Towards a Political Economy of Ukraine: Selected Essays 1990–2015*, ibidem Verlag, Stuttgart, 2020, pp. 99–106, 109–12.

29 Mark Edele, 'The Impact of War and the Costs of Superpower Status', in Simon Dixon (ed.), *The Oxford Handbook of Modern Russian History*, online edn, Oxford University Press, Oxford, 2015; Mark Harrison, *One Day We Will Live without Fear: Everyday Lives under the Soviet Police State*, Hoover Institution Press, Stanford, 2016; and James Heinzen, 'Soviet Entrepreneurs in the Late Socialist Shadow Economy: The Case of the Kyrgyz Affair', *Slavic Review*, vol. 79, no. 3, 2020, pp. 544–65.

30 Plokhy, *Lost Kingdom*, p. 261; and Brandon Schechter, '"The People's Instructions": Indigenizing the Great Patriotic War among "Non-Russians"', *Ab Imperio*, no. 3, 2012, pp. 109–33.

31 Kivelson and Suny, *Russia's Empires*, p. 361.

32 Yitzhak M Brudny, *Reinventing Russia: Russian Nationalism and the Soviet State*, Harvard University Press, Cambridge, 1998, p. 7.

3 Ukraine since 1991: The Struggle for Democracy

1 Soviet census of 1989—raw data available here: *Demoscope*, 21 March 2013, http://www.demoscope.ru/weekly/ssp/sng_nac_89.php?reg=2 (accessed April 2023).

2   Seventeen Moments in Soviet History: An On-line Archive of Primary Sources, 'Ukrainian Independence Referendum, 1 December 1991', https://soviethistory.msu.edu/1991-2/the-end-of-the-soviet-union/the-end-of-the-soviet-union-texts/ukrainian-independence-declaration/ (accessed April 2023).

3   Andreas Kappeler, *Kleine Geschichte der Ukraine*, 4th edn, C. H. Beck, Munich, 2014, pp. 265–66.

4   Marko Bojcun, *Towards a Political Economy of Ukraine: Selected Essays 1990–2015*, ibidem Verlag, Stuttgart, 2020, p. 112. On the economic costs of separation and transition: ibid., pp. 114–44.

5   ME Sarotte, *Not One Inch: America, Russia, and the Making of Post-Cold War Stalemate*, Yale University Press, New Haven, 2021, p. 158.

6   Bojcun, *Towards a Political Economy of Ukraine*, p. 91.

7   Ibid., p. 93. On the Soviet background history and the Russian situation, see Stephen Lovell, *Summerfolk: A History of the Dacha, 1719–2000*, Cornell University Press, Ithaca and London, 2003.

8   Olga Onuch, 'Why Ukrainians Are Rallying around Democracy', *Journal of Democracy*, vol. 33, no. 4, 2022, p. 39.

9   Simon Troktington, 'Ukraine's Economy Will Shrink By Almost Half This Year, Says World Bank', *World Economic Forum*, 22 April 2022, https://www.weforum.org/agenda/2022/04/ukraine-economy-decline-war/ (accessed November 2022).

10 Onuch, 'Why Ukrainians Are Rallying around Democracy', p. 40.

11 *Aljazeera*, 'Pandora Papers: Ukraine Leader Seeks to Justify Offshore Accounts', 4 October 2021, https://www.aljazeera.com/news/2021/10/4/pandora-papers-ukraine-leader-seeks-to-justify-offshore-accounts (accessed January 2022).

12 Freedom House, 'Expanding Freedom and Democracy', http://www.freedomhouse.org (accessed April 2023).

13 William Partlett and Herbert Küpper, *The Post-Soviet as Post-Colonial: A New Paradigm for Understanding Constitutional Dynamics in the Former Soviet Empire*, Edward Elgar Publishing, Cheltenham, 2022, quotation p. 30; on Ukraine's development: pp. 81, 85.

14 Partless and Küpper, *The Post-Soviet as Post-Colonial*, p. 81. For the comparison with Russia: Kappeler, *Kleine Geschichte der Ukraine*, p. 259.

15 *Polit.ru*, 'Ukrainskaia politicheskaia sistema: slishkom mnogo partii', 11 October 2022, https://polit.ru/news/2002/10/11/575466 (accessed April 2023).

16 Aleksandr Kynev, 'Osobennosti sistemy politicheskikh partii Ukrainy: evolutsiia i perspektivy', *Polit.ru*, 11 October 2002, https://polit.ru/article/2002/10/11/473556 (accessed April 2023).

17 Kappeler, *Kleine Geschichte der Ukraine*, p. 258.

18 Paul D'Anieri, 'Ethnic Tensions and State Strategies: Understanding the Survival of the Ukrainian State', in Taras Kuzio (ed.), *Democratic Revolution in Ukraine: From Kuchmagate to Orange Revolution*, Routledge, London, 2009, pp. 44–5.

19 Plokhy, *The Gates of Europe*, p. 327; on religion: p. 328.

20 Bálint Magyar and Bálint Madlovics, *A Concise Field Guide to Post-Communist Regimes: Actors, Institutions, and Dynamics*, Central European University Press, Budapest, 2022, pp. 227–9.

21 Ibid.

22 Ibid., p. 229; and Gwendolyn Sasse, *Der Krieg gegen die Ukraine: Hintergründe, Ereignisse, Folgen*, C. H. Beck, Munich, 2022, p. 41.

23 Andrew Wilson, *Ukraine's Orange Revolution*, Yale University Press, New Haven and London, 2005.

24 Owen Matthews, *Overreach: The Inside Story of Putin's War against Ukraine*, Mudlark, London, 2022, p. 75.

25 Kappeler, *Kleine Geschichte der Ukraine*, pp. 297–306.

26 On the use of live ammunition, see the reporting by *Kyiv Post*, 19 February 2014, https://www.kyivpost.com/article/content/ukraine-politics/renewed-violence-breaks-out-today-near-ukraines-parliament-at-least-one-injured-336993.html (accessed January 2022).

27 Mikhail Zygar, *All the Kremlin's Men: Inside the Court of Vladimir Putin*, Public Affairs, New York, 2016, p. 268.

28 Bojcun, *Towards a Political Economy of Ukraine*, pp. 269–70; and Sasse, *Der Krieg gegen die Ukraine*, p. 55.

29 Samuel Charap and Timothy Colton, *Everyone Loses: The Ukraine Crisis and the Ruinous Contest for Post-Soviet Eurasia*, Routledge, 2017, p. 124.

30 David R Marples, 'Russia's Perceptions of Ukraine: Euromaidan and Historical Conflicts', *European Politics and Society*, vol. 17, no. 4, 2016, pp. 425, 432.

31 Prezident Rossii, 'Obrashchenie Presidenta Rossiiskoi Federatsii', official Kremlin transcript, 18 March 2014, http://kremlin.ru/events/president/news/20603 (accessed April 2023).

32 Vyacheslav Likhachev, 'The "Right Sector" and Others: The Behavior and Role of Radical Nationalists in the Ukrainian Political Crisis of Late 2013–Early 2014', *Communist and Post-Communist Studies*, vol. 48, 2015, pp. 260, 263, 264, 265, 266.

33 Volodymyr Ishchenko, 'Far Right Participation in the Ukrainian Maidan Protests: An Attempt of Systematic Estimation', *European Politics and Society*, vol. 17, no. 4, 2016, pp. 453–72, quotations pp. 453, 462. The author copped much unfair criticism for a thoughtful, if far-left, critique of nationalist identity politics. It does show him as a person of the left, but certainly not as a Russian stooge: Volodymyr Ishchenko, 'Ukrainian Voices?', *New Left Review*, vol. 138, November/December 2022, https://newleftreview.org/issues/ii138/articles/volodymyr-ishchenko-ukrainian-voices (accessed April 2023).

34 Kyiv International Institute of Sociology, 'Vid Maydanu-taboru do Maydanu-sichi: shcho zminylosia?', 6 February 2014, https://www.kiis.com.ua/?lang=ukr&cat=reports&id=226&page=1&y=2014&m=2 (accessed April 2023).

35 Likhachev, 'The "Right Sector" and Others', pp. 265, quotation p. 266. For more on the National Minority Monitoring Group, which focuses on monitoring expressions of anti-Semitism in Ukraine, see its website: https://www.noa-project.eu/project/national-minority-rights-monitoring-group (accessed April 2023).

36 Onuch, 'Why Ukrainians Are Rallying around Democracy', pp. 37, 38.

37 Ibid., 42.

38 Kyiv International Institute of Sociology, 'Demokratiia, prava i svobody hromadian ta mediaspozhyvannia v umovah viiny', July 2022, https://www.kiis.com.ua/materials/pr/20220817_z/Дослідження%20Демократія%2C%20права%20i%20свободи%20громадян%20та%20медіаспоживання%20в%20умовах%20війни.pdf (accessed April 2023).

39 Vyacheslav Likhachev, 'Far-right Extremism as a Threat to Ukrainian Democracy', Freedom House Analytical Brief, 2018,

https://freedomhouse.org/report/analytical-brief/2018/far-right-extremism-threat-ukrainian-democracy (accessed December 2022).

40 Ibid.; Likhachev, 'The "Right Sector" and Others', pp. 260, 269; and Michael Colborne, 'The Far Right Just Got Humiliated in Ukraine's Election—but Don't Write It off Just Yet', *Haaretz*, 22 July 2019, https://www.haaretz.com/world-news/europe/.premium-the-far-right-just-got-humiliated-in-ukraine-s-election-but-don-t-write-it-off-1.7563138 (accessed April 2023).

41 Shaun Walker, 'Comedian Wins Landslide Victory in Ukrainian Presidential Elections', *The Guardian*, 22 April 2019, https://www.theguardian.com/world/2019/apr/21/zelenskiy-wins-second-round-of-ukraines-presidential-election-exit-poll (accessed April 2023).

42 Stephen Burgen, 'Exiled Chief Rabbi Says Jews Should Leave Russia While They Can', *The Guardian*, 30 December 2022, https://www.theguardian.com/world/2022/dec/30/exiled-chief-rabbi-jews-should-leave-russia-while-they-can-pinchas-goldschmidt-war-ukraine (accessed April 2023).

43 Tetjana Bezruk and Andreas Umland, 'Der Fall Azov: Freiwillingenbataillone in der Ukraine', *Osteuropa*, vol. 645, nos 1–2, 2015, pp. 33–5.

44 Ibid., 35; symbols: pp. 39–40.

45 Andreas Umland, 'Bad History Doesn't Make Friends', *FP*, 25 October 2016, https://foreignpolicy.com/2016/10/25/bad-history-doesnt-make-friends-kiev-ukraine-stepan-bandera (accessed April 2023).

46 Gillian Brockell, 'Putin Says He'll "Denazify" Ukraine: Its Jewish President Lost Family in the Holocaust', *The Washington Post*, 25 February 2022, https://www.washingtonpost.com/history/2022/02/25/zelensky-family-jewish-holocaust (accessed November 2022).

47 Likhachev, 'The "Right Sector" and Others', p. 263; see Yuriy Yuzych, '"Glory to Ukraine!": Who and When Was the Slogan Created?', *istorichna pravda*, 4 October 2018, https://www.istpravda.com.ua/eng/articles/2018/10/4/153036 (accessed November 2022).

48 State Statistic Committee of Ukraine, 'All-Ukrainian Population Census 2001, National Structure', 2001, http://2001.ukrcensus.gov.ua/eng/results/general/nationality (accessed December 2022).

49 President Ukrainy, 'Konstytutsiia Ukrainy', Ofitsiyne internet pre-dstavnytstvo, https://www.president.gov.ua/documents/constitution (accessed December 2022).

50 Paul D'Anieri, 'Ethnic Tensions and State Strategies: Understanding the Survival of the Ukrainian State', in Taras Kuzio (ed.), *Democratic Revolution in Ukraine: From Kuchmagate to Orange Revolution*, Routledge, London, 2009, esp. pp. 39–40. On the policies in the Baltics, see Lewis H Siegelbaum and Leslie Page Moch, *Making National Diasporas: Soviet Migration Regimes and Post-Soviet Consequences*, Cambridge University Press, Cambridge, forthcoming.

51 For data on the rise of civic nationalism during the Orange Revolution and Euromaidan, see Grigore Pop-Elches and Graeme Robertson, 'Revolutions in Ukraine. Shaping Civic Rather than Ethnic Identities', PONARS Eurasia Policy Memo no. 510, February 2018; on the further rise in 2017–18 as well as the role of Zelensky's civic vs Poroshenko's ethnic nationalism in the 2019 election: Sasse, *Der Krieg gegen die Ukraine*, pp. 41–2, 90–1.

52 Marko Pavlyshyn, 'Motivating Ideas, Images and Narratives of Resistance to Invasion', paper presented at webinar titled 'Resistance: Russia's War on Ukraine', Melbourne Eurasianist Seminar Series, University of Melbourne, 13 May 2022, recording available at https://blogs.unimelb.edu.au/shaps-research/2022/05/13/resistance-russias-war-on-ukraine-part-i (accessed April 2023).

53 See YouTube, 2014, https://www.youtube.com/watch?v=kgOSrw 9Q8rc (accessed April 2023).

4 Russia since 1991: Failed Decolonisation

1 Geoffrey Hosking, 'The Freudian Frontier', *The Times Literary Supplement*, 10 March 1995, p. 27.

2 Peter C Purdue in *The Journal of American-East Asian Relations*, vol. 14, nos 1–2, 2009, p. 102.

3 Cf. Samuel Charap and Timothy Colton, *Everyone Loses: The Ukraine Crisis and the Ruinous Contest for Post-Soviet Eurasia*, Routledge, London, 2017, pp. 52–3.

4 Serhii Plokhy, *The Last Empire: The Final Days of the Soviet Union*, Basic Books, New York, 2014, pp. 389–99.

5 Dmitri Trenin, *Post-Imperium: A Eurasian Story*, Carnegie Endowment for International Peace, Washington, DC, 2011, pp. 41, 233.

6 Yegor Gaidar, *Collapse of an Empire: Lessons for Russia*, Brookings Institution Press, Washington, DC, 2007, pp. ix, xi, xii, xiv.

7 ME Sarotte, *Not One Inch: America, Russia, and the Making of Post-Cold War Stalemate*, Yale University Press, New Haven, 2021, pp. 128–9.

8 Jeffrey Mankoff, 'The War in Ukraine and Eurasia's New Imperial Moment', *The Washington Quarterly*, vol. 45, no. 2, 2022, p. 139.

9 Serhii Plokhy, *Lost Kingdom: The Quest for Empire and the Making of the Russian Nation, from 1470 to the Present*, Basic Books, New York, 2017, p. 309.

10 Ibid., p. 314.

11 William Partlett and Herbert Küpper, *The Post-Soviet as Post-Colonial: A New Paradigm for Understanding Constitutional Dynamics in the Former Soviet Empire*, Edward Elgar Publishing, Cheltenham, 2022, p. 33.

12 Plokhy, *Lost Kingdom*, p. 314.

13 Zbigniew Brzeszinski, 'The Premature Partnership', *Foreign Affairs*, vol. 73, no. 2, 1994.

14 Vladimir Putin, *First Person: An Astonishingly Frank Self-Portrait of Russia's President*, Public Affairs, New York, 2000, pp. 139–40.

15 Valerie A Kivelson and Ronald Grigor Suny, *Russia's Empires*, Oxford University Press, Oxford, 2017, p. 337; Mankoff, 'The War in Ukraine and Eurasia's New Imperial Moment', p. 139; Charap and Colton, *Everyone Loses*, p. 56; Decree of President of the Russian Federation of 14.09.1995, no. 940 http://kremlin.ru/acts/bank/8307 (accessed November 2022); and Anna Arutunyan, *Hybrid Warriors: Proxies, Freelancers and Moscow's Struggle for Ukraine*, Hurst, London, 2022, p. 142.

16 Mark Edele, 'Fighting Russia's History Wars: Vladimir Putin and the Codification of World War II in Russia', *History and Memory*, vol. 29, no. 2, 2017, pp. 90–124.

17 Arutunyan, *Hybrid Warriors*, p. 99.

18 Ibid., pp. 97–8.

19 Ibid., pp. 99–100.

20 Masha Gessen, *The Man without a Face: The Unlikely Rise of Vladimir Putin*, 3rd edn, Riverhead Books, New York, 2022, p. 290.

21 Peter Reddaway and Dmitri Glinski, *The Tragedy of Russia's Reforms: Market Bolshevism against Democracy*, United States Institute of Peace Press, Washington, DC, 2001, p. 2.

22 Robert Sharlet, 'Russian Constitutional Crisis: Law and Politics under Yeltsin', *Post-Soviet Affairs*, vol. 9, no. 4, 1993, pp. 317–19.

23 Arutunyan, *Hybrid Warriors*, p. 86.

24 Sarotte, *Not One Inch*, p. 172.

25 Kivelson and Suny, *Russia's Empires*, pp. 364–5, 367.

26 Gessen, *The Man without a Face*, pp. 177, 181.

27 Ibid., p. 190. Elections for governors were reintroduced in 2012.

28 Kivelson and Suny, *Russia's Empires*, p. 370.

29 Partlett and Küpper, *The Post-Soviet as Post-Colonial*, ch. 2. On the status of Russian and the Russians: art. 68.1, 'Novyi tekst Konstitutsii RF s popravkami 2020', http://duma.gov.ru/news/48953 (accessed April 2023).

30 *Demoscope*, 'Russian Census of 2002, National composition', http://www.demoscope.ru/weekly/ssp/rus_nac_02.php (accessed April 2023).

31 President of Russia, 'Stenographic Report of Meeting with History Teachers!', 21 June 2007, http://kremlin.ru/events/president/transcripts/24359 (accessed January 2022).

32 On the processes which created the Russian diaspora all over the post-Soviet space, see Lewis H Siegelbaum and Leslie Page Moch, *Making National Diasporas: Soviet Migration Regimes and Post-Soviet Consequences*, Cambridge University Press, Cambridge, forthcoming.

33 The quotation is from the critical journalist Anna Arutunyan, who left Russia for political reasons after the 2022 invasion; see her *Hybrid Warriors*, p. 29.

34 Owen Matthews, *Overreach: The Inside Story of Putin's War against Ukraine*, Mudlark, London, 2022, pp. 4–5.

35 Ibid., p. 63. On Kohl: Ian Kershaw, *Personality and Power: Builders and Destroyers of Modern Europe*, Penguin, London, 2022, ch. 12.

36 US Energy Information Administration, 'Oil and Petroleum Products: Where Our Oil Comes from',16 September 2022, https:// www.eia.gov/energyexplained/oil-and-petroleum-products/where-our-oil-comes-from.php (accessed April 2023).

37 Shaun Walker, 'Unequal Russia: Is Anger Stirring in the Global Capital of Inequality?', *The Guardian*, 25 April 2017, https://www.theguardian. com/inequality/2017/apr/25/unequal-russia-is-anger-stirring-in-the-global-capital-of-inequality (accessed April 2023).

38 Robert Horvath, *Putin's Preventive Counter-Revolution: Post-Soviet Authoritarianism and the Spectre of Velvet Revolution*, Routledge, London, 2013. On the turn towards the right: Matthews, *Overreach*, ch. 4.

39 Levada-Center, 'Russia and NATO', 10 June 2022, https://www. levada.ru/en/2022/06/10/russia-and-nato (accessed April 2023).

40 Marc Trachtenberg, 'The United States and the NATO Non-extension Assurances of 1990', *International Security*, vol. 45, no. 1, 2020/21, pp. 162–303; Genscher quotation: p. 175.

41 Manfred Wörner, 'The Atlantic Alliance and European Security in the 1990s', NATO On-line Library, 17 May 1990, https://www.nato. int/docu/speech/1990/s900517a_e.htm (accessed April 2023).

42 Most importantly, Mark Kramer, 'The Myth of a No-NATO-Enlargement Pledge to Russia', *The Washington Quarterly*, vol. 32, no. 2, 2009, pp. 39–61.

43 Sarotte, *Not One Inch*, pp. 19–106.

44 Ibid., p. 161. 'Demand-driven': Andreas Basekamp, 'An Uncertain Journey to the Promised Land: The Baltic States' Road to NATO Membership', *Journal of Strategic Studies*, vol. 43, nos 6–7, 2020, pp. 869–96.

45 Sergey Radchenko, '"Nothing but Humiliation for Russia": Moscow and NATO's Eastern Enlargement, 1993–1995', *Journal of Strategic Studies*, vol. 43, nos 6–7, 2020, pp. 769–815, quotation p. 772.

46 Sarotte, *Not One Inch*, p. 154.

47 Ibid., pp. 189–90, 241, 251–2.

48 Radchenko, 'Nothing but Humiliation', pp. 776–77.

49 Sarotte, *Not One Inch*, ch. 8.

50 Vladimir Putin, 'Speech and the Following Discussion at the Munich Conference on Security Policy', President of Russia, 2007, http://en.kremlin.ru/events/president/transcripts/copy/24034 (accessed April 2023).

51 Henri de Grossouvre, 'The NATO Summit in Bucharest: Origins and Consequences for Europe of a Historic US Defeat', *World Affairs*, vol. 12, no. 3, 2008, pp. 84–92.

52 *Unian*, 'Text of Putin's Speech at NATO Summit Bucharest, April 2, 2008', 18 April 2008, https://www.unian.info/world/111033-text-of-putin-s-speech-at-nato-summit-bucharest-april-2-2008.html (accessed April 2023).

53 NATO, 'Bucharest Summit Declaration', 3 April 2008, https://www.nato.int/cps/en/natolive/official_texts_8443.htm (accessed April 2023).

54 Independent International Fact-Finding Mission on the Conflict in Georgia, *Report*, September 2009, vol. 1: pp. 22–24.

55 Matthews, *Overreach*, p. 184.

56 Mikhail Zygar, *All the Kremlin's Men: Inside the Court of Vladimir Putin*, Public Affairs, New York, 2016, pp. 253–70.

57 David R Marples, 'Russia's Perceptions of Ukraine: Euromaidan and Historical Conflicts', *European Politics and Society*, vol. 17, no. 4, 2016, pp. 425–7, quotation p. 427.

58 Ibid., pp. 425, 426.

59 Ibid., p. 428.

60 Charap and Colton, *Everyone Loses*, p. 127; Robert Person and Michael McFaul, 'What Putin Fears Most', *Journal of Democracy*, vol. 33, no. 2, 2022, pp. 18–19.

61 Marko Bojcun, *Towards a Political Economy of Ukraine: Selected Essays 1990–2015*, ibidem Verlag, Stuttgart, 2020, pp. 277–9.

62 Matthews, *Overreach*, pp. 99–104, quotation p. 102.

63 Charap and Colton, *Everyone Loses*, pp. 127–31; and Matthews, *Overreach*, p. 97.

64 Arutunyan, *Hybrid Warriors*, ch. 2 for the polling data, p. 32; and Kyiv International Institute of Sociology, 'How Relations between Ukraine and Russia Should Look Like', 4 March 2014, https://www.

kiis.com.ua/?cat=reports&id=236&lang=eng (accessed April 2023). Quotation: Matthews, *Overreach*, p. 102.

5 Vladimir the Great

1 Gwendolyn Sasse, *Der Krieg gegen die Ukraine: Hintergründe, Ereignisse, Folgen*, C. H. Beck, Munich, 2022, p. 82.

2 For an introduction to the debate: James R Harris, 'Was Stalin a Weak Dictator?', *The Journal of Modern History*, vol. 75, 2003, pp. 375–86.

3 Anna Arutunyan, *Hybrid Warriors: Proxies, Freelancers and Moscow's Struggle for Ukraine*, Hurst, London, 2022, pp. 125, 196; and Philip Short, *Putin*, Henry Holt, New York, 2022, pp. 273, 425, 615–25, 640. On the workload: pp. 459–61; 'too early': p. 294.

4 Arutunyan, *Hybrid Warriors*, pp. 123, 124.

5 Ibid., pp. 138–9; European Council, 'Timeline: EU Restrictive Measures against Russia over Ukraine', https://www.consilium. europa.eu/en/policies/sanctions/restrictive-measures-against- russia-over-ukraine/history-restrictive-measures-against-russia-over- ukraine (accessed November 2022); and US Department of State, 'Ukraine and Russia Sanctions', https://2009-2017.state.gov/e/eb/ tfs/spi/ukrainerussia/index.htm (accessed November 2022).

6 Arutunyan, *Hybrid Warriors*, p. 140.

7 Ibid., p. 167. On the presence of regular troops by August, see also Nikolay Mitrokhin, 'Infiltration, Instruction, Invasion: Russia's War in the Donbass', *Journal of Soviet and Post-Soviet Politics and Society*, vol. 1, no. 1, 2015, pp. 219–49.

8 'Putin in Hiding; Russia', *The Economist*, 2 October 2021, p. 45; and Owen Matthews, *Overreach: The Inside Story of Putin's War against Ukraine*, Mudlark, London, 2022, pp. 173–82. An alternative interpretation of the increasingly erratic behaviour of Putin since 2020 is provided by Short, *Putin*, p. 657.

9 Vladimir Putin, 'The Real Lessons of the 75th Anniversary of World War II', *The National Interest*, 18 June 2020, https://nationalinterest. org/feature/vladimir-putin-real-lessons-75th-anniversary-world- war-ii-162982 (accessed April 2023).

10 Luke Harding, *Invasion: Russia's Bloody War and Ukraine's Fight for Survival*, Guardian Faber, London, 2022, p. 26.

11 Vladimir Putin, 'On the Historical Unity of Russians and Ukrainians', President of Russia, 12 July 2021, http://en.kremlin.ru/events/president/news/66181 (accessed March 2022).

12 Short, *Putin*, p. 653.

13 Sarah Rainsford, 'Why Russia May Not Be Planning the Invasion that Ukraine Fears', *BBC News*, 15 April 2021, https://www.bbc.com/news/world-europe-56746144 (accessed April 2023).

14 Mykhaylo Zabrodskyi, Jack Watling, Oleksandr V Danylyk and Nick Reynolds, *Preliminary Lessons in Conventional Warfighting from Russia's Invasion of Ukraine: February–July 2022*, Royal United Services Institute for Defence and Security Studies, London, 2022, p. 7.

15 *Aljazeera*, 'Ukraine May Seek Nuclear Weapons if Left out of NATO: Diplomat', 16 April 2021, https://www.aljazeera.com/news/2021/4/16/ukraine-may-seek-nuclear-weapons-if-left-out-of-nato-diplomat (accessed April 2023); and *Politico*, 'White House Freezes Ukraine Military Package that Includes Lethal Weapons', 18 June 2021, https://www.politico.com/news/2021/06/18/white-house-ukraine-military-lethal-weapons-495169 (accessed April 2023).

16 Short, *Putin*, p. 648.

17 Matthews, *Overreach*, p. 194.

18 Samir Puri, *Russia's Road to War with Ukraine: Invasion amidst the Ashes of Empires*, Biteback Publishing, London, 2022, p. 199.

19 Mykhailo Minakov, 'Just Like All the Others: The End of the Zelensky Alternative?', Wilson Center, 2 November 2021.

20 Levada-Center, 'Putin's Approval Rating', https://www.levada.ru/en/ratings (accessed November 2022).

21 See the discussion in Mark Edele, *Debates on Stalinism*, Manchester University Press, Manchester, 2020, pp. 218–21, quotation 219.

22 Zabrodskyi et al., *Preliminary Lessons in Conventional Warfighting*, p. 7.

23 Mark Galeotti, *Putin's Wars: From Chechnya to Ukraine*, Osprey Publishing, Oxford, 2022, p. 347.

24 *The Kyiv Independent*, 'Ukrainian Intelligence: Putin Postponed Ukraine Invasion Date Three Times', 19 December 2022, https://kyivin

dependent.com/news-feed/ukrainian-intelligence-putin-postponed-ukraine-invasion-date-three-times (accessed April 2023).

25 'Dogovor mezhdu Rossiiskoi Federatsiei i soedinennymi shtatami Ameriki o garantiiakh bezopasnosti. Proekt', 17 December 2021, https://mid.ru/tv/?id=1790818&lang=ru (accessed April 2023).

26 Matthews, *Overreach*, p. 205; and Harding, *Invasion*, p. 4.

27 Andrew Roth, 'Russia Issues List of Demands It Says Must Be Met to Lower Tensions in Europe', *The Guardian*, 18 December 2021, https://www.theguardian.com/world/2021/dec/17/russia-issues-list-demands-tensions-europe-ukraine-nato (accessed April 2023).

28 Matthews, *Overreach*, pp. 22–4.

29 A transcript of the session is available here: President of Russia, 'Security Council Meeting. The President Held a Meeting of the Russian Federation Security Council at the Kremlin', 21 February 2022, http://en.kremlin.ru/events/president/news/67825 (accessed November 2022).

30 Matthews, *Overreach*, p. 12.

31 Mark Galeotti, 'The Personal Politics of Putin's Security Council Meeting', *The Moscow Times*, 22 February 2022, https://www.themoscowtimes.com/2022/02/22/the-personal-politics-of-putins-security-council-meeting-a76522 (accessed November 2022).

32 Short, *Putin*, p. 657.

33 Shaun Walker, 'Putin's Absurd, Angry Spectacle Will Be a Turning Point in His Long Reign', *The Guardian*, 22 February 2022, https://www.theguardian.com/world/2022/feb/21/putin-angry-spectacle-amounts-to-declaration-war-ukraine (accessed November 2022).

34 On the earlier expression of these views, see, for example, Short, *Putin*, pp. 223–32.

35 Prezydent Ukrainy, 'Stratehiia voennoi bezpeky Ukrainy'. Ofitsiine internet-predstavnutstvo, approved by decree of the President of Ukraine, 25 March 2021, https://www.president.gov.ua/documents/1212021-37661 (accessed April 2023).

36 President of Russia, 'Address by the President of the Russian Federation', The Kremlin, 21 February 2022, http://en.kremlin.ru/events/president/news/67828 (accessed April 2023).

37 Short, *Putin*, p. 239.

38 NATO, 'Relations with Ukraine', 28 October 2022, https://www.nato.int/cps/en/natohq/topics_37750.htm (accessed April 2023).

39 Matthews, *Overreach*, pp. 185–6.

40 Robert Horvath, *Putin's 'Preventive Counter-Revolution': Post-Soviet Authoritarianism and the Spectre of Velvet Revolution*, Routledge, Milton Park, 2013; Robert Person and Michael McFaul, 'What Putin Fears Most', *Journal of Democracy*, vol. 33, no. 2, 2022; and Tetiana Sydoruk and Viktor Pavliuk, 'Rozshyrennia NATO iak fal'shyvyi pryvid dlia vypravdannia viiny Rosii proty Ukrainy', *Stratehichna Panorama*, special issue, 2022, pp. 35–44.

41 John Mearsheimer, 'Why the West Is Principally Responsible for the Ukrainian Crisis', *The Economist*, 11 March 2022.

42 NATO Newsroom, 'Brussels Summit Communique', 14 June 2021, https://www.nato.int/cps/en/natohq/news_185000.htm (accessed February 2023).

43 Sheila Fitzpatrick, 'The Ukraine War: Does Anyone Want It to End?', *Australian Foreign Affairs*, 15 July 2022, pp. 90–102, quotation p. 96.

44 'U.S-Ukraine Charter on Strategic Partnership', 10 November 2021, section II, preamble; section III, paragraph 1, https://www.state.gov/u-s-ukraine-charter-on-strategic-partnership (accessed April 2023).

45 'Dogovor mezhdu Rossiiskoi Federatsiei i soedinennymi shtatami Ameriki o garantiiakh bezopasnosti. Proekt'.

46 This point has also been made by Peter Clement, 'Analysing Russia, Putin, and Ukraine at the CIA and Columbia', *Harriman Magazine*, fall 2022, p. 39.

47 Arutunyan, *Hybrid Warriors*, p. 37. On Putin's sense of mission and preoccupation with history, see Fiona Hill and Clifford G Gaddy, *Mr Putin: Operative in the Kremlin*, Brookings Institution, Washington, DC, 2013.

48 Vladimir Putin, 'The Real Lessons of the 75th Anniversary of World War II', *The National Interest*, 18 June 2020, https://nationalinterest.org/feature/vladimir-putin-real-lessons-75th-anniversary-world-war-ii-162982 (accessed April 2023).

49 Edele, *Debates on Stalinism*, ch. 8; and Stephen M Norris, 'Memory for Sale: Victory Day 2010 and Russian Remembrance', *Soviet & Post-Soviet Review*, vol. 38, no. 2, 2011, pp. 201–29.

50 Mikhail Zygar, 'How Vladimir Putin Lost Interest in the Present', *The New York Times*, 10 March 2022.

51 Short, *Putin*, p. 650.

52 Carlo JV Caro, 'Vladimir Putin's "Orthodoxy, Autocracy and Nationality"', Center for Ethics and the Rule of Law, University of Pennsylvania, 31 August 2022, https://www.penncerl.org/the-rule-of-law-post/vladimir-putins-orthodoxy-autocracy-and-nationality (accessed April 2023).

53 Andrew Roth, 'Putin Compares Himself to Peter the Great in Quest to Take Back Russian Lands', *The Guardian*, 10 June 2022, https://www.theguardian.com/world/2022/jun/10/putin-compares-himself-to-peter-the-great-in-quest-to-take-back-russian-lands (accessed April 2023).

54 Matthews, *Overreach*, p. 69.

55 Kremlin.ru, 'Address by the President of the Russian Federation', 24 February 2022, http://en.kremlin.ru/events/president/news/67 843 (accessed April 2023).

56 On the dangers of using historical analogies for contemporary decision-making, see Yuen Foong Khong, *Analogies at War: Korea, Munich, Dien Bien Phu, and the Vietnam Decisions of 1965*, Princeton University Press, Princeton, 1992.

57 Putin, 'The Real Lessons of the 75th Anniversary of World War II'.

58 See, for example, Mark Edele, 'Who Won the Second World War and Why Should You Care? Reassessing Stalin's War 75 Years after Victory', *Journal of Strategic Studies*, vol. 43, nos 6–7, 2020, pp. 1039–62; or the roundtable on Sean McMeekin's misleading book, *H-Diplo*, 26 September 2022, https://hdiplo.org/to/RT24-5 (accessed April 2023).

59 Maybe 250 000 Ukrainians served in German formations; between 25 000 and 200 000 served in the UPA, but 4.5 million donned Red Army uniforms: Petro Sodol, 'Ukrainian Insurgent Army', *Internet Encyclopedia of Ukraine*, http://www.encyclopediaofukraine.com/

display.asp?linkpath=pages%5CU%5CK%5CUkrainianInsurgent
Army.htm (accessed April 2023); Lev Shankovsky, 'Soviet Army',
Internet Encyclopedia of Ukraine, http://www.encyclopediaofukraine.
com/display.asp?linkpath=pages%5CS%5CO%5CSovietArmy.htm
(accessed April 2023); and Olesya Khromeychuk, 'Ukrainians in the
German Armed Forces during the Second World War', *History*, no.
5, 2015, pp. 704–24.

60 The quotations are from Elizabeth A Wood's cutting 'Hypermasculinity
as a Scenario of Power: Vladimir Putin's Iconic Rule, 1999–2008',
International Feminist Journal of Politics, vol. 18, no. 3, 2016, pp. 329–50.
The link to the 2022 war has also been made by historian Rebecca
Friedman: 'Macho, Macho Man: Russia's Politics of Manhood Drive
Putin's Invasion of Ukraine', *SIPA News*, 20 March 2022, https://
sipanews.fiu.edu/2022/03/10/opinion-macho-macho-man-russias-
politics-of-manhood-drive-putins-invasion-of-ukraine (accessed April
2023). On homophobia: Dan Healey, *Russian Homophobia from
Stalin to Sochi*, Bloomsbury, London, 2017; and Tatiana Klepikova,
Homophobia: Soviet and Post-Soviet, Cambridge University Press,
Cambridge, forthcoming.

61 Cf. Short, *Putin*, pp. 480–2, 650.

62 Arutunyan, *Hybrid Warriors*, p. 225.

63 ME Sarotte, *Not One Inch: America, Russia, and the Making of Post-Cold
War Stalemate*, Yale University Press, New Haven, 2021, p. 16.

64 Short, *Putin*, p. 15.

65 Matthews, *Overreach*, pp. 63, 360–1.

6 The Future

1 Heli Simola, 'What Effects Have Sanctions Had on the Russian
Economy?', World Economic Forum, 22 December 2022, https://
www.weforum.org/agenda/2022/12/sanctions-russian-economy-
effects (accessed April 2023).

2 For an optimistic assessment: Department of the Treasury,
Department of Commerce, Department of State, United States
of America, 'Impact of Sanctions and Export Controls on Russia's

Military-Industrial Complex', 14 October 2022, https://home. treasury.gov/system/files/126/20221014_russia_alert.pdf (accessed April 2023).

3 Anton Hrushetskyi, 'Geopolitical Orientations of Residents of Ukraine; Result of a Telephone Survey Conducted on July 6–20, 2022', Kyiv International Institute of Sociology, https://www.kiis.com.ua/?lang=e ng&cat=reports&id=1125&page=2 (accessed April 2023).

4 The quotations are from one of the main critics of applying the term: Marlene Laruelle, 'So, Is Russia Fascist Now? Labels and Policy Implications', *The Washington Quarterly*, vol. 45, no. 2, 2022, pp. 149–68.

5 Levada-Center, 'Conflict with Ukraine: September 2022', 7 October 2022,https://www.levada.ru/en/2022/10/07/conflict-with-ukraine -september-2022 (accessed April 2023).

6 Philip Short, *Putin*, Henry Holt, New York, 2022, p. 670.

7 Moira Fagan and Sneha Gubbala, 'Positive Views of European Union Reach New Highs in Many Countries', Pew Research Center, 13 October 2022, https://www.pewresearch.org/fact-tank/2022/10/13/positive-views-of-european-union-reach-new-highs-in-many-countries (accessed April 2023).

8 Richard Wike, Janell Fetterolf, Moira Fagan and Sneha Gubbala, 'International Attitudes toward the US, NATO and Russia in a Time of Crisis', Pew Research Center, 22 June 2022, https://www. pewresearch.org/global/2022/06/22/positive-ratings-for-nato (accessed April 2023).

9 The World Bank, 'Military Expenditure % of GDP', https://data. worldbank.org/indicator/MS.MIL.XPND.GD.ZS (accessed April 2023).

10 Mykhaylo Zabrodskyi, Jack Watling, Oleksandr V Danylyk and Nick Reynolds, *Preliminary Lessons in Conventional Warfighting from Russia's Invasion of Ukraine: February–July 2022*, Royal United Services Institute for Defence and Security Studies, London, 2022, p. 1.

11 On Putin's views on the 'near abroad' in the early to mid-1990s, see Short, *Putin*, pp. 222–32.

12 Shaun Walker, @shaunwalker7, *Twitter*, 2 March 2022, https://twitter.com/shaunwalker7/status/1498764691384020995 (accessed April 2023). Albats has meanwhile left Russia.

13 Zabrodskyi et al., *Preliminary Lessons*, p. 2.

14 *Global Firepower*, 'Comparison of Ukraine and Russia: Military Strengths 2023', https://www.globalfirepower.com/countries-comparison-detail.php?country1=ukraine&country2=russia (accessed January 2023).

15 Levada-Center, 'Russia–Ukraine Relations', 2 November 2020, https://www.levada.ru/en/2020/11/02/russia-ukraine-relations-7 (accessed April 2023).

16 'Simnadtsiate zahalnonatsionalne opytuvannia: identychnist', patriotyzm, tsinnisti 17–18 serpnia 2022, Reiting, 23 August 2022, https://ratinggroup.ua/research/ukraine/s_mnadcyate_zagalnonac_onalne_opituvannya_dentichn_st_patr_otizm_c_nnost_17-18_serpnya_2022.html (accessed April 2023).

GUIDE TO FURTHER READING

Putin's War? An Introduction

A quick overview of the fighting until June 2022 is provided by Mark Galeotti, *Putin's Wars: From Chechnya to Ukraine*, Osprey Publishing, Oxford, 2022, chapter 29. The best-informed account of the first months is Mykhaylo Zabrodskyi, Jack Watling, Oleksandr V Danylyk and Nick Reynolds, *Preliminary Lessons in Conventional Warfighting from Russia's Invasion of Ukraine: February–July 2022*, Royal United Services Institute for Defence and Security Studies, London, 2022, but readers need to be tolerant of military jargon and rapid-fire acronyms. More readable are two early accounts by journalists: Owen Matthews, *Overreach: The Inside Story of Putin's War against Ukraine*, Mudlark, London, 2022; and the shorter Luke Harding, *Invasion: Russia's Bloody War and Ukraine's Fight for Survival*, Guardian Faber, London, 2022. A detailed, and ongoing, military history of this war is available from the Institute for the Study of War: see https://www.understandingwar.org.

This book suggests that contemporary Ukraine is 'postcolonial' and Russia 'neo-imperial'. Such an approach has become quite fashionable, but some scholars have engaged in it for decades. A classic is Marko Pavlyshyn, 'Post-Colonial Features in Contemporary Ukrainian Culture', *Australian Slavonic and East-European Studies*, vol. 6, no. 2, 1992, pp. 41–55. A useful comparative history of empires is Jane Burbank and Frederick Cooper, *Empires in World History: Power and the Politics of Difference*, Princeton University Press, Princeton, 2010. A good introduction to the conceptual and theoretical issues involved is Valerie A

Kivelson and Ronald Grigor Suny, *Russia's Empires*, Oxford University Press, Oxford, 2017, chapter 3.

There is a whole library of studies on the 'invention' or 'construction' of nations. A landmark was Eric Hobsbawm and Terence Ranger (eds), *The Invention of Tradition*, Cambridge University Press, Cambridge, 1983. An important counterpoint was Anthony D Smith, *The Ethnic Origins of Nations*, Wiley-Blackwell, Oxford, 1991. This book's approach is more influenced by the latter than the former.

For a good introduction to the basic assumptions of 'realism', written by a prominent proponent, see John J Mearsheimer, 'Structural Realism', in Tim Dunne, Milja Kurti and Steve Smith (eds), *International Relations Theories: Discipline and Diversity*, 4th edn, Oxford University Press, Oxford, 2016, pp. 51–67. The best contributions to analysing the origins of the war against Ukraine from a 'realist' perspective apportion blame to both sides. Most sophisticated is the thoughtful book by Samuel Charap and Timothy Colton, *Everyone Loses: The Ukraine Crisis and the Ruinous Contest for Post-Soviet Eurasia*, Routledge, Abington, 2017. Less convincing are Richard Sakwa, *Frontline Ukraine: Crisis in the Borderlands*, updated edn, I.B. Tauris, London, 2016; and Samir Puri, *Russia's Road to War with Ukraine: Invasion amidst the Ashes of Empire*, Biteback Publishing, London, 2022. Puri does not like to be labelled an international relations scholar: Samir Puri, 'Ashes of Empire', *Inside Story*, 23 November 2022, https://insidestory.org.au/ashes-of-empires/ (accessed November 2022). For a polemical counterpoint to such interpretations, see Keir Giles, *Russia's War on Everybody: And What it Means for You*, Bloomsbury, London, 2023.

Chapter 1—Ukraine: A Short History to 1991

To gain a sense of Ukraine's history, readers might begin with Paul Robert Magocsi's slim but informative *Ukraina Redux: On Statehood and National Identity*, 2nd rev. edn, Kashtan Press, Kingston, Ontario, 2023; and Serhy Yekelchyk's equally punchy *Ukraine: What Everyone Needs to Know*, 2nd edn, Oxford University Press, Oxford, 2020 (3rd edn expected 2023). You might then graduate to his more in-depth *Ukraine: Birth of a Modern Nation*, Oxford University Press, Oxford, 2007; Serhii

Plokhy's comprehensive *The Gates of Europe: A History of Ukraine*, Basic Books, New York, 2015; or Andrew Wilson's *The Ukrainians: Unexpected Nation*, 5th edn, Yale University Press, New Haven, 2022. Plokhy's more recent *The Russo-Ukrainian War* (Penguin, London, 2023) appeared too late to be considered for this book.

A summary of more recent research on the realm of the Rus can be found in Valerie A Kivelson and Ronald Grigor Suny, *Russia's Empires*, Oxford University Press, Oxford, 2017, chapter 1. An essential political, social and cultural history is Simon Franklin and Jonathan Shepard, *The Emergence of Rus 750–1200*, Longman, London and New York, 1996. A good introduction, despite the misleading title, to the traditional story of 'Kyivan Rus' rise and fall' is Janet Martin, *Medieval Russia 980–1584*, Cambridge University Press, Cambridge, 1995, chapters 1–4. An empirical critique of such 'Kyiv-centric' history of the Rus is summarised by Simon Franklin, 'Kievan Rus' (1015–1125)', in Maureen Perrie (ed.), *The Cambridge History of Russia*, vol. 1: *From Early Rus' to 1689*, Cambridge University Press, Cambridge, 2008, pp. 778–97. The period of the alleged disintegration of Kyiv is covered in Martin Dimnik, 'The Rus' principalities (1125–1246)', in the same volume: pp. 98–126. Essential reading on medieval and early modern East Slav identities (including 'Ukrainian') is Serhii Plokhy, *The Origins of the Slavic Nations: Premodern Identities in Russia, Ukraine, and Belarus*, Cambridge University Press, Cambridge, 2009.

A synthesis of research on the first half of the twentieth century is George Liber, *Total Wars and the Making of Modern Ukraine, 1914–1954*, University of Toronto Press, Toronto, 2016. For a summary of the latest research on the 1932–33 famine, see Anne Applebaum, *Red Famine: Stalin's War on Ukraine*, Doubleday, New York, 2017; and the roundtable in *Contemporary European History*, vol. 27, no. 3, 2018, pp. 432–81. An introduction to the debate on how to explain and classify the famine is Mark Edele, *Debates on Stalinism*, Manchester University Press, Manchester, 2020, chapter 9.

Essential reading on World War II is Karel Berkhoff, *Harvest of Despair: Life and Death in Ukraine under Nazi Rule*, Harvard University Press, Cambridge, MA, 2004. For a broad-ranging introduction to the lively debate about the OUN, including whether or not this organisation was 'fascist', see the special sections edited by Andreas Umland and Yulia Yurchak in the *Journal of Soviet and Post-Soviet Politics and Society*, vol. 3, no. 2, 2017; vol. 4, no. 2, 2018; vol. 6, no. 2, 2020; vol. 7, no. 1, 2021; and vol. 7, no. 2, 2021. On the role in the Holocaust, see John-Paul Himka, *Ukrainian Nationalists and the Holocaust: OUN and UPA's Participation in the Destruction of Ukrainian Jewry, 1941–1944*, ibidem Verlag, Stuttgart, 2021. On the memory, see David R Marples, *Heroes and Villains: Creating a National History in Contemporary Ukraine*, Central European University Press, Budapest, 2007.

A snapshot of Ukraine just before independence is David R Marples, *Ukraine under Perestroika: Ecology, Economics and the Workers' Revolt*, London, Palgrave Macmillan, 1991. The best study of the breakdown is Vladislav Zubok, *Collapse: The Fall of the Soviet Union*, Yale University Press, New Haven, 2021. The role of Ukraine is highlighted in Serhii Plokhy, *The Last Empire: The Final Days of the Soviet Union*, Basic Books, New York, 2014.

Chapter 2—Russia: A Short History to 1991

Essential reading for the pre-Soviet period is Andreas Kappeler, *The Russian Empire: A Multi-Ethnic History*, Traylor and Francis, Hoboken, NJ, 2014. The entire period is covered in Serhii Plokhy, *Lost Kingdom: The Quest for Empire and the Making of the Russian Nation, from 1470 to the Present*, Basic Books, New York, 2017; and Geoffrey Hosking, *Russia and the Russians: A History*, Harvard University Press, Cambridge, MA, 2001. Geoffrey Hosking also provides a deeper dive into the Soviet period: *Rulers and Victims: The Russians in the Soviet Union*, Harvard University Press, Cambridge and London, 2006.

A good guide to scholarly debates, together with a thought-provoking interpretation of the long sweep of Russian history, is Valerie A Kivelson and Ronald Grigor Suny, *Russia's Empires*, Oxford University Press, Oxford, 2017. A useful attempt to cross the 1917 divide which traditionally marked the literature is Theodore R Weeks, *Across the Revolutionary Divide: Russia and the USSR, 1861–1941*, Wiley-Blackwell, Chichester, 2011.

On the role of Siberia in Russian and Soviet history, see W Bruce Lincoln, *The Conquest of a Continent: Siberia and the Russians*, Cornell University Press, Ithaca and London, 1994. The history of the encounter with Central Asia is more complex than could be outlined here. A good introduction to some of the complexities is Daniel Brower, *Turkestan and the Fate of the Russian Empire*, Routledge, London, 2003. A good overview of conquest and rule is Adeeb Khalid, *Central Asia: A New History from the Imperial Conquests to the Present*, Princeton University Press, Princeton, 2021, chapters 5 and 6. The most complete history of the Caucasus is James Forsyth, *The Caucasus: A History*, Cambridge University Press, Cambridge, 2013. A closer focus on the North Caucasus is provided by Jeronim Perović, *From Conquest to Deportation: The North Caucasus under Russian Rule*, Oxford University Press, Oxford, 2018.

Russification policies were often quite contradictory. For an introduction, see Theodore Weeks, *Nation and State in Late Imperial Russia: Nationalism and Russification on the Western Frontier, 1863–1914*, Northern Illinois University Press, DeKalb, IL, 1996. For a thorough intellectual history of attempts to come to terms with empire and nation in the Russian context (and their failure), see Vera Tolz, *Russia*, Arnold, London, 2001. For a case study involving Ukraine, see Faith Hillis, *Children of Rus': Right Bank Ukraine and the Invention of a Russian Nation*, Cornell University Press, Ithaca, NY, 2013.

Good recent overviews of the late tsarist and revolutionary periods are provided by SA Smith, *Russian in Revolution: An Empire in Crisis, 1890 to 1928*, Oxford University Press, Oxford, 2017; and Beryl Williams, *Late Tsarist Russia, 1881–1913*, Routledge, New York, 2021. An excellent introduction to the complex political, social and cultural world of the late empire is Wayne Dowler, *Russia in 1913*, Northern Illinois University Press, DeKalb, IL, 2010. For the period of wars, revolutions and civil wars, see Jonathan Smele, *The 'Russian' Civil Wars, 1916–1926: Ten Years that shook the World*, Oxford University Press, Oxford, 2016; and Laura Engelstein, *Russia in Flames: War, Revolution, Civil War, 1914–1921*, Oxford University Press, Oxford, 2018. A broader framework is provided by Sheila Fitzpatrick, *The Russian Revolution*, 3rd rev. edn, Oxford

University Press, Oxford, 2008. For the Stalin years, see Mark Edele, *Stalinist Society, 1928–1953*, Oxford University Press, Oxford, 2011.

The classical studies of the making of the Soviet empire are Richard Pipes, *The Formation of the Soviet Union: Communism and Nationalism, 1917–1923*, 2nd rev. edn, Harvard University Press, Cambridge, MA, 1997; and Terry Martin, *The Affirmative Action Empire: Nations and Nationalism in the Soviet Union, 1923–1939*, Cornell University Press, Ithaca and London, 2001. An overview of nationality policy for the entire Soviet period is provided by Jeremy Smith, *Red Nations: The Nationalities Experience in and after the USSR*, Cambridge University Press, Cambridge, 2013.

An overview of the Soviet Union in World War II is provided by Mark Edele, *Stalinism at War: The Soviet Union in World War II*, Bloomsbury, London, 2021. On the impact of the war and the postwar decades, see Stephen Lovell, *The Shadow of War: Russia and the USSR, 1941 to the Present*, Wiley-Blackwell, Chichester, 2010.

An excellent one-chapter sketch of Gorbachev's conundrums is provided by Ian Kershaw, *Personality and Power: Builders and Destroyers of Modern Europe*, Penguin, London, 2022, chapter 11; the standard biography is William Taubman, *Gorbachev: His Life and Times*, Simon & Schuster, London, 2017. The most up-to-date exploration of the breakdown of the Soviet Union is Vladislav Zubok, *Collapse: The Fall of the Soviet Union*, Yale University Press, New Haven, 2021; and a systematic overview of the legacies of the Soviet-Russian empire is provided by Jeffrey Mankoff, *Empires of Eurasia: How Imperial Legacies Shape International Security*, Yale University Press, New Haven, 2022, pp. 16–79.

Chapter 3—Ukraine since 1991: The Struggle for Democracy

The overviews listed under chapter 1 are as relevant for this chapter as they are for the longer prehistory. For concise introductions to the political system and its transformations, see Bálint Magyar and Bálint Madlovics, *A Concise Field Guide to Post-Communist Regimes: Actors, Institutions, and Dynamics*, Central European University Press, Budapest, 2022. For the political economy, see Marko Bojcun, *Towards a Political Economy of Ukraine: Selected Essays 1990–2015*, ibidem Verlag, Stuttgart, 2020.

On the Orange Revolution and its prehistory, see Andrew Wilson, *Ukraine's Orange Revolution*, Yale University Press, New Haven and London, 2005; and Taras Kuzio (ed.), *Democratic Revolution in Ukraine: From Kuchmagate to Orange Revolution*, Routledge, London, 2009.

An excellent collection of analyses on the Revolution of Dignity is David R Marples and Frederick V Mills (eds), *Ukraine's Euromaidan: Analyses of a Civil Revolution*, ibidem Verlag, Stuttgart, 2015. For a study of social self-organisation from a distinctly far-left perspective, see Emily Channell-Justice, *Without the State: Self-Organization and Political Activism in Ukraine*, University of Toronto Press, Toronto, 2022. A broader overview is provided by Natalia Shapovalova and Olga Burlyuk (eds), *Civil Society in Post-Euromaidan Ukraine: From Revolution to Consolidation*, ibidem Verlag, Stuttgart, 2018. On the far right, see Michael Colborne, *From the Fires of War: Ukraine's Azov Movement and the Global Far Right*, ibidem Verlag, Stuttgart, 2022. On the causes and consequences of the Donbas war (2014–21), see also Dominique Arel and Jesse Driscoll, *Ukraine's Unnamed War: Before the Russian Invasion of 2022*, Cambridge University Press, Cambridge, 2023.

Chapter 4—Russia since 1991: Failed Decolonisation

For a general overview, see Stephen Lovell, *Destination in Doubt: Russia since 1989*, Zed Books, New York, 2006. The political system is sketched in Bálint Magyar and Bálint Madlovics, *A Concise Field Guide to Post-Communist Regimes: Actors, Institutions, and Dynamics*, Central European University Press, Budapest, 2022. The centrality of postcoloniality to state-building in the post-Soviet space has been effectively elucidated by William Partlett and Herbert Küpper, *The Post-Soviet as Post-Colonial: A New Paradigm for Understanding Constitutional Dynamics in the Former Soviet Empire*, Edward Elgar Publishing, Cheltenham, 2022. An effective overview of the post-Soviet space at large is Peter Rutland, 'Thirty Years of Nation-Building in the Post-Soviet States', *Nationalities Papers*, vol. 51, no. 1, 2023, pp. 14–32.

On the emergence and techniques of preventive counter-revolution in 2005–07, see Robert Horvath, *Putin's Preventive Counter-Revolution: Post-Soviet Authoritarianism and the Spectre of Velvet Revolution*, Routledge, London,

2013; on the deepening of the counter-revolution and the relationship to the far right, see the same author's *Putin's Fascists: Russkii Obraz and the Politics of Managed Nationalism in Russia*, Routledge, Abingdon, 2021.

A forensic and well-argued investigation of the available evidence on the assurances regarding NATO expansion is Marc Trachtenberg, 'The United States and the NATO Non-Extension Assurances of 1990', *International Security*, vol. 45, no. 1, 2020/21, pp. 162–303. A somewhat more readable overview is in William Taubmann, *Gorbachev: His Life and Times*, Simon & Schuster, London, 2017, pp. 545–54. Essential reading for any informed discussion about how and why NATO expansion came about are ME Sarotte, *Not One Inch: America, Russia, and the Making of Post-Cold War Stalemate*, Yale University Press, New Haven, 2021; and Sergey Radchenko, '"Nothing but Humiliation for Russia": Moscow and NATO's Eastern Enlargement, 1993–1995', *Journal of Strategic Studies*, vol. 43, nos 6–7, 2020, pp. 769–815. Sarotte's research is well summarised in her '"Not One Inch": Unpicking Putin's Deadly Obsession with the Details of History', *Financial Times*, 17 February 2023. On the discussions within the Bush administration, see Joshua R Itzkowitz Shifrinson, 'Eastbound and Down: The United States, NATO Enlargement, and Suppressing the Soviet and Western European Alternatives, 1990–1992', *Journal of Strategic Studies*, vol. 43, nos 6–7, 2020, pp. 816–46; as well as Liviu Horovitz and Elias Götz, 'The Overlooked Importance of Economics: Why the Bush Administration Wanted NATO Enlargement', *Journal of Strategic Studies*, vol. 43, nos 6–7, 2020, pp. 847–68. Attempts by Eastern European countries to join preceded these discussions, however: see Kimberly Marten, 'Reconsidering NATO Expansion: A Counterfactual Analysis of Russia and the West in the 1990s', *European Journal of International Security*, vol. 3, no. 2, 2017, pp. 140–1.

Chapter 5—Vladimir the Great

The best biographies in English include Fiona Hill and Clifford G Gaddy, *Mr. Putin: Operative in the Kremlin*, Brookings Institution Press, Washington, DC, 2013; and Philip Short, *Putin*, Henry Holt, New York, 2022. Putin's immediate political environment is explored in Mikhail Zygar, *All the Kremlin's Men: Inside the Court of Vladimir Putin*,

Public Affairs, New York, 2016; and Catherine Belton, *Putin's People: How the KGB Took Back Russia and Then Took on the West*, Farrar, Straus and Giroux, New York, 2020. The radicalisation of Putinism since 2014 is discussed in Owen Matthews, *Overreach: The Inside Story of Putin's War against Ukraine*, Mudlark, London, 2022.

Russia's annexation of Crimea and the following war in Donbas are well covered by Anna Arutunyan, *Hybrid Warriors: Proxies, Freelancers and Moscow's Struggle for Ukraine*, Hurst, London, 2022.

On Russia's politics of memory, which can also serve as a guide to further reading, see Mark Edele, *Debates on Stalinism*, Manchester University Press, Manchester, 2020, chapter 8. The classic on the topic is Nina Tumarkin, *The Living & the Dead: The Rise and Fall of the Cult of World War II in Russia*, Basic Books, New York, 1994.

Chapter 6—The Future

On the question of whether or not Russia is fascist, see Marlene Laruelle, 'So, Is Russia Fascist Now? Labels and Policy Implications', *The Washington Quarterly*, vol. 45, no. 2, 2022, pp. 149–68; and her earlier *Is Russia Fascist? Unraveling Propaganda East and West*, Cornell University Press, Ithaca, NY, 2021. On the other side of the argument is Timothy Snyder, 'We Should Say It: Russia Is Fascist', *New York Times*, 19 May 2022, https://www.nytimes.com/2022/05/19/opinion/russia-fascism-ukraine-putin.html (accessed April 2023); and his earlier *The Road to Unfreedom: Russia, Europe, and America*, Tim Duggan Books, New York, 2018; as well as Alexander Motyl, 'Yes, Putin and Russia Are Fascist: A Political Scientist Shows How They Meet the Textbook Definition', *The Conversation*, 30 March 2022, https://theconversation.com/yes-putin-and-russia-are-fascist-a-political-scientist-shows-how-they-meet-the-textbook-definition-179063 (accessed April 2023).

On Russian public opinion and the war, see, for example, Kseniya Kizlova and Pippa Norris, 'What Do Ordinary Russians Really Think about the War in Ukraine?', *LSE Blog*, 17 March 2022, https://blogs.lse.ac.uk/europpblog/2022/03/17/what-do-ordinary-russians-really-think-about-the-war-in-ukraine (accessed April 2023).

INDEX